Reading Victorian Poetry

Reading Poetry

The books in this series include close readings of well known and less familiar poems, many of which can be found in the Blackwell Annotated Anthologies. Each volume provides students and interested faculty with the opportunity to discover and explore the poetry of a given period, through the eyes of an expert scholar in the field.

The series is motivated by an increasing reluctance to study poetry amongst undergraduate students, born out of feelings of alienation from the genre, and even intimidation. By enlisting the pedagogical expertise of the most esteemed critics in the field, the volumes in the *Reading Poetry* series aim to make poetry accessible to a diversity of readers.

Published:

Reading Sixteenth-Century Poetry
Patrick Cheney, Penn State University

Reading Paradise Lost
David Hopkins, University of Bristol

Reading Eighteenth-Century Poetry
Patricia Meyer Spacks, University of Virginia

Reading Romantic Poetry
Fiona Stafford, Oxford University

Reading Victorian Poetry
Richard Cronin, Glasgow University

Reading Modernist Poetry
Michael Whitworth, Oxford University

Reading Postwar British and Irish Poetry
Michael Thurston, Smith College
and Nigel Alderman, Mount Holyoke College

Forthcoming:

Reading Shakespeare's Poetry
Dympna Callaghan, Syracuse University

Reading Seventeenth-Century Poetry
Michael Schoenfeldt, University of Michigan

Reading Victorian Poetry

Richard Cronin

WILEY Blackwell

This paperback edition first published 2016

Edition history: John Wiley & Sons Ltd (hardback, 2012)

Registered Office
John Wiley & Sons Ltd, The Atrium, Southern Gate, Chichester, West Sussex, PO19 8SQ, UK

Editorial Offices
350 Main Street, Malden, MA 02148-5020, USA
9600 Garsington Road, Oxford, OX4 2DQ, UK
The Atrium, Southern Gate, Chichester, West Sussex, PO19 8SQ, UK

For details of our global editorial offices, for customer services, and for information about how to apply for permission to reuse the copyright material in this book please see our website at www.wiley.com/wiley-blackwell.

Library of Congress Cataloging-in-Publication Data

Cronin, Richard, 1949–
Reading Victorian poetry / Richard Cronin.
p. cm.
Includes bibliographical references and index.
ISBN 978-1-4051-9392-4 (cloth) – ISBN 978-1-1191-2141-1 (paper)
1. English poetry–19th century–History and criticism. 2. Literature and society–Great Britain–History–19th century. 3. Poetics–History–19th century. I. Title.
PR591.C76 2012
821′.809–dc23

2011031525

A catalogue record for this book is available from the British Library.

Cover image: *An Open Book*, by Albert Joseph Moore. Watercolour, ca. 1884.
© V & A Images / Alamy

Set in 10/13pt Galliard by SPi Global, Pondicherry, India

1 2016

For Clare and Alexandra

Contents

Acknowledgments

I am grateful to Emma Bennett at whose suggestion this book was written, to the whole editorial team at Blackwell and to Dan Leissner the freelance copy editor. This book, sometimes directly, sometimes indirectly, is the product of conversations, conversations that have taken place over many years, some of them with my colleagues, but most of them with my students. It would be impossible to list all the students to whom I have been indebted in that time, but in this, which is likely to be my last book before my retirement, I would like to acknowledge at least some of those from whom I have learned so much and who have made teaching such a pleasure for almost forty years. I am especially grateful to Anna Barton, Alison Chapman, Carol Collins, Gavin Corbett, Thomas Docherty, Rebecca Domke, Jennie Donald, George Donaldson, Gillian Dow, John Gardner, Misty Gonzalez, Michael Heyman, David Kinloch, Simon Kovesi, Hieronim Kwiatkowski, Tom Leonard, Kyung Ook Lee, Maureen McCue, Chantelle MacPhee, Susan Miller, Katie Murphy, Hye-Young Park, Chankil Park, Rajeswari Rajan, Sumita Roy, Veronika Ruttkay, Jane Stabler, David Stewart, Iain Vaughan, and Ya-Feng Wu, almost all of whom are now teachers themselves. My greatest debt as always is to Dorothy, my best reader.

1

Introduction: The Victorian Poetry Palace

There is no style that Victorian poets share, one reason for which is that they had too many to choose from. They had available to them, as their predecessors did not, the full history of English poetry. They were the heirs, as George Saintsbury puts it, of materials that had been 'furnished by the thought and work of a score of generations of English poets, by the growth and development of seven centuries of English language and English literature'.[1] Saintsbury's claim might be extended. The first scholarly edition of *Beowulf* which probably dates from the ninth century was published by Tennyson's friend, J.M. Kemble, in 1833, and Victorian poets were not familiar only with English literature. Shelley had to teach himself Greek after some lessons from his friend, Thomas Love Peacock, but his successors were, many of them, classically educated at their public schools to a level that neither earlier nor later poets could reach, and some of their female contemporaries such as Elizabeth Barrett and Augusta Webster matched their achievements. Many were also widely read in the poetry of continental Europe and beyond. D.G. Rossetti translated the early Italian poets, Swinburne translated from the medieval French of François Villon, and introduced his countrymen to the contemporary French of Charles Baudelaire. Edward FitzGerald's translation from the eleventh-century Persian of Omar Khayyam became, after initial neglect, one of the century's more unlikely best-sellers. Tennyson's 'Locksley Hall' (1842) with its vision of 'the great world' spinning 'for ever down the ringing grooves of change' (The short-sighted Tennyson explained, 'When I went by the first train from Liverpool to Manchester I thought that the wheels ran in a groove') is properly recognized as a quintessentially

Reading Victorian Poetry, First Edition. Richard Cronin.

Victorian poem, but its idiosyncratic eight-stress trochaic line, 'slides the bird o'er lustrous woodland, swings the trailer from the crag,' (162) was probably borrowed by Tennyson from his Cambridge contemporary, Richard Chenevix Trench, who had himself found it employed in a German translation of a poem by another Persian poet, Omar Khayyam's younger contemporary, Sa'adi Shirazi.[2] The British poets of the nineteenth century recognized, too, their debts to their American contemporaries. Arthur Hugh Clough who, because of his family's American connections, was known to his Oxford friends as Yankee Clough, acknowledged that his own experiments with English hexameters were inspired by a reading of Longfellow's *Evangeline*, and the metres of Swinburne and Hopkins bear the impress of their reading of Whitman.

Nineteenth-century poets lay claim to a far wider historical and geographical range than their predecessors. Felicia Hemans is in this respect typical. In her 1828 volume, *Records of Woman with Other Poems*, she speaks as Sappho in the sixth century BC, as the wife of Hasdrubal at the end of the third, as the wife of Rudolph von Wart in the fourteenth century, the wife of Charles V in the sixteenth, and as Arabella Stuart in the seventeenth. Her geographical range is equally wide, from American Indians to those of the sub-continent, from the Russia of 'Ivan the Czar' to the tropical island home that the exile dreams of in 'The Palm Tree'. Nineteenth-century poets were conscious, as their predecessors had not been, that their poems had to find a place within a great poetry museum, which was, rather like the British Museum itself, remarkable for the breadth and the miscellaneousness of its collections. I begin with three poems, one from the beginning of the period, one from its middle and one from its end, all of which concern museums. All three are poems that reflect upon the state of British poetry in the nineteenth century, and all three poets seem tempted to represent that poetry as defined, rather like the space occupied by the Victorian museum, by its separation from the workaday world.

In Tennyson's 'The Palace of Art' the palace is inhabited by a solitary 'Soul' who gains access, through its collections, to what Tennyson describes as 'the supreme Caucasian mind' (126). The phrase is indebted to an essay in which Arthur Hallam, Tennyson's closest Cambridge friend and the friend he was to memorialize in *In Memoriam*, records his delight in contemplating 'the bonds by which the Law of the Universe has fastened me to my distant brethren of the same Caucasian race' (the expression is not for Tennyson and Hallam racially exclusive in the manner it has since become: for Hallam, for example, one of the principal constituents of the Caucasian mind is 'the Oriental, derived from the Arabians, and circulating especially through those provinces of Europe least remote from the extensive territories of their splendid domination').[3] In Tennyson's palace the tapestries, paintings and stained glass make up a visual inventory of the contents of this mind, but in the version of the poem first published in his *Poems* of 1833 (it was heavily revised for its publication in the *Poems* of 1842: the earlier text can be recovered from Ricks' edition of Tennyson's poems) what impresses most about the character of this mind is how everything exists in it higgledy-piggledy. The stained glass windows, for example, seem over-crowded:

> And in the sunpierced Oriel's coloured flame
>   Immortal Michael Angelo
> Looked down, bold Luther, largebrowed Verulam,
>   The king of those who know.
>
> Cervantes, the bright face of Calderon,
>   Robed David touching holy strings,
> The Halicarnasseän, and alone,
>   Alfred, the flower of kings,
>
> Isaïah with fierce Ezekiel,
>   Swarth Moses by the Coptic sea,
> Plato, Petrarca, Livy, and Raphaël,
>   And Eastern Confutzee.

There may be an attempt here at cultural comprehensiveness, but the selection seems merely random. It recalls the tables at Vivian-place in which the products of 'every clime and age' are displayed:

> Jumbled together, celts and calumets,
> Claymore and snowshoe, toys in lava, fans
> Of sandal, amber, ancient rosaries,
> Laborious orient ivory in sphere,
> The cursed Malayan crease, and battle-clubs
> From the isles of palm.
> (*The Princess* (1847), 'Prologue', 17–22)

Hallam suggested finding a place in the Palace for Goethe, and Tennyson himself considered adding Pyrrho, Averröes, Virgil, and Cicero, but however many the additions it would still resemble a curiosity shop rather than a museum, and the effect would remain Cole Porterish rather than studiously encyclopaedic:

> You're the top! You're the Coliseum.
> You're the top! You're the Louvre Museum.
> You're the melody from a symphony by Strauss.
> You're a Bendel bonnet,
> A Shakespeare sonnet,
> You're Mickey Mouse!

The stained glass windows offer the Soul pictures of Cervantes and Livy, not their works. What she relishes is culture reduced to a series of illustrations, as in a child's picture book. But even this seems at times too substantial to suit her taste. She often prefers to sit on a dais that offers her a perspective from which the pictures dissolve into a play of many-coloured light: 'rose, amber, emerald, blue / Flushed in her temple and her eyes' (169–70). At moments like this the palace is like a kaleidoscope, fragmenting and multiplying impressions until the world is reduced to a pattern of colour. The palace only pretends to be the Soul's university, and pretends so even less successfully than the foundation established by Tennyson's Ida in *The Princess*. The Soul delights in it not because she wants to learn anything, but because its contents are so varied that she is able to find something to match 'every mood / And change of [her] still soul' (59–60).

The Soul is one of a succession of enclosed maidens in early poems by Tennyson, taking her place beside Mariana enclosed in her moated grange, the sleeping beauty enclosed in years-long slumber, and Oenone secluded within her Idalian valley. Lionel Stevenson surmises that all of these women derive from Shelley's 'To a Skylark' in which the bird reminds the poet of a 'high-born maiden' enclosed in 'a palace tower' as well as 'a poet hidden / In the light of thought.'[4] But what kind of poet does Tennyson's Soul put one in mind of? She is first of all, to borrow a distinction made by Hallam in a review of Tennyson's *Poems, Chiefly Lyrical* of 1830, a poet of sensation rather than reflection. For the poets of sensation, for Keats, Shelley, and Tennyson, 'so vivid was the delight attending the simple exertions of eye and ear, that it became mingled more and more with their trains of active thought, and tended to absorb their whole being into the energy of sense.' Tennyson, Hallam insists, bears 'no more resemblance to Byron or Scott, Shelley or Coleridge, than to Homer or Calderon, Firdúsí, or Calidasa,' but the form of the claim, by so clearly recalling a window in the Palace of Art that Tennyson had neglected to describe, contradicts its substance. Poets of sensation emerge, Hallam admits, only when the 'first raciness and juvenile vigor of literature' has vanished, 'never to return'. But in losing its juvenile vigour, literature has gained a history. 'The energy of sense' that Hallam celebrates in the new school is generated less by the objects represented in the poems than by the thick literary medium through which they are glimpsed. If the senses of the poets of sensation 'told them a richer and ampler tale than most men could understand',[5] then the principal reason was that they had read more poems. Tennyson's Soul in 1832 feasts herself

> With piles of flavorous fruits in basket-twine
> Of gold, upheapèd, crushing down
> Muskscented blooms – all taste – grape, gourd or pine –
> In bunch, or singlegrown –

But the flavours of these fruit are very evidently intensified by the Keatsian medium through which they are seen (compare, for example, the spread prepared by Porphyro for Madeleine in *The Eve of St Agnes* (1820).

Christopher Ricks finds sources for Tennyson's Palace in *Ecclesiastes*, in *Luke*, in George Herbert's 'The World', in Bacon's *Advancement of Learning*, George Sandys's *Travels*, Sir William Jones's *The Palace of Fortune*, and in three poems by Shelley, but it is a poem so literary that the list might be extended almost indefinitely. The quatrain that Tennyson uses in which two ten syllable lines are separated by a line of eight syllables before the stanza closes with a six syllable line suggests that this is a poem that has its origin in the library as much as in life. It is the stanza of Henry Vaughan's 'They are all gone into the world of light'. Christopher Ricks believes that the stanza was 'independently developed' by Tennyson, an entirely reasonable supposition given that Vaughan's poem was not reprinted until the 1840s, but *The Palace of Art* is dedicated to Richard Chenevix Trench, and it is surely more than a coincidence that in the summer of 1831, shortly before returning to Cambridge where he met Tennyson for the first time, Trench wrote of his 'especial desire' to read Vaughan's poems.[6] Tennyson himself might well have been irritated by any suggestion that he borrowed his stanza from Vaughan. 'They allow me nothing,' he complained to H.D. Rawnsley of his critics, and illustrated his point by adducing a celebrated line from 'Ulysses', 'The deep / Moans round with many voices' (54–5) : '"The deep", Byron; "moans", Horace; "many voices", Homer; and so on.'[7] Tennyson, far more intricately than

Vaughan, exploits the rhythmic possibilities of the stanza. He seems especially interested in finding how many metrical variations he can devise for the stanza's short final line. The effects are often very fine, as in the desert landscape:

> One seemed all dark and red – a tract of sand,
>   And some one pacing there alone,
> Who paced for ever in a glimmering land,
>   Lit with a low large moon.
>
> (65–8)

The metre is adjusted to the sense so exquisitely that the attention is seized less by the scenery than the display of metrical skill. But, as so often in Tennyson, the display is not empty: it carries the poem's meaning. It is one of the principal ways in which Tennyson tempts his readers to imitate the Soul by responding to the world as if it was offered to them simply for their fastidious aesthetic contemplation.

This all seems very unlike the other most celebrated Victorian poet, Robert Browning, the rough texture of whose verse was from the first contrasted with Tennyson's smoothness, not least by Tennyson himself ('He can conceive of grand dramatic situations, but where's the music?'[8]). But Browning too focuses attention on his metrical effects even when these are quite different from Tennyson's. He draws attention, for example, to the doggerel movement of *Christmas-Eve* (1850) as assertively as Tennyson focuses attention on the silky movement of his quatrains in *The Palace of Art* (like Tennyson in *Locksley Hall*, Browning finds in the railway the most powerful emblem of modernity):

> A tune was born in my head last week,
> Out of the thump-thump and shriek-shriek
> Of the train, as I came by it, up from Manchester;
> And when, next week, I take it back again,
> My head will sing to the engine's clack again,
> While it only makes my neighbour's haunches stir,
> – Finding no dormant musical sprout
> In him, as in me, to be jolted out.
>
> (249–56)

Browning asks his reader to relish a rhythm made out of the 'engine's clack', which reminds us that just as much as Tennyson, he needed to fabricate his style. He set about it very much in the manner of his own Sordello engaged in the task that Dante would complete of inventing a new language for vernacular Italian poetry. Sordello 'slow re-wrought' the language of poetry, 'welding words into the crude / Mass from the new speech round him, till a rude / Armour was hammered out' (*Sordello*, 2, 574–7). This seems a self-conscious reflection by Browning on the manner in which he had forged his own poetic style, but the analogy is pointed by the contrast. Sordello in Mantua at the beginning of the thirteenth century stands at the very beginning of a poetic tradition: Browning, in a poem that he published in 1840, looks at Sordello through the long expanse of literary history that has intervened between them, a literary history that includes, for example, all the Elizabethan and Jacobean drama that was so important to Browning when he set about hammering out his own style.

It was sly of Tennyson to choose that particular quotation from 'Ulysses' when he wanted to mock scholarly source hunters, 'the deep / Moans round with many voices'. He chose it surely because it is so unmistakably Tennysonian. Robert Douglas Fairhurst traces the line back to the stanza of *The Palace of Art* comparing the Soul to a traveller who 'A little before moon-rise hears the low / Moan of an unknown sea,' (279–80) and forward to the 'moanings of the homeless sea' of the 1850 *In Memoriam* (XXXV, 9), the 'phantom circle of a moaning sea' in *The Passing of Arthur* of 1869 (87), and 'the waves that moan about the world' in *Demeter and Persephone* (63), a poem published in 1889, just three years before Tennyson's death.[9] When John Churton Collins classed Tennyson amongst the 'essentially imitative poets', and supported the claim by adducing sources, classical, Italian, or English, for many of his most famous passages, Collins stood revealed, Tennyson told Edmund Gosse, as 'a louse upon the locks of literature'. But Collins claimed that Tennyson's was a trait common to all literatures 'at a certain point in their development.' Tennyson and his contemporaries had 'inherited the splendours of Greece, of Rome, of Italy, and of the illustrious dynasties of English genius.' They were, in a phrase that Collins courteously borrowed from Tennyson himself, 'the heirs of all the ages' ('Locksley Hall', 178), which made it inevitable that their poems should be admirable for their refinement rather than their originality.[10] Isobel Armstrong makes a similar point when she describes Victorian poetry as 'overwhelmingly secondary' in its character.[11] The Victorian poet, it seems, is as enclosed in the history of literature as is Tennyson's Soul in her palace, and like the Soul, the belated poets of the nineteenth century took their colour from the masterpieces of the past that they moved amongst. But the violence of Tennyson's response to such suggestions is an index of the very high value that was attached in the period to originality.

Victorian poetry may be 'overwhelmingly secondary', but style, many Victorians believed, should express the individual personality of the poet. In consequence much Victorian poetry has a paradoxical character of the kind nicely exemplified in the career of Robert Browning. So much of his poetry is dramatic in character, as if he were entirely willing to speak in the voices of others, and yet Browning manufactures, like his own Sordello, and like other Victorian poets such as Swinburne and Christina Rossetti and Hopkins, a poetic manner startlingly and unmistakably idiosyncratic. As the passage from *Sordello* suggests, Victorian poetic styles tend to be forged rather than found, and one result is that the poetic styles so energetically developed often seem like performances, as if poets had found their own voices when they had shown themselves to be their own best impersonators. When Everard Hall, the poet of Tennyson's *Morte d'Arthur* reads, 'mouthing out his hollow oes and aes,' ('The Epic', 50) Tennyson, although he probably wrote the poem in 1837–8, before he was thirty, is already so aware of himself as a Tennysonian poet that he could make a quiet joke of it ('He is', Hopkins wrote of Tennyson in a revealing joke, 'one must see it, what we used to call Tennysonian'[12]). Swinburne more flamboyantly ended his volume of parodies, *The Heptalogia* (1880) with 'Nephelidia', in which he contrives the most accomplished Victorian parody of his own poetic manner, singing from 'the depth of the dreamy decline of the dawn through a notable nimbus of nebulous moonshine' (1). In 'Poeta Loquitur' (published posthumously in 1918) he matches this achievement by launching an attack on his own verse that effortlessly outdoes even his most belligerent critics such as Robert Buchanan:

> Mad mixtures of Frenchified offal
> With insults to Christendom's creed,
> Blind blasphemy, schoolboylike scoff, all
> These blazon me blockhead indeed.
> (25–8)

Tennyson's Soul wanders through her Palace, the rooms of which are 'fitted to every mood / And change of [her] still soul'. Nothing in the palace or in its accoutrements impinges on her perfect self-absorption. And yet there is also a sense in which the Soul has no self, existing only in so far as she reflects the objects that she moves amongst, 'a manyfacèd glass'. These might seem antithetical, if equally disturbing, ways of figuring the artist's role, and the poets of the century seem to oscillate between them. Browning, for example, introducing in 1852 a volume of newly discovered letters by Shelley (the letters, it later emerged, were forged), was driven to ponder the relationship between the person of the poet and the character of the poems, and came to the conclusion that there were two quite different kinds of poet. There were objective poets whose work was wholly independent of their personalities, and subjective poets whose work was inexplicable unless read as an expression of those personalities. Browning imagined that a perfect poet might combine the qualities of both, rather as Aristotle had imagined that the same dramatist might excel in both tragedy and comedy. It was clearly the ambition that he harboured for himself, but the essay leaves it unclear quite how the two poetic characters might be reconciled.[13]

For most of its length *The Palace of Art* describes the galleries through which the Soul wanders. The organizational problem that seems most to exercise Tennyson is the question of where each stanza will show best, where it might most effectively be hung. In 1833, for example, the stanza describing the 'maid-mother', the Virgin with child, was daringly followed by a Venus, but Tennyson seems quickly to have decided that this arrangement was vulgar. In a version of the poem preserved in the Heath manuscript he inserts a stanza on the Magi, before allowing the Virgin to find her counterpart in another virgin, the traitress Tarpeia, and in 1842 we glide from the 'maid-mother' to Saint Cecily before we encounter a 'group of Houris' gracefully preparing to solace a 'dying Islamite'. The hanging decisions are usually intelligent, and yet they remain provisional. It would be rash to claim that any version of the poem achieved finality. Tennyson's decisions as to which stanzas to include and which to exclude from the poem seem equally casual. The poem's earliest readers, Tennyson's Cambridge friends, felt free to offer their advice. Hallam wrote to Tennyson: 'I hear that Tennant has written to dissuade you from publishing Kriemhilt, Tarpeia, and Pendragon. Don't be humbugged, they are very good.'[14] In 1832 even the reader of the printed text is allowed to participate in this exercise. Tennyson includes notes in which he gives supplementary stanzas, inviting the reader to judge whether room should have been found for them in the printed poem. He admits into his poem a circumstantial description of the architecture of the palace, and yet the poem that results serves only to underwrite Arnold's charge that contemporary poetry lacked the architectonic power that for him was most powerfully embodied in the Greek drama. Tennyson seems to have made the poem piecemeal, as he made *In Memoriam* and as he made his *Idylls of the King*. But in this he was, as Arnold allowed, the true representative of the century's poetry, even of Arnold's own.

The Palace of Art ends when description is replaced by narrative. The Soul's life of luxuriant ease breeds self-loathing, her solitude leaves her shrieking for very loneliness: 'No voice breaks through the stillness of this world' (259). She bitterly repents the life she has lived in the Palace: '"Make me a cottage in the vale," she said, / "Where I may mourn and pray."' (291–2) It seemed to John Sterling, a close associate of Tennyson's, a regrettable instance of monkish asceticism:

> The writer's doctrine seems to be that the soul, while by its own energy surrounding itself with all the most beautiful and expressive images that the history of mankind has produced, and sympathising with the world's best thought, is perpetrating some prodigious moral offence for which it is bound to repent in sackcloth and ashes.[15]

The poem ends by repudiating the 'beautiful and expressive images' that make up the greater part of the poem. It is a gesture that several of Tennyson's contemporaries repeated. One thinks of Arnold devoting so much of the preface to his *Poems* of 1853 to an explanation of why he had chosen to exclude from the volume the major poem that he had published only the previous year, *Empedocles on Etna*, or Elizabeth Barrett ending *Aurora Leigh* (1857) by allowing her heroine to acknowledge the limitations of her masterpiece, a poem that is clearly very like *Aurora Leigh*. Hopkins's anxiety that his priestly and his poetic vocations might be incompatible is obviously a special case, and yet his anxiety, as the self-loathing of Tennyson's Soul suggests, was not as idiosyncratic as might be assumed. But *The Palace of Art* is not quite so conflicted as a summary of its plot suggests. The Soul delights in her palace, and loathes it, and leaves it, with an impartial gusto. The sequence of her actions mimes a moral progress, but our understanding of the import of her gestures is at every stage diverted into an appreciation of their charming, charade-like theatricality. It is somehow entirely appropriate that even the account of how the Soul is stricken by self-contempt yields a landscape as hauntingly beautiful as any hung in the palace's picture galleries. The Soul comes to see herself as

> A still salt pool, locked in with bars of sand,
> Left on the shore; that hears all night
> The plunging seas draw backward from the land
> Their moon-led waters white.
>
> (249–52)

It is, as John Sterling would say, a beautiful and expressive image, a memory of the Lincolnshire coast near which Tennyson grew up, but a memory so vivid that it slips the lead of the solemn moral truth that it seems intended to figure. In the introductory lines presenting the poem to Trench, Tennyson describes it as 'a sort of allegory' carrying the moral that 'Beauty, Good, and Knowledge, are three sisters' that 'never can be sundered without tears'. But in the poem that follows the sisters seem strangers to one another. As John Sterling rather stiffly points out, the poem's beauty seems almost wholly disconnected from the knowledge that it is supposed to impart.

The Palace of Art was prompted, Tennyson recalls, by Trench's remark, 'Tennyson, we cannot live in art.' It is the lesson learned in the poem by the Soul, but when she abandons her palace for prayer and a cottage, she asks that the Palace not be demolished:

> Yet pull not down my palace towers, that are
> So lightly, beautifully built:
> Perchance I may return with others there
> When I have purged my guilt.
>
> (293–6)

The Soul's repudiation of the palace and of the life that she has lived there seems less than wholehearted. There may be an implication that the pleasures that the Palace offers are guilty only if their enjoyment is solitary. Tennyson described the poem as 'the embodiment of [his] own belief that the Godlike life is with man and for man,'[16] but it seems more appropriately described as the embodiment of his own radical uncertainty as to what the poet's civic responsibilities might be. A letter from J.W. Blakesley offered Tennyson naively robust encouragement to step forward as a social commentator:

> The present race of monstrous opinions and feelings which pervade the age require the arm of a strong Iconoclast A volume of poetry written in a

> proper spirit, a spirit like that which a vigorous mind indues by the study of Wordsworth and Shelley, would be, at the present juncture, the greatest benefit the world could receive. And more benefit would accrue from it than from all the exertions of the Jeremy Benthamites and Millians, if they were to continue for ever and a day.[17]

Blakesley's reference is presumably to James Mill. His son, John Stuart Mill, took a rather different view. He distinguished writing addressed directly to its reader, writing that he termed eloquence, from poetry, which, he suggested, its reader only ever overheard.[18] *The Palace of Art* does not choose unequivocally between the two kinds of writing, and it is precisely in its equivocations that it exemplifies a good deal of the century's poetry. It is a poem, like the two other museum poems that I will discuss in this chapter, preoccupied and puzzled by the relationship that poets should establish with their societies.

Tennyson's Palace accommodates an imaginary exhibition space (although the palace's architecture, as has often been noticed, is loosely based on Tennyson's Cambridge college, Trinity). D.G. Rossetti's, 'The Burden of Nineveh', a poem that he began in 1850, first published in the *Oxford and Cambridge Magazine* in 1856, and revised for its inclusion in the *Poems* of 1870, is set on the steps of the British Museum. The museum's impressive neoclassical façade looking onto Great Russell Street was completed only in 1848, and the main gates and forecourt still later, in 1852. But for Rossetti, despite the ongoing building work, it is a space almost as distant from the 'London dirt and din' (7) as Tennyson's palace:

> In our Museum galleries
> To-day I lingered o'er the prize
> Dead Greece vouchsafes to living eyes, —
> Her Art for ever in fresh wise
> From hour to hour rejoicing me.
>
> (1–5)

Greek art is at once 'for ever' and 'fresh', a thought that establishes Rossetti as the heir not only of classical sculptors, but of English poets. He has been lingering, as Keats had before him, over the Elgin marbles, and has been taught the lesson that Keats rehearses in his 'Ode on a Grecian Urn' (1820), that the paradoxical power of art is that it may be at once in time and out of it, 'For ever panting, and for ever young'. But that is how

Rossetti began his poem in 1870. In 1856, in its first printing in the *Oxford and Cambridge Magazine*, the contents of the Museum had inspired less reverence, and Rossetti had scarcely lingered. He stays only an hour:

> I have no taste for polyglot:
> At the Museum 'twas my lot,
> Just once, to jot and blot and rot
> In Babel for I know not what.
> I went at two, I left at three.
>
> (1–5)

The contents of the Museum in mid-century were even more chaotically eclectic than the contents of Tennyson's Palace. It was, for William Cobbett, 'the old curiosity shop'.[19] For Rossetti in 1856 it seems a cacophonous Tower of Babel. The museum's main staircase, for example, was dominated by three stuffed giraffes. The museum had its origin in the decision to purchase Sir Hans Sloane's collections for the nation in 1753, collections which, Horace Walpole observed, were highly valued by 'anybody who loves hippopotamuses, sharks with one ear, and spiders as big as geese' (the animals were not removed to the newly built Natural History Museum until the 1880s).[20] In the poorly lit reading room (construction of the great circular Reading Room did not begin until 1854) scholars were far outnumbered by novel readers, all the museum's British antiquities were displayed in four cases in a single room, and the treasures unearthed by Sir Austin Henry Layard in his Assyrian excavations, amongst them the 'wingèd beast from Nineveh' (10) that Rossetti witnessed as it was being hoisted up the museum's steps, were first displayed, for lack of space, in the basement.

In 1856 the Museum had not impressed Rossetti as offering any kind of haven from the city streets outside. Once the Assyrian bull-god is installed, the 'kind of light' that falls on it will be the light that 'London takes the day to be':

> Here cold-pinch'd clerks on yellow days
> Shall stop and peer; and in sun-haze
> Shall clergy crimp their eyes to gaze;
> And misses titter in their stays
> Just fresh from 'Layard's Nineveh'.
>
> (66–70)

Layard's dashing account of his excavations, *Nineveh and its Remains* (1848–9), became a best-seller. Layard succeeded in making the ancient history of Assyria a nineteenth-century craze. In a rather similar way, despite its Ionic façade, Sir Robert Smirke's museum was an emphatically Victorian building, equipped with revolving doors (in 1870, as Rossetti leaves, he makes 'the swing-door spin' (8)). Even for the serious students of the antique who take their lunch there, art is not a joy for ever so much as a branch of the fashion industry. In their lunchtime conversations 'Art' is 'slang'd o'er cheese and hunch' (72) (a hunch is a thick slice, a hunk, of bread), and the conversation centres on the attack on the Royal Academy by Rossetti and his associates, the self-named Pre-Raphaelite Brotherhood:

Whether the great R.A.'s a bunch
Of gods or dogs, and whether Punch
Is right about the P.R.B.
(73–5)

Art in such conversations is emphatically not 'for ever': it is simply material for the gossip of the day. In the1870 version of the poem, the Museum is presented more respectfully, but traces of the 1856 irreverence are preserved. Rossetti, for example, still imagines the Assyrian sculpture viewed by 'school-foundations in the act / Of holiday' (a devastatingly precise turn of phrase) who will vaguely connect it with popular anti-Catholic sentiment,

As a fact
Connected with that zealous tract:
'Rome, – Babylon and Nineveh'.
(78–80)

What clinches the joke here is that Rossetti himself will choose at the last not to look at the Assyrian bull-god as he looked at the museum's Greek sculpture, alert to its capacity to be at once 'fresh' and 'for ever', but with a gaze that more closely resembles the stupefied gaze of those schoolchildren as they are guided by their teachers through the Museum's galleries in their regimented crocodiles.

In 1870 Rossetti begins by offering his tribute to the art of Greece, but he does so in a stanza that decisively links his poem not with the Elgin marbles or a Grecian urn, but with the strange, grotesque 'wingèd beast' that, as he leaves the Museum, is being hoisted in. The proper comparison here is with the graceful 10-line stanzas of Keats's odes, 'Ode on a Grecian

Urn' or 'Ode to a Nightingale', in which an interlocking quatrain is followed by some variation on the sestet of an Italian sonnet. Keats's metre is equally graceful: the iambic pentameters may be clipped to a trimeter, 'And leaden-eyed despairs', or overflow into an alexandrine, 'And with thee fade away into the forest dim' ('Ode to a Nightingale', 28 and 20). Rossetti's ten-line stanza is unvaryingly octosyllabic, so that it is always threatening to break into the scamper of the opening lines in 1856, 'Just once, to jot and blot and rot' (3). The stanza consists of two groups of four rhyming lines inexpertly sewn together by rhyming the fifth with the final, tenth line, which, inevitably, given that each stanza ends with the word 'Nineveh', is an approximate rather than a full rhyme. It is like the stanza of a Keats ode caricatured by a hostile critic, and its effect is decisively to align Rossetti's poem not with the Greek sculpture that he has just been lingering over, but with the grotesque Assyrian bull that is being carried into the museum as he makes his exit. The poem has its origin in the event that Rossetti witnessed and in the stanza that he fashioned to record it. That stanza was already established in the poem's very earliest draft, two stanzas dating, William Rossetti recalled, from 1850 (they became the fifth and sixth stanzas of the poem in 1870). The stanzas describe the shadow that the beast casts, a shadow so dark that it admits '[n]o light, no shade', and so unvarying that it is 'shed the same' on London streets as it had been on the streets of 'Sardanapalus' Nineveh'. Greek art is a joy for ever because it has the power from hour to hour to rejoice the human spirit 'in fresh wise'. The 'wingèd beast' from Assyria seems its antithesis: the shadow it casts is unchanging and impenetrable.

Whereas Greek art frees the imagination, Assyrian art seems to mark its limit. It is as inscrutable as Blake's 'Tyger' (1794). Blake had asked, 'In what distant deeps or skies / Burnt the fire of thine eyes', and Rossetti echoes him: 'Ah! In what quarries lay the stone / From which this pigmy pile has grown' (91–2). Rossetti responds to the question, unlike Blake, by trying to domesticate the statue. The print that the statue still bears of its 'first rush-wrapping' prompts questions that recall the questions prompted in Keats by the Grecian Urn and the questions evoke forms of worship much like those that Keats imagines his Psyche deprived of:

> What song did the brown maidens sing,
> From purple mouths alternating
> When that was woven languidly?
>
> (23–5)

Keats's 'pale-mouthed prophet dreaming' becomes the Assyrian priests who '[y]earned pale in bitter ecstasy' (85). But the statue has a recalcitrant strangeness that refuses to be appropriated in this way:

A human face the creature wore,
And hoofs behind and hoofs before,
And flanks with dark runes fretted o'er.
'Twas bull, 'twas mitred Minotaur,
A dead disbowelled mystery.
(11–5)

Those runes are not translatable into Rossetti's Keatsian idiom. The shadow cast by the statue remains darkly obscure.

In the version of the poem published in 1856, Rossetti describes the beast as the 'elder' of any god of Greece, or Egypt, or Rome, prompting his brother to object that 'Egyptian civilization and art are far *older* than Ninevite'. Rossetti made the correction in his 1870 revision, and yet it is a revealing mistake. In 1856 Rossetti had whimsically imagined brown maidens singing from their purple mouths as the 'colour'd Arab straw-matting / Half-ripp'd' (21–2) was woven in which the beast was wrapped for the voyage that took it from the banks of the Euphrates to London. In 1870 the matting has impressed its pattern on the beast's flanks, so that there is no need to imagine a rush mat surviving through the centuries. But it remains a poem about the collapsing together of different times, a poem appropriate to the new British Museum, in which classical architecture is reproduced in an otherwise entirely modern building, and to the moment that the poem records, in which the winged beast casts on London stones the selfsame shadow that it had cast centuries before on the courts of Nineveh. A very similar conceit brings the poem to an end. Rossetti imagines London itself become, like Nineveh, an archaeological site, and the 'Great Bull' disinterred again by Australasian excavators who will view it as 'a relic now / of London, not of Nineveh!' (179–80) At once the statue, its flanks fretted with 'dark runes' that had resisted Rossetti's best attempts to read them, becomes all too legible:

Those heavy wings spread high,
So sure of flight, which do not fly;
That set gaze never on the sky …
(192–4)

Rossetti is reduced to a single, troubled question: 'O Nineveh was this thy God, – / Thine also, mighty Nineveh?' (199–200) The statue becomes fraught with meaning, but only when Rossetti stops looking at it as a work of art, and agrees to understand it simply as a symptom of the society that produced it, as a commodity rather like the 'corpulent, straggling epergne' that graces Mr Podsnap's dining table in Chapter XI of Dickens's *Our Mutual Friend*, and so perfectly embodies his philosophy of life that all his dinner guests feel as if it is being thrust down their throat with every morsel they eat. One impulse common amongst Victorian poets was to insist, just as stridently as the poets of the 1930s, that poets choose their subject matter from the here and now. It is a demand rehearsed robustly by Elizabeth Barrett Browning in her own aggressively modern epic, *Aurora Leigh*:

> Nay, if there's room for poets in this world
> A little overgrown (I think there is),
> Their sole work is to represent the age,
> Their age, not Charlemagne's,— this live, throbbing age,
> That brawls, cheats, maddens, calculates, aspires,
> And spends more passion, more heroic heat,
> Betwixt the mirrors of its drawing-rooms,
> Than Roland with his knights at Roncesvalles.
> (*Aurora Leigh*, 5, 200–7)

But it countered another impulse, often, even for Elizabeth Barrett Browning, just as strong, to define poetry by its distance from the modern world, which might be an imaginative distance as in 'The Palace of Art' or a historical distance as in 'The Burden of Nineveh'. Those poems, like Rossetti's, in which the far off and the here and now collide seem especially characteristic.

The treasures that Layard excavated from Nineveh and transported to the British Museum inspired the Nineveh Court in the Crystal Palace when it opened in 1854, after being transported from Hyde Park where the building had housed the Great Exhibition. John Davidson would not have inspected the reproductions of Layard's bull-gods when he visited the Palace in 1905 in the company of Max Beerbohm, and commemorated the event in a poem, because the Nineveh Court had been destroyed by fire on December 30, 1866, and was not rebuilt. Tennyson's Palace is built according to an architecture of the mind. The British Museum was designed by Robert Smirke, the leading neoclassical architect of his day.

The Crystal Palace by contrast was less a product of architecture than of engineering. In its first incarnation it had been erected in Hyde Park at a speed and at a cost possible only because it was constructed from factory-made, endlessly reproducible parts. It was the brainchild of Joseph Paxton, who brought to the task his experience of designing the great conservatory at Chatsworth. Tennyson's Palace expresses an idea of culture as the possession of the individual, the enclosed Soul, but the Soul is already conscious that its enjoyments might be construed as self-indulgent. She dreams, after she abandons the building, that she might one day return to it with 'others'. When the British Museum was opened for the first time on a public holiday, on Easter Monday, 1837, it attracted 23 895 visitors, an impressive number but one that shrinks into insignificance beside the six millions who bought tickets for the Crystal Palace in the six months in 1851 when it housed the Great Exhibition. These are crude figures but they point to one of the most significant stories of the nineteenth century, the story of the democratization of culture, made possible by national education, restricted working hours, and the provision of public libraries, museums and galleries. It is a process that Tennyson seems to look forward to in 'The Palace of Art' and still more in the 1840s when he wrote *The Princess* in which the tale of the foundation of a university for women is framed by an account of a Mechanics' Institute fete in the gardens of a country house. Almost a quarter of a century later, Rossetti seems conscious only of his difference from his fellow visitors to the Museum, the 'cold-pinch'd clerks', the minor clergy crimping their eyes at the exhibits, and the 'misses' tittering 'in their stays'. Even when he revised his poem for its 1870 publication he insisted on the difference between his own response to the museum's treasures, and the dim responses of the compact files of schoolchildren three abreast. The great majority of the poets of the century failed to benefit from the new mass readership that supported the earnings of novelists such as Dickens and George Eliot. No doubt that economic discrepancy encouraged poets to cultivate a certain disdain for the popular, but they seem also to have felt a real anxiety. Joseph Paxton met successfully what must have seemed the all but impossible demand that he complete in nine months and at minimal cost a building six times the size of St Paul's by making his building from industrially produced sheets of plate glass and cast iron rods and girders. The anxiety was that the demands of the new reading public could be met only by writers just as willing to mechanise their methods of production. These are not fears one would have expected John Davidson to harbour when he visited the

Crystal Palace. He was after all a Scot, brought up in modest circumstances in Greenock, an unlovely industrial town on the Clyde,

> where hammers clang
> On iron hulls, and cranes in harbour creak
> Rattle and swing, whole cargoes on their necks.
> ('A Ballad in Blank Verse'
> (1894), 26–8)

But in 'The Crystal Palace' (1908) Davidson far outruns Rossetti in his disdain for the populace.

The poem begins abruptly, 'Contraption, – that's the bizarre, proper slang, / Eclectic word' (1–2). 'Contraption' had once been a west-country dialect word. It only developed its modern sense in which it denotes an unadmired mechanical device during the nineteenth century. In the poem it is the just word for Hiram Maxim's 'captive flying machine', a 'portentous toy' that had been erected outside the Crystal Palace in 1904, the year before Davidson's visit. Maxim, best known for his invention of the Maxim gun that was to prove so effective in World War One, also experimented unsuccessfully with flying machines of which the captive flying machine was a by-product. The decline from the dream of powered flight to the provision of sophisticated fairground rides (in 1904 captive flying machines were installed at Earl's Court, Blackpool and Sydenham) is itself a neat indication of what happened when the Crystal Palace was moved from Hyde Park to its new site south of the river. The building designed to house the Great Exhibition, which had been planned by Prince Albert to illustrate how science and art might be applied to industrial purposes and to demonstrate to the world Britain's technological supremacy, became when it was re-erected in Sydenham the world's first theme park. More pertinently, Davidson's opening line alerts the reader to the fact that his own poem is a contraption at least as bizarre as Hiram Maxim's. The whole poem is written in a 'bizarre, proper slang' that finds its proper emblem in Maxim's flying machine, or, as the poem later describes it (Tibetans have been imagined to mistake the machine for an advanced kind of prayer wheel), 'the Tartar's volant oratory' (67). The poet attempts to fix the flying machine as the object of his derision, but contrives somehow to manufacture a phrase so strange that it resembles the machine more persuasively than it mocks it.

In 'The Burden of Nineveh' chronology puckers: an Assyrian shadow falls on London stone. Something similar seems to happen in 'The Crystal

Palace'. The building still seemed aggressively modern even in 1905. It is 'a shed / Intended for a palace' that recalls the 'fossil of a giant myriapod' (21–3). The thought is suggested, perhaps, by the Palace's Dinosaur Court that housed the first dinosaur sculptures in the world. But for Davidson the building itself is like a fossil because it seems independent of time: it resembles the prehistoric because it is posthistoric:

> no mood
> Can make your glass and iron beautiful.
> Colossal ugliness may fascinate
> If something be expressed; and time adopts
> Ungainliest stone and brick and ruins them
> To beauty; but a building lacking life,
> A house that must not mellow or decay? –
> 'Tis nature's outcast.
>
> (28–35)

On the face of it, nothing could be more distant from the austere simplicity of Paxton's architecture than the style of Davidson's poem that so consistently calls attention to itself by its sheer oddity. Davidson, it is true, freely admits technical terms, a crustacean's 'gannoid skeleton' (18) (the word is more usually spelt ganoid), a mason's 'ashlar' (38), which might bring his poem into alignment with a building in which architecture is so firmly subordinated to engineering. The difference is that Davidson's technical terms are decorative, constituting not so much a rejection as a parodic reinstatement of poetic diction. A slice of lemon, for example, becomes a 'starred bisection' (193). Paxton's was a democratic building, suspicious of replicating the hierarchical spatial orders of conventional architecture (though these are not wholly avoided). The primary function of Davidson's diction, by contrast, is to secure his distance from the crowd, the mob, that, in Davidson's idiolect are denied even the tiny distinction of a definite article, 'here's crowd, here's mob' (42), 'For this is Mob, unhappy locust-swarm' (132), 'Crowd; Mob; a blur of faces featureless / Of forms inane' (144–5). Rossetti's amused detachment from the typical museum visitor has hardened into a fierce, proto-Modernist disdain. Davidson looks more sympathetically, perhaps, at the flush on the cheeks of the young slum-dwellers with their '[t]orn coats and ragged dresses' (91) as they cling together on the dance floor, 'solemn youths / Sustaining ravished donahs!' (86–7). He even borrows from them the vocabulary that he uses to describe them. 'Donahs' is a slang term for sweethearts that derives from the Spanish or Portuguese and seems to have been first introduced by circus people. But Davidson accommodates such words within a syntax that maintains by its formality his distance from the dancers. So too do his rhythms. Davidson made large claims for his versification ('I use blank verse newly as Wagner did music'), and what he most prided himself on was not writing verse at all likely to make his readers tap their feet: 'You can't sing-song my blank verse'.[21]

It seems odd that John Davidson, who had left the west of Scotland where he was an underpaid schoolteacher to become an impoverished journalist in London, whose most famous poem, 'Thirty Bob a Week', celebrates the unnoticed heroism of the underpaid clerk, should so far outdo Tennyson and Rossetti in his contempt for the people. He presents the Crystal Palace, in an unusually flat phrase, as the 'Victorian temple of commercialism' (14), which he defines as the antithesis of the temple of art in which he is himself a worshipper. But if he points the antithesis more stridently than Tennyson or Rossetti, that may be because he was still less able than them to secure a living by the practice of his art. The visitors to the Palace are 'wedged / So tightly' they can 'neither clap nor stamp' (285–6), and yet the library is almost empty: 'Three people in the silent Reading room / Regard us darkly as we enter' (293–4). It is a mordant comment on the place of literature in English cultural life at the beginning of the twentieth century. Davidson parades rather ostentatiously a power of aesthetic discrimination that the designers of the exhibitions have failed to match. They have placed side by side in the sculpture gallery reproductions of Cellini's Perseus and 'a stupid thing' by Canova (258–9), 'Verrochio's Coleone' (270) (the spelling of neither word is standard, and one wonders whether Davidson's connoisseurship is quite so assured as he pretends), and an 'absurd' equestrian statue by Clesinger (268–9). But such supposed lapses of taste mean nothing to the '[c]ourageous folk' who dance a cakewalk 'beneath / The brows of Michael Angelo's Moses' (290–2) (folk who may have lingered in the mind of T.S. Eliot, an admirer of Davidson, when his women come and go, talking of Michelangelo). Success is available in such a world only to those like the curate encountered in the deserted billiard room who 'undertakes / to entertain and not to preach' (238–9):

> It's with the theatre and the music-hall,
> Actor and artiste, the parson must compete.
> (240–1)

The man of letters is in the same unhappy predicament, but Davidson clearly finds the curate's cynicism shocking (like many nineteenth-century atheists he can often seem more pious than any but the most devout believer). Artistic integrity, it seems, does not allow such compromises, but Davidson's relationship with the Palace and its other visitors is more complex than this suggests.

It is a society of consumers. For visitors to the Palace '[t]he business and the office of the day' is '[t]he eating and the drinking', and in this, if in little else, Davidson joins the crowd. He still claims to be distinguished by the refinement of his taste, but this becomes a disconcertingly literal claim when exemplified in his enjoyment of a grilled sole that he accompanies with a choice claret 'a decade old; not more' (203):

> The delicate texture of the foam-white fish,
> Evolving palatable harmony
> That music might by happy chance express.
> (197–9)

All that distinguishes him from the vulgar diners seems to be that he has, for once in his life at least, the funds to be choosier. The crowd is attracted to the Crystal Palace by the exhibits. Davidson signals his superiority by inspecting the crowd as if it was itself the most striking object in the exhibition. But the superiority that he claims is precarious. In the end, 'The Crystal Palace', like 'The Palace of Art' and 'The Burden of Nineveh' works to problematise rather than to define the relationship between poets and the people, or between art and society.

This book will offer an introduction to Victorian poetry, that is, to the poetry written in the years that separated Romanticism from the Modernist poetry that began to be written in the second decade of the twentieth century. The descriptive labels that I have used suggest one way in which it differs from the poetry that preceded and followed it. Romanticism and Modernism denote literary programmes as much as they denote literary periods, even if they were programmes never clearly agreed by those supposed to have established them, and even if literary scholars have disputed ever since how those programmes might best be defined. Victorian poetry, on the other hand, denotes only a period. It refers simply to the poetry written in the reign of a particular queen. It is a very long period. Victoria remains the longest-reigning British monarch, although it is a distinction that she seems likely soon to lose. I have selected the three poems on which I have focused in this chapter in part because to move from one to the other calls attention to that long lapse of years. For Arthur Hallam, Tennyson is a member of the same poetic school as Keats and Shelley. When John Davidson looks at revellers dancing the cakewalk beneath a cast of Michelangelo's Moses, he seems almost contemporary with T.S. Eliot. Rossetti, on the other hand, may gaze at a relic of Nineveh that seems to mock the passage of time, but he gazes at it, especially in the first version of the poem, from an emphatically mid-century London pavement. The statue had only recently been unearthed by Henry Layard, and the topic of conversation amongst the students taking their lunch at the Museum is the challenge to the authority of the Royal Academy newly orchestrated by Rossetti and his friends. Another of my reasons for choosing the three poems is that they all describe collections remarkable for the heterogeneousness of their contents. The cultural museums represented in all three closely resemble curiosity shops, and in this they accurately figure the poetry of the period. One of my aims in the chapters that follow is to represent as best I can the sheer variety of Victorian poetry. But I want also to suggest some of the qualities that seem characteristic of Victorian poetry, or at least a large number of Victorian poems. Any one of these qualities might, I am aware, be located in poetry of other periods. It is their co-presence in so much of the period's poetry that underpins my claim that they are representative, but I advance all such claims only tentatively.

The variousness of Victorian poetry might itself, I want to suggest, be thought of as a distinctive Victorian quality, and not just because Victoria reigned for so long. Variety is predictable in the work of poets who had internalized, as earlier poets had not, the long history of English poetry, a history which was supplemented for most of them by poetry in a number of other languages both ancient and modern. This is a book about British poetry. Indeed, it is very largely a book about English poetry, but in the nineteenth century that term was already ambiguous, signifying either the poetry of a particular nation or the poetry written in a particular language. I have registered that second sense not only by including some Scottish and Irish poets, such as John Davidson in this chapter, but also by accepting that a poet such as Toru Dutt, born in Calcutta, might also be thought of as Victorian poet. I have even admitted American poems when it seemed appropriate. This is not because I wish to join my voice to those who have argued that Victorian poetry is best thought of as an Atlantic phenomenon, but because an interest in America is so characteristic of Victorian England and its poets. It was not just because of his family connections with America that Arthur Hugh Clough was known as Yankee Clough. Claude, the hero of *Amours de Voyage*, his finest poem, is a very English figure who cannot be understood without reference to the great English institution, the University of Oxford, that produced him, and yet Clough's poem was first published in a Boston magazine, the *Atlantic Monthly*. There was no English edition in Clough's lifetime. G.K. Chesterton's *Robert Browning*, first published in 1903, is the first great study of a Victorian poet, and Chesterton insists on Browning's emphatic Englishness, but Chesterton does not think that Englishness compromised by Browning's many American friends, nor by the fact that his poems were for many years more widely read in America than in his own country, which is why it seems so natural that Chesterton, when selecting a poet with whom to compare him, should so often happen on Walt Whitman. There is surely no more English a Victorian novel than Thomas Hughes's *Tom Brown's Schooldays*, and yet Hughes, when he selected the verse epigraphs with which he introduces his chapters, chose, as well as two quotations from Tennyson, two quotations from James Russell Lowell.

I have already suggested that the poems by Tennyson, Rossetti and Davidson seem all to imagine a vexed relationship between art and its consumers. All three poems seem to have had their origin in exclusive (and, as it happens, exclusively male) gatherings of the like-minded. 'The Palace of Art', long before it was published, was celebrated amongst Tennyson's closest university friends, almost all of whom were members of the select Cambridge society known as the Apostles. 'Only think of an "Apostolic" dinner next Friday', wrote James Spedding to another member. 'Only think of 'The Palace of Art".[22] Rossetti first published his poem in the *Oxford and Cambridge Magazine*, so that it seemed a by-product of his exuberant collaboration with the magazine's editor, William Morris, and Burne Jones in the production of murals for the Oxford Union. Davidson's 'The Crystal Palace' is the outcome of a more unlikely meeting, between the alcoholic Scottish poet and the dandiacal Max Beerbohm. But the exclusivity of those meetings prompts all three poets to consider their relationship with the wider public. Tennyson's Soul is inspired to make a high-minded promise that if she returns to her palace it will be 'with others'. This seems very unlike John Davidson's blustering disdain for the populace ('For this is Mob, unhappy locust-swarm' (132)), but the two have in common and share with many poets of the century a preoccupation with their relationship with the anonymous public that read, but still more often did not read, their poems. All three poems exemplify the odd collisions that so many Victorian poems effect between the present and the past, between the modern world and those vanished worlds with which the poems of the past have to do. The three poems seem to me representative of the century's poetry, too, in their self-consciousness, a self-consciousness evident in their verse forms, in their rhythms and in their diction as much as in their self-reflexiveness. It is the self-consciousness of Victorian poetry that I will turn to in my next chapter.

Endnotes

1. George Saintsbury, *A History of English Prosody*, 3 vols (London: Macmillan, 1910), 3, p. 351.
2. See Robert Cummings (1992) 'Tennyson, Trench, Tholuck and the "Oriental" Metre of *Locksley Hall*, *Translation and Literature*, **1**, 127–33.
3. See Arthur Hallam, 'The Influence of Italian upon English Literature', collected in *The Writings of Arthur Hallam*, ed. T.H. Vail Motter (London: Oxford University Press, 1943), pp. 216 and 218.
4. See Lionel Stevenson, 'The "High-Born Maiden" Symbol in Tennyson', in *Critical Essays on the Poetry of Tennyson*, ed. John Killham (London: Routledge and Kegan Paul, 1960).
5. Arthur Hallam, 'On Some of the Characteristics of Modern Poetry, and on the Lyrical Poems of Alfred Tennyson'
6. Richard Chenevix Trench, *Letters and Memorials*, ed. Mary Chenevix Trench, 2 vols (London: Kegan Paul and Trench), 1, p. 93.
7. Quoted in *Tennyson: Interviews and Recollections*, ed. Norman Page (Basingstoke: Macmillan, 1983), p. 71.
8. *Tennyson: Interviews and Recollections*, ed. Norman Page, p. 64.
9. Robert Douglas-Fairhurst, *Victorian Afterlives: The Shaping of Influence in Nineteenth-Century Literature* (Oxford: Oxford University Preess, 2002), pp. 6–8.
10. John Churton Collins (1880) 'A New Study of Tennyson', *Cornhill Magazine*, **41** (January), 36–50. Tennyson annotated the article indignantly.
11. Isobel Armstrong: *Victorian Poetry: Poetry, Poetics and Politics* (London and New York: Routledge, 1993), p. 3.
12. *Further Letters of Gerard Manley Hopkins*, ed. Claude Colleer Abbott (London: Oxford University Press, 1956), p. 219.
13. Browning's essay is reprinted in Robert Browning, *The Poems*, ed. John Pettigrew and Thomas J. Collins, 1, 999–1013.
14. *The Letters of Arthur Hallam*, ed. Jack Kolb (Columbus, Ohio: Ohio State University Press, 1981), pp. 661–2.

15. *Tennyson: The Critical Heritage*, ed. John D. Jump (London: Routledge and Kegan Paul, 1967), p. 121.
16. Hallam Tennyson, *Alfred Lord Tennyson: A Memoir*, 2 vols (London: Macmillan, 1897), 1, pp. 118–9.
17. Hallam Tennyson, *Alfred Lord Tennyson: A Memoir*, 1, 68.
18. In 'What is Poetry?' (1833), *John Stuart Mill: Essays on Poetry*, ed. F. Parvin Sharpless (Columbia, South Carolina: University of South Carolina Press, 1976), p. 12.
19. Quoted in J. Mordaunt Crook, *The British Museum* (London: Allen Lane, 1972), p. 62.
20. *Yale Edition of Horace Walpole's Correspondence*, ed. W.S. Lewis, 48 vols, 20 (London: Oxford University Press, 1960), pp. 358–9.
21. *The Poems of John Davidson*, ed. Andrew Turnbull (Edinburgh and London: Scottish Academic Press, 1973), p. xxxi.
22. Hallam Tennyson, *Alfred Lord Tennyson: A Memoir*, 1, 85.

2

The Divided Self and the Dramatic Monologue

Keats has claims to be the single most pervasive influence on Victorian poetry. His claim might be challenged by Wordsworth, but Wordsworth would never have offered, as did Keats, a warning that '[n]ot one word I ever utter can be taken for granted as an opinion growing out of my identical nature.'[1] And yet Wordsworth is a poet of memory, and memory is as likely to issue in a sense of self-division as in a consoling sense of continuity. When he remembers, Wordsworth writes, he sometimes seems 'Two consciousnesses, conscious of myself / And of some other Being' (*Prelude*, 1850, 2, 32–3). Browning, as might be expected, insisted in his advertisement to *Dramatic Lyrics* that his poems were 'dramatic in principle, and so many utterances of so many imaginary persons, not mine' (1842), but Swinburne too, in a defence of his own *Poems and Ballads* (1866), made a similar claim when he stipulated that 'no utterance of enjoyment or despair, belief or unbelief, can properly be assumed as the assertion of its author's personal feelings or faith.'[2] Some of his critics granted his case, but remained unreassured. 'Confusing … the lyrical and the dramatic,' one of them observed, 'has a decided tendency to pruriency and vice'.[3] Elegy, even more pressingly than other kinds of lyric, might seem to demand of elegists that they maintain, if only as a polite fiction, that the emotions they feel are continuous with the emotions that they express, but that was not Tennyson's view in *In Memoriam* (1850). At the very beginning of the sequence, he opens up a gap between himself and his words. Far from expressing his grief, his verses are the best means he has of distracting himself from it:

> But, for the unquiet heart and brain,
> A use in measured language lies;
> The sad mechanic exercise,
> Like dull narcotics, numbing pain.
>
> (v, 5–8)

Reading Victorian Poetry, First Edition. Richard Cronin.

As Isobel Armstrong observes, the Victorians characteristically produced double poems, by which she means poems that offer themselves at once as the medium through which the reader is invited to gaze at the world, and as themselves the objects of that gaze.[4] It is a peculiarly suggestive remark. Indeed, almost the whole of this book is an attempt to unpack the various senses that the expression accommodates.

On one level the phrase recognizes that Victorian poets often record an awareness that in the act of composition they experience a sense of being divided from themselves. The lyric 'I' is for them a compound rather than a simple subject, 'My Heart and I', as Barrett Browning expresses it in the title of one of her poems (1862). It is a thought that Tennyson accommodates in a late section of *In Memoriam*, when he asks, 'What find I in the highest place, / But mine own phantom chanting hymns?' (cviii, 9–10) In Victorian poems, as Augusta Webster warns in her essay 'Poets and Personal Pronouns' (1878), 'as a rule, I does not mean I'.[5] For Arthur Symons that lack of coincidence between the self and the self is one reason for the close affinity between poetry and the music hall, a favourite venue for the poets of the 1890s. He shares John Davidson's humiliating sense that the poet just as much as the parson is a public entertainer who must compete with every other variety of public entertainment, and the thought works to make him into the detached spectator of his own performance:

> My life is like a music-hall,
> Where in the impotence of rage,
> Chained by enchantment to my stall,
> I see myself upon the stage
> Dance to amuse a music-hall.
> ('Prologue' to *London Nights*
> (1895), 1–5)

He regards the performers with an amused superiority, and yet he recognizes in them the 'vacancy' that he feels in himself. As he lounges in his seat, smoking, and laughs 'for vacancy' as he watches the dancers, he is aware, 'It is my very self I see / Across the cloudy cigarette' (9–10). His inner vacancy is deftly voiced by a stanza in which the final line empties rather than completes the measure, by dissolving rhyme into repetition. His poem, he acknowledges, is as much an 'empty song' (13) as those he sees performed on stage.

A similar experience is rendered very differently in Augusta Webster's 'Faded' (1870, first published 1893). A woman contemplates a youthful portrait of herself, and finds that the experience dissolves rather than confirms her grasp of her own identity: 'Myself has faded from me; I am old.' (36) As she gazes at the portrait , she experiences no Wordsworthian confidence that the days of her life are 'bound each to each' ('My heart leaps up' (1807), 9), only a bleak confirmation that she is separated from her youthful self as abruptly as the dead are separated from the living. She can bring herself to gaze at her youthful portrait only at the brief, precarious moment of twilight, in the 'hushed, hueless light' (10) when 'we too a little time are one' (17). The poem is a dramatic monologue in which Webster, who was in her early thirties, married, and mother to a young daughter, speaks as a woman who, in remaining single, has missed 'a woman's destiny and sole hope.' (103) Such women are 'irretrievable bankrupts of [their] very selves,' (70) their fate predicted in a dream that the speaker remembers from when she was young, a nightmare in which she found herself in the midst of her family, speaking to them, hugging them, but all unnoticed, because, as a voice explains to her, she is dead. Webster was a supporter of the woman's suffrage movement and an acquaintance of Frances Power Cobbe and John Stuart Mill. In 'Faded' she is addressing her interest in the lot of unmarried women in the nineteenth century, but also, if less evidently, in the lot of Victorian poets. Aged speakers, and characters like Tennyson's Tiresias (1885, though first drafted 1833), Tithonus (1860) and Enoch Arden (1864), condemned to a posthumous life, proved oddly congenial even to youthful Victorian poets, presumably because through them they could express a sense that they were practising an art of the past, an art that in the modern world might, it seemed, soon become obsolete. In 'Faded', the portrait, unlike its subject, does not age, but this does not figure for Webster the power of art to transcend time. The painted woman's cheeks may preserve their 'gloss of almond-bloom' (26), but the speaker knows that it is only a matter of time before the portrait like the sitter is superseded, consigned to the attic, its place usurped by some newer model. Only then will the woman and her portrait become 'one again,' (164) reunited in neglect.

Other poems address the poet's lot more directly, but, as in 'Faded', the effect is often to divide the poem's speakers from themselves. Tennyson's *Morte d'Arthur* (1842), for example, is enclosed in a frame that offers the poem not as the work of Tennyson but of another university poet, Everard Hall, who dismisses his poem as '[m]ere chaff and draff, much better burnt' ('The Epic', 40). When Everard agrees to read the poem aloud, his college friends listen rapt, but the parson, the representative of the older generation, offers his own silent commentary on the poem's merits by falling asleep. A.H. Clough similarly encloses his *Dipsychus* (1865, but probably drafted in 1850) in a prose frame in which the poem is read by its author to his uncle, who is not much impressed: 'I won't say I didn't drop into a doze while the young man was drivelling through his later soliloquies'. The irony in both cases seems nervously defensive, an attempt to forestall hostile responses, but similar devices are employed by poets much less given to self-deprecation.

In the 1850s there was a short-lived fashion, closely associated with the group of poets who became known as the Spasmodics, for the composition of poems about poets. *Maud* (1855) was widely identified as Tennyson's own Spasmodic poem, but *Blackwood's* was thankful that in one respect at least Tennyson had preserved his difference: his speaker 'is not – let us be grateful – a poet'.[6] Young poets anxious to win fame wrote ambitious poems that took as their subject a young poet's struggle to write the poem that would make him famous. The young poets were admirers of Philip Bailey's *Festus* (1837, revised and expanded in successive editions until Bailey's death), a poem of ever-increasing length that inspired in many nineteenth-century readers an enthusiasm that more recent readers have failed to share. In one crucial scene an aspiring poet comes to Festus looking for instruction, and Festus recommends to him the work of a poet friend, who 'wrote amid the ruins' of his own heart, 'They were his throne and theme' (I quote from the 1848 edition of the poem in which the lines are not numbered). His poem is remarkable for the vastness of its theme and the looseness of its construction ('It has a plan, but no plot. Life hath none'), and it is predictable that Festus should confess at last (p. 266) that he is himself that poet. It is equally unsurprising that the poem that he describes seems indistinguishable from *Festus* itself.

In the 1850s the example of Bailey was supplemented by that of Wordsworth, whose *Prelude*, belatedly published after Wordsworth's death in 1850, made of the 'Growth of a Poet's Mind' the central poetic topic. But the differences between Wordsworth and his Victorian successors are more interesting than the similarities. For Wordsworth becoming a poet is indistinguishable from becoming himself. He makes of blank verse a metre so adept in representing the activity of the reflective mind that the turns of the lines seem identical with the turns of thought that they map. By contrast, the blank verse of Alexander Smith in his *Life-Drama* (1853) insistently obtrudes itself on the reader's attention. A reminiscence of a young poet who, stung by a rebuff, 'foamed at God and died', prompts an invitation to 'rain similes upon his corse like tears' (in the first edition from which I quote the lines are not numbered). He is a frail, March flower, a 'Lapland fool' who runs mad because his own poor hut cannot match in grandeur the aurora borealis. At that point a less reverent speaker interrupts to compare him to a 'ginger-beer bottle burst' (pp. 139–40). Smith is dryly mocking the frenetically figurative character of his own poetic manner, and the effect is to open up a gap between himself and his style.

The character of Wordsworth's blank verse is appropriate to a narrative in which the poet's acquisition of technical skills is wholly subsumed into an account of the growth of his mind. The poem concludes on the summit of Snowden as Wordsworth ordains himself the poet-priest that his age demands. The business of becoming a poet is made to seem all but independent of the business of writing poems, and completely independent of the business of having them published (a posture reinforced by the long-delayed publication of the *Prelude* itself). In the poems of the 1850s things are very different. Sydney Dobell's Balder is given to quoting from his own poems at tedious length, chief amongst them his 'early planned, / Long meditate, and slowly written epic!', (p. 24) a work that seems very similar to *Balder* (1853). J. Westland Marston's Gerald, in the poem named after him (1842), is also a poet. He is embittered by neglect, and only saved from suicide by a visit from Lord Roxmore, who wishes on behalf of himself and his wife to thank the author of the poem that has transformed their lives. Gerald dies young, but not before the appearance of newspaper articles belatedly recognizing his greatness. John Stanyan Biggs's *Night and the Soul* (1854, the lines are not numbered) ends with Alexis reading one of his poems to his friends. They are unlikely to be surprised when he explains, 'The Poet's mighty mission is its theme' (p. 183). At the end of Smith's *A Life-Drama* Walter, the poet-hero, embarks on a life of domestic contentment with the woman that he has raped and then abandoned, but not before he has recorded his agonies of remorse in a poem that becomes a publishing sensation. 'That was a hit!' one of his friends assures us: 'The world is murmuring like a hive of bees; / He is its theme' (p. 182). The relationship between Walter's poem and *A Life Drama* is teasing in a manner that exactly matches the relationship between Walter and Alexander Smith. When he published *A Life Drama*, Smith, who had left school at the age of ten, was still employed as a designer in a Glasgow textile factory. His hero, Walter, has an estate in Kent, and is confident enough of his social position to refer to a tenant as 'one of my peasants' (p. 86). And yet, within the poem, Walter admits that one of his tales is his own life story 'tricked out in a quaint disguise' (p. 145), and intermittently throughout the poem the disguise slips. Whenever it does so, Walter is revealed as a quite different person, someone indistinguishable from Smith himself: 'Within a city One was born to toil / Whose heart could not mate with the common doom' (p. 131). His hero, it seems, is Alexander Smith tricked out in 'a quaint disguise', and his poem a fiction to which Smith's reader is invited to respond as Violet does to Walter's poems:

> you shine though each disguise;
> You are a masker in a mask of glass,
> You've such transparent sides, each casual eye
> May see the heaving heart.
>
> (p. 145)

The vocabulary of masks and disguises works at once to suggest that the author is identical to his character and to preserve a difference between them.

The major Victorian poem of this kind is Elizabeth Barrett Browning's *Aurora Leigh* (1856) in which the twenty-seven-year-old Aurora at last succeeds in writing her 'long poem' (5, 1213), the 'unscrupulously epic' work that was needed if ever the 'full-veined, heaving, double-breasted Age' she lived in was to be adequately represented. (5, 214–6) The book is a critical success, winning the respect of friends such as the painter, Vincent Carrington, and so admired by its young female readers that one of them, Carrington's fiancée, insists that he paint her wearing a cloak like Aurora's with Aurora's 'last book folded in her dimpled hands' (7, 607). Romney Leigh, her cousin, had mocked Aurora when she declared her vocation, confidently assuring her, even as he was asking for her hand in marriage, that, though women may make 'doating mothers, and perfect wives' they will never make a poet (2, 222). But after reading the new poem, he is persuaded to make a humble recantation and then to renew his marriage proposal. The success of Aurora's poem anticipates the success of *Aurora Leigh*, but the relation between the two poems remains problematical. Elizabeth Barrett Browning's husband had thought her earlier work distinguished from his own by her willingness to speak in her own voice: 'You speak out, *you*, – I only make men and women speak – give you truth broken into prismatic hues, and fear the pure white light.'[7] But *Aurora Leigh* seems committed to an aesthetic of division, which is an aesthetic that Barrett Browning and her husband held in common.

Its first five books constitute a poetic autobiography. Aurora reviews the events of the past that have made her the woman and the poet that she has become. As in the *Prelude* the reader is invited to identify the first-person narrative with the 'long poem' with which Aurora marks her achievement of poetic maturity. But the *Prelude* ends in rapt self-contemplation, as Wordsworth gazes from the peak of Snowden and sees above him the 'Moon hung naked in a firmament / Of azure', at his feet 'a silent sea of hoary mist' unbroken but for a single 'rift' through which

> Mounted the roar of waters, torrents, streams
> Innumerable, roaring with one voice!

He recognizes the landscape as 'the emblem of a mind / That feeds upon infinity', which is at once his own mind and the mind the growth of which his poem has charted. (*Prelude*, 1850, 14, 40–70) When Aurora achieves her poetic maturity she does not feel her sense of her own personal identity confirmed. She feels it melt away:

> Most like some passive lump of broken salt
> Dropt in by chance to a bowl of oenomel,
> To spoil the drink a little and lose itself,
> Dissolving slowly, slowly, until lost.
> (7, 1308–11)

The poem's second part is as discordant with its first as that salt is with the honeyed wine. Aurora no longer writes as someone in control of her story. Past are interrupted by present tenses as the narrative is delivered piece-meal, and has to be constructed by the reader from a series of diary entries. Aurora is no longer claiming and pursuing her own vocation, but is all at sea – sometimes literally so, as when she crosses the Channel and when she voyages from Marseilles to Genoa. In Paris she recognizes Marian Erle, the young woman of the working classes who had jilted her cousin, Romney Leigh, on their wedding day. Romney had proposed to Marian after being rejected by Aurora, seeking a marriage that would effect a symbolic reconciliation between the classes, but Marian had been persuaded by the villainous Lady Waldemar that such a marriage would disgrace him. At Lady Waldemar's instigation, Marian is given into the care of a woman who had once dressed Lady Waldemar's hair, taken to France, inveigled into a brothel, drugged, and raped. She succumbs to madness, only to find on her recovery that she has fallen pregnant. Aurora believes until she listens to Marian's story that Marian's status as an unmarried mother constitutes incontestable evidence of her disgrace. It is one of a number of misapprehensions of which she must be disabused. She believes that, after being jilted by Marian, Romney had married Lady Waldemar. When Romney travels to Italy and arrives at the house she has taken outside Florence she believes him to be a married man. She does not even notice that he has been blinded in the fire when Leigh Hall was burnt down by the joint efforts of Romney's neighbours who are outraged that he has converted his house into an Owenite commune for the urban dispossessed, and the dispossessed themselves, the beneficiaries of Romney's charity who have found his austere high-mindedness constraining.

A poem that for half its length seems to follow Wordsworth in identifying as the epic theme of the modern age the growth of the poet's own mind suddenly performs an about-turn, and finds that the true epics of the modern age are not its poems but its novels. The poem begins to model itself on prose fiction rather than on epic poetry, fiction from Richardson's *Clarissa* to the industrial novels of the 1840s and *Jane Eyre*. The epic task for the poet, it now seems, is not to look inwards at her own mind, nor even to find a place for herself in the long poetic tradition of Western Europe as Aurora sets out to do in Book Five. The pressing task is now to look outwards at the world, and to find materials for poetry in what that world has to offer; drawing-room treacheries, urban prostitution, railways and class conflict:

> Nay, if there's room for poets in this world
> A little overgrown (I think there is),
> Their sole work is to represent the age,
> Their age, not Charlemagne's, – this live, throbbing age,
> That brawls, cheats, maddens, calculates, aspires,
> And spends more passion, more heroic heat,
> Betwixt the mirrors of its drawing-rooms,
> Than Roland with his knights at Roncesvalles.
>
> (5, 200–7)

If *Aurora Leigh* is epic it is 'unscrupulously epic' (5, 214), challenging the epic tradition still more radically than Wordsworth, who could plausibly claim that in locating the epic action within the mind he was completing a lengthy process of generic evolution that had been instigated by Milton. Hers is, as she described it to Robert Browning, 'a sort of novel-poem', but it is a poem that seems to reinforce as much as it challenges the difference between novels and poems.

Elizabeth Barrett Browning, like her Romantic predecessors, often indulged her nostalgia for a world of undifferentiated unity, an unfallen world where the divisions that rack the world as we experience it no longer obtain:

We divide
This apple of life, and cut it through the pips:
The perfect round which fitted Venus' hand
Has perished as utterly as if we ate
Both halves.
(*Aurora Leigh*, 7, 769–73)

The division she has in mind here is between nature and spirit. The poem ends when that division disappears in 'the thought of perfect noon', with the building on earth of the New Jerusalem:

'Jasper first,' I said,
'And second, sapphire; third, chalcedony;
The rest in order, – last, an amethyst.'
(9, 962–4)

But even as Browning offers the apple as the 'perfect round', the figure for unfallen unity, she admits that for her it remains a fruit made up of two halves. The claim that nature and spirit are indistinguishable fades repeatedly into the notion that they are distinct but complementary, two worlds rather than one, as when she confesses the belief that she draws from Swedenborg (and, it may be, from her interest in séances and mediums) that the material world has a spiritual counterpart:

There's not a flower of spring
That dies ere June, but vaunts itself allied
By issue and symbol, by significance
And correspondence, to that spirit-world

> Outside the limits of our space and time,
> Whereto we are bound.
>
> (5, 120–5)

Aurora Leigh is built out of a long sequence of divisions; between men and women and between the head and the heart – 'Men and women make / The world, as head and heart make human life', (2, 132–3) Romney assures Aurora, who has jibbed at the notion that the headache is 'too noble for [her] sex' (it is the heartache that is 'the woman's special, proper ache' (2, 110–2)) – between the classes, between Italy and England, between Aurora's art with its appeal to the inner being and Romney's political economy that ministers only to the outward person, and divisions within Aurora herself, between the woman and the artist. The poem attempts to resolve them, but they survive. The world, as Elizabeth Barrett Browning represents it in *Aurora Leigh* is defined by its divisions. It is a 'twofold sphere' inhabited by a 'twofold man' (7, 777), and the true poet is the individual who experiences that twofoldedness most intensely:

> O sorrowful great gift
> Conferred on poets, of a twofold life,
> When one life has been found enough for pain!
>
> (5, 380–2)

The self-divisions that might seem to disable Aurora are in fact what qualify her to write the epic of her age. It is, in Aurora's words, a 'full-veined, heaving, double-breasted Age' (5, 216). It is an age, then, of which the epic poet must be a woman, but that is because the women of the nineteenth century have a more intimate experience than their male contemporaries of the fractured (or doubled) subjectivity that qualifies them to represent a divided world. 'Shine out for two, Aurora' (9, 910), Romney urges. He means that he is blind, so that Aurora must shine for him too, but he also manages, even if unconsciously, to pay tribute to the double vision that makes Aurora a poet.

The poem's blank verse shares its divided character. Metaphors are consistently insubordinate, regularly going beyond their explanatory function to claim a frenetic life of their own. In *Aurora Leigh* the poem's events and its figures of speech seem to exist on distinct, though connected, planes. It is, as Romney understands by the time that he journeys to Italy, the artist's peculiar function to make connections between the spiritual and material worlds:

> Art's a service – mark:
> A silver key is given to thy clasp,
> And thou shalt stand unwearied, night and day,
> And fix it in the hard, slow-turning wards,
> To open, so, that intermediate door
> Betwixt the different planes of sensuous form
> And form insensuous.
>
> (9, 915–21)

In defiance of what he means to say, he fixes Aurora, freezes her in a single position, turning a key that will only ever be about to open a passage from the 'sensuous' world to the 'insensuous'. One reason that the door never quite opens is the metaphor that Browning deploys. The lock with its 'hard, slow-turning wards' separates rather than connects the two worlds. It resists the attempt to dissolve it into an idea even more stoutly than the wards resist the key. The lines that Romney speaks are representative of a good deal of the poem: they read as if language had been arrested at a point just as it was about to turn into poetry. That is what some of its first reviewers objected to, and it is what made the poem unreadable for most readers in the early twentieth century, but it is perhaps the only language in which Browning's 'novel-poem', her unscrupulous epic, could be written.

Browning claims for her poem the virtue that Romney Leigh recognized in Aurora's own long poem: 'But, in this last book, / You showed me something separate from yourself'. (8, 605–6) When the poem was half completed, she described it to her mentor, John Kenyon, as the 'autobiography of a poetess – (not me).'[8] In the dash and the bracketed phrase Browning marks the difference between her poem and the *Prelude*, and she marks too the poem's Victorian character. That same distinction or something very like it was frequently insisted on by her contemporaries. Given Tennyson's close friendship with Arthur Hallam, it is almost startling that he should warn the reader of *In Memoriam*, '"I" is not always the author speaking of himself.'[9] A humdrum example may be still more revealing. The afterlife of Macaulay's 'Horatius' (1842) was as a stirring recitation piece: it was once much favoured by histrionic schoolmasters at elementary schools for boys. The poem takes its story from an event of the sixth century B.C. recorded by the Roman historian Livy. The poem is, as Macaulay puts it in his subtitle, 'A Lay made about the Year of the City

CCCLX.' (1842) The numerals insist that the material is Roman, and that the poem is designed to meet a taste in Victorian men formed by the Latin lessons of the schoolroom, but Macaulay is anxious to widen the appeal of his material. The word 'Lay' associates the poem with Walter Scott's medievalizing ballads, *The Lay of the Last Minstrel* (1805) (which may be a poem sung by a warrior minstrel, but it is sung to an audience of women) and its successors, an association confirmed by the poem's metre and by its manner. Romans and Etruscans do battle as in Scott's poems the English and the Scots wage war on one another, each side ever willing to act as the admiring audience of the other's valour. When Horatius displays his heroism, single-handedly defending the bridge against an army, 'even the ranks of Tuscany / Could scarce forbear to cheer.' (508–9) It is an ethics of the playing field, common to Scott, to Rudyard Kipling in a poem such as 'Fuzzy-Wuzzy' (1892) and to Macaulay here, except that Macaulay prefaced his poem with a dry note: 'The author seems to have been an honest citizen, proud of the military glory of his country, sick of the disputes of factions, and much given to pining after good old times which had never really existed.' Macaulay was a Whig, of course, and anxious no doubt to dissociate himself from the Tory assumptions embedded in Walter Scott's variety of medievalism, and so he offers his poem as dramatic. But it is also a note that fixes the Victorian character of the poem.

D.G. Rossetti made the first draft of 'Jenny', his brother William Rossetti recalled, 'before the end of 1847', but that first draft was very different from the poem that Rossetti finally published in 1870: it was 'short, and was merely in the nature of general reflection – not (as now) of semi-dramatic monologue'.[10] 'Jenny' was one of the poems violently attacked by Robert Buchanan in his paper for the *Contemporary Review*, 'The Fleshly School of Poetry'.[11] It is, Buchanan allows, 'in some respects the finest poem in the volume', a poem 'suggested', he observes with a truly remarkable effrontery, by poems of Buchanan's own, especially 'Artist and Model' (1867). Nevertheless, Rossetti's poem is vitiated by the complexity of its speaker's responses to the young prostitute. Buchanan pities Jenny's plight when 'such a poet as this comes fawning over her, with tender compassion in one eye and aesthetic enjoyment in the other!' That response is acute enough, and in his reply Rossetti does not quarrel with it. Instead, he argues that Buchanan has mistaken the genre of the poem. It is not, as Buchanan supposes and as William Rossetti suggests that it had been in its first draft, a 'soliloquy'. Rossetti recognizes that even friendly readers (Ruskin for one) would have preferred it had he delivered his thoughts on prostitution while dispensing with 'the situation which', in the poem as published, 'serves it as framework'. The poem is spoken after the speaker has returned with Jenny to her room, as she falls asleep with her head on his knee. Rossetti defends his decision to write the poem as a monologue by insisting that the poem demanded 'an *inner* standing-point': 'the self-questionings and all-questionings' that the situation prompts 'can come with full force only from the mouth of one alive to its whole appeal, such as the speaker put forward in the poem, – that is, of a young and thoughtful man of the world. To such a speaker, many half-cynical revulsions of feeling and reverie, and a recurrent presence of the impressions of beauty (however artificial) which first brought him within such a circle of influence, would be inevitable features of the dramatic relation portrayed'.[12] Rossetti accepts, and repeats in more turgid prose, Buchanan's account of how the poem works. He insists only that Buchanan has failed to recognize its dramatic character.

In the earliest draft of the poem that survives, a text that probably dates from 1860, Rossetti has already introduced the 'situation' that serves as the 'framework' of the poem, and the '*inner* standing point', but both are developed far more fully in the text that Rossetti finally published in 1870. The room to which Jenny has brought the young man is realized with painful clarity when dawn breaks to reveal a 'pier-glass scrawled with diamond rings' (322):

Glooms begin
To shiver off as lights creep in
Past the gauze curtains half drawn-to,
And the lamp's doubled shade grows blue.
(311–14)

That double shadow is rendered with a fine painterly precision, and the same quality informs the '*inner* standing point' too, as when the young man looks at Jenny as if she were a High Renaissance Madonna:

Fair shines the gilded aureole
In which our highest painters place
Some living woman's simple face,
And the still features thus descried
As Jenny's long throat droops aside, –
The shadows where the cheeks are thin,
And pure wide curve from ear to chin, –

With Raffael's or Da Vinci's hand
To show them to men's souls, might stand,
Whole ages long, the whole world through,
For preachings of what God can do.
(230–40)

His artist's eye is just as evident when he sees her as a woman of quite another kind, a Magdalen rather than a Madonna,'Your silk ungirdled and unlac'd / And warm sweets open to the waist' (48–9) It is when he sees her as pitiable, as the victim of male lust, that his vision becomes blurred:

Fresh flower, scarce touched with signs that tell
Of Love's exuberant hotbed: – Nay,
Poor flower left torn since yesterday
Until tomorrow leave you bare;
Poor handful of bright spring-water
Flung in the whirlpool's shrieking face.
(12–7)

The lack of clarity (the wild flowers and hothouse flowers, the stream and the whirlpool reveal the speaker's confusion more clearly than they illuminate Jenny's situation) seems defensive. The imprecision helps him to avoid implicating himself in the behaviour that he condemns. The speaker never manages to resolve his conflicting responses, and looks at Jenny throughout the poem, to borrow Buchanan's devastating statement of the case, 'with tender compassion in one eye and aesthetic enjoyment in the other!'

It cannot be otherwise because Jenny is at once a person and a commodity. When she falls asleep with her head on his knee, she claims the protection to which her trust in him entitles her, and yet her body is what he has paid for. Jenny's room cannot be, like the room in Donne's 'The Sunne Rising', an erotic space perfectly sealed against the outside world. At dawn noises begin to intrude into the room, amongst them the sound of 'an early wagon drawn / To market' (304–5), but the sound fails to alert the young man to the fact that market values operate within the room just as ruthlessly as outside it.

The poem's 'framework' and its 'inner standing-point', it emerges, are thoroughly entangled. The speaker cherishes the flimsy, self-exculpatory fiction that Jenny might be equally fond of sex and money, that the economic and the erotic might be complementary. In the very first lines of the poem the thought becomes catchy:

> Lazy, laughing, languid Jenny,
> Fond of a kiss and fond of a guinea.
> (1–2)

Two extra unstressed syllables in the second line, two dactyls instead of two trochees, give it a jaunty swing. In Jenny's dreams, he guesses, men and money feature all but interchangeably:

> Whose person or whose purse may be
> The lodestar of your reverie?
> (20–1)

The thought remains with him in the poem's conclusion. He places coins in Jenny's hair as she sleeps and imagines how they will tumble about her when she rises, a 'Danaë for a moment there'. (376) Danaë was impregnated by Zeus when he defeated her father's security measures by transforming himself into a shower of gold, but the allusion serves only to accentuate the social distance between the speaker and his subject. Jenny, after all, is very unlikely to be familiar with classical mythology. The thought prompts another heartless pun – 'Jenny, my love rang true!' (377) –, from which even the perpetrator flinches, achieving as he does so at long last a fragile self-knowledge: 'And must I mock you to the last, / Ashamed of my own shame?' (380–1).

He leaves the money for Jenny even though he has not had sex with her (he rather prides himself on his self-restraint). He imagines her thankful that he has not been 'drunk or ruffianly' and has allowed her just to rest with her head upon his knee. (66–7) Denying himself the pleasure of penetrating her body, he has occupied himself during the night by attempts to penetrate her mind. He imagines her thoughts, her history, and, when she falls asleep, her dreams. She is, in a repeated metaphor, a book, a book that he spends the night reading. If he were to speak aloud his thoughts, 'the pages of her brain' might open, but only momentarily, as 'a volume seldom read / Being opened halfway shuts again' (158–61). As he gazes at her, he thinks,

> You know not what a book you seem,
> Half-read by lightning in a dream!
> (51–2)

Later, it is the book's contents rather than the light that it is read by that seem lurid. Women, the speaker admits, might be better qualified to read Jenny than he is himself, because their gaze would be uncomplicated by desire. But in the world as it is constituted she is a text that they are forbidden from looking into. Her heart is like a rose pressed within the pages of a pornographic book,

> Where through each dead rose-leaf that clings,
> Pale as transparent psyche-wings,
> To the vile text, are traced such things
> As might make lady's cheek indeed
> More than a living rose to read.
>
> (257–61)

A very different kind of book comes to mind when the cheeks of Aurora Leigh's strait-laced aunt are said to have a colour 'like a rose in a book / Kept more for ruth than pleasure' (2, 285–6), but in *Aurora Leigh* just as persistently as in 'Jenny' people are likened to books. Romney Leigh, Aurora tells him with some astringency, is a 'holy book', '[r]eserved for mild-eyed saints to pore upon' (2, 837–8), whereas she is herself '[t]oo light a book for a grave man's reading!' (5, 41). Lady Waldemar's over-familiarity prompts a more extended metaphor:

> Sweet heaven, she takes me up
> As if she had fingered me and dog-eared me
> And spelled me by the fireside half a life!
>
> (5, 1053–5)

People are like books in these poems because understanding them requires an act of interpretation, and it is often an act of some complexity. When Rossetti's speaker compares Jenny to a book, he inevitably offers himself too as a text that the reader is invited to construe, and the process does not stop there. Robert Buchanan read the poem as a text through which he could divine Rossetti's own character, and Rossetti was appalled by the interpretative methods that he deployed, but it would be hard to claim that Buchanan's project was in itself illegitimate.

In *Aurora Leigh* there is a teasing relationship between Elizabeth Barrett Browning's poem and Aurora's poem that at last brings her the fame that she has sought. In Rossetti's poem relationships are still more vexed. The poem's instability is nicely caught by William Rossetti when he describes it as a 'semi-dramatic monologue'. Some lines are spoken to Jenny on the assumption that she is awake:

> Well, handsome Jenny mine, sit up,
> I've filled our glasses, let us sup.
> (89–90)

Other lines seem spoken, but to a Jenny believed to be sleeping: 'Why, Jenny, you're asleep at last!' (171). Still other lines are presented as unspoken thoughts:

> Suppose I were to think aloud, –
> What if to her all this were said?
> (156–7)

But the status of a large majority of the poem's lines is unfixed, and offered to the reader to puzzle over. The same might be said of the poem's tetrameter couplets. In poems that distinguish between poet and speaker, the verse form employed has to be assigned to one or the other. The Duke in Browning's 'My Last Duchess' (1842), for example, is surely, despite the suggestions of some critics to the contrary, unaware that he is speaking in couplets. The verse form, so muffled by enjambment that it all but defeats the ear, stands as a formal guarantee of the distinction between the Duke's speech and the poem that Browning makes of it. The couplets frame the Duke for the reader's appalled and delighted inspection. When Browning's Fra Lippo Lippi (1855) breaks into couplets, on the other hand, they are his rather than Browning's:

> Flower o'the quince,
> I let Lisa go, and what good in life since?
> (55–6)

It is Lippo Lippi who chooses to punctuate his speech with these 'whifts of song' (52) that, just as powerfully as his style of painting, express his outlook on life. 'A Grammarian's Funeral' (1855) is a more complex example, which may be why the poem has puzzled its readers as to whether Browning shares or satirizes the admiration that the students who speak the poem claim to feel for their master. The poem is a marching song, sung by the grammarian's students as they carry the body of their master to its proper resting place on the summit of a mountain, elevated high above the humble dwellers on the plain. 'Step to a tune', (25) they urge each other, claiming the poem's metre as their own. In its interlocked quatrains, iambic pentameters alternate with dimeter lines made up of a dactyl followed by a trochee. The dimeters are almost wholly regular, but the pentameters are so various that it is little more than an act of faith to describe them as iambic. The swing of the poem is repeatedly threatened by lines, to quote the poem, of 'Accents uncertain' (54), which might express the difficulty of the climb ('Step two abreast, the way winds narrowly' (91)), but seem more tellingly to betray a lurking suspicion that the grammarian's life of scholarship does not inspire in his students the single-minded admiration that they profess. The young scholars' song has an exuberance that makes them unlikely celebrants of a life lived 'Dead from the waist down' (132). But do the poem's iambic lines that seem to reach after 'New measures, other feet' (39), betray the suspicion that the students cannot quite bring themselves to make explicit that the life of the mind is not much of a life after all, or do they signal Browning's dry suspicion that the young men find it easier to praise such a life than to emulate it?

'Jenny' raises similar problems. Its tetrameter couplets are not clearly assigned either to the speaker or the poet. The opening couplet may have a jaunty, aphoristic quality that it seems easier to ascribe to the speaker, but elsewhere the couplets seem, as in 'My Last Duchess', to offer a formal guarantee that the poem is subject to a control of which the speaker is quite unaware. Rossetti has a tendency, for example, to muffle a rhyme by dividing a single couplet between verse paragraphs, and he sometimes uses rhymes so approximate that they can scarcely be heard (the most extreme example rhymes 'bare' with 'spring-water' (15–6)). By contrast, he also finds place for a number of obtrusively rhymed triplets:

> Poor little Jenny, good to kiss, –
> You'd not believe by what strange roads
> Thought travels when your beauty goads
> A man to-night to think of toads!
>
> (299–302)

Such uncertainties may simply point to the history of the poem's composition, revealing the poem as a palimpsest, a reflective lyric incompletely rewritten as a dramatic poem, but they also work more positively. They keep the reader constantly alert to the status of the poem as text, and to the act of reading as an act of interpretation. The poem's speaker is a student, a reader, his room unlike Jenny's 'full of books' (23), and yet Jenny's room offers him no escape from print:

> All golden in the lamplight's gleam, –
> You know not what a book you seem.
> (51–2)

And if Jenny is a book to the young man, so he is to the poem's reader, and a book just as elusive, a book that, just like Jenny herself, 'opened halfway shuts again'. (159)

When John Ruskin accused him of obscurity, Robert Browning mounted a vigorous self-defence. He encouraged Ruskin 'to keep pace with the thought tripping from ledge to ledge', and 'not stand poking your alpenstock into the holes, and demonstrating that no foot could have stood there – suppose it sprang over them?' Browning was describing a poetic style defined not by connections but by gaps, and, as he recognized, the most significant gap was between the poet and his speaker. The relationship, he admitted, might be uncertain, he might 'put Robert Browning' into his speakers: 'If so, *peccavi* [I have sinned]: but I don't see myself in them at all events.'[13] The challenge with which Victorian poets present their readers very often has its origin in the decision, common to so many Victorian poems, from Elizabeth Barrett Browning's *Aurora Leigh* to Tennyson's *Maud* to D.G. Rossetti's 'Jenny', to distinguish poet and speaker. The most distinctive generic innovation made by Victorian poets is, as everyone has recognized, the dramatic monologue, but it has proved impossible to define just what is distinctive about it. Either the qualifications for membership are so strict (in a famous article Ina Sessions argued that the perfect dramatic monologue must display seven distinct features[14]) that only a handful of poems, almost all of them by Browning, qualify, or Victorian poems with fictitious speakers become impossible to distinguish from poems with fictitious speakers written in any other period. But looked at in a different way the problem disappears. The dramatic monologue is the exemplary Victorian verse form because so many Victorian poems share some of its characteristics.

The poem most often identified as the first Victorian dramatic monologue, Tennyson's 'St Simeon Stylites', was written in 1833, some years before the Queen's accession. The use by poets of fictitious speakers was already common, as, for example, in Felicia Hemans's *Records of Woman* (1828), in which many of the poem's titles, such as 'Arabella Stuart' and

'Properzia Rossi', simply name their speakers. Tennyson's difference is signalled in Edward FitzGerald's recollection of how he would recite the poem 'with grotesque Grimness, especially at such passages as "Coughs, Aches, Stitches, etc." laughing aloud at times.'[15] The dramatic monologue, as FitzGerald intimates, is commonly a performance. The reader of 'St Simeon Stylites', for example, is invited to examine the self-delusion of a man who believes that he equips himself for heaven by choosing to spend his life on a pillar, on the assumption that sainthood is available for purchase by the man prepared to pay the price in self-mortification, but he is invited still more strongly to relish the gusto with which Tennyson assumes the character:

> Good people you do ill to kneel to me.
> What is it I can have done to merit this?
> I am a sinner viler than you all.
> It may be I have wrought some miracles,
> And cured some halt and maimed; but what of that?
> (131–5)

Tennyson's friend, W.H. Thompson was concerned that the poem might be thought 'unwholesome', 'the description of [Simeon's] sufferings being too minute for any but those whom the knowledge of the Art holds above the subject.' But in this, as in most dramatic monologues, the reader is given little opportunity to forget the poet's 'Art'. St Simeon on his latest, and as he hopes his last pillar, is raised sixty feet above the ground, from where he looks down on those on whose behalf he suffers:

> But thou, O Lord,
> Aid all this foolish people; let them take
> Example, pattern: lead them to thy light.
> (218–20)

He is a grotesque compound of egotism and vanity, shut up in a hallucinatory world in which weird shapes 'with colt-like whinny and with hoggish whine' (174) drown out his prayers, and yet he never loses sight of how he is regarded by the admiring spectators, amongst whom he seems to include not only the 'good people' down below but God and all his angels. The poem is satirical, but, for all that, there is an odd complicity between the poet and his speaker. The fierceness of Tennyson's mockery of Simeon, performing with so much energy his own saintliness, cannot quite prevent the reader from noticing that Tennyson is playing the role of Simeon, and playing it just as vigorously. Odd complicities of this kind are characteristic of the dramatic monologue. Browning's first dramatic monologue, 'Johannes Agricola' (1836), was probably written two years after 'St Simeon Stylites', but Tennyson's poem was not published until 1842. It must be a coincidence, then, that Tennyson and Browning should both have chosen as the speakers of their first monologues a religious fanatic (Johannes Agricola, the first of the antinomians, held that the elect were exempt from the moral law). In the 1830s Wordsworth stood unchallenged at the head of the profession that Tennyson and Browning aspired to join, and it is possible to read these, the very first Victorian monologues, as a mordant response to the belief so closely associated with Wordsworth that the poet's true function was as the dispenser of religious truths.

The speaker of Browning's second monologue, 'Porphyria's Lover' (1836), is a murderer. So too is the speaker of the monologue of his that critics have agreed on identifying as the most perfect representative of the genre, 'My Last Duchess'. He is a murderer at any rate if that is how the Duke's nonchalant remark should be interpreted (Browning himself suggested, surely disingenuously, that he might simply have ordered that his wife be shut up in a convent):

> I gave commands;
> Then all smiles stopped together. There she stands
> As if alive.
>
> (45–7)

Dramatic monologues are very often spoken from the margins, from what Tennyson's Tithonus (1860) calls the 'limit of the world' (7), whether those margins be ethical or social or geographical or historical. Browning's Duke, for example, is not only a murderer, but an aristocrat, the bearer of a 'nine-hundred-years-old-name', and the ruler of a city state in late Renaissance Italy, in all which respects he would have been as marginal to most of Browning's readers as to Browning himself. Enjambment is so extreme that the ear scarcely registers that the poem is written in pentameter couplets. Rhyme and metre serve formally to secure the difference between the poet and the speaker, but they do not build between the two a fence high enough to keep them quite apart. The charge that the poem brings against the Duke is that he found it intolerable that his wife responded with a 'spot / Of joy' on the cheek to each and every instance of the vital beauty that she admired in everything around her, the selfsame beauty for which she herself, although she seems quite unconscious of it, was remarkable:

> The dropping of the daylight in the West.
> The bough of cherries some officious fool
> Broke in the orchard for her, the white mule
> She rode with round the terrace.
>
> (26–9)

The free play of her responses is itself an outrage to the Duke's demand that she find her only satisfaction in being the object of his regard. In death, when 'the faint / Half-flush that dies along her throat' (18–9) persists only in its reproduction by Fra Pandolf, the portrait painter, her behaviour has at last been brought into conformity with her husband's demands. Now she is dead, her image is displayed as, when, and to whom the Duke chooses, 'since none puts by / The curtain I have drawn for you, but I' (9–10). By the Duke's command the Duchess has been reduced to her painted reproduction, but the Duke's deadening hand has fallen on himself too. The poem ends as the Duke and the envoy go downstairs together, the Duke pointing out another prized item from his collection:

> Notice Neptune, though,
> Taming a sea horse, thought a rarity,
> Which Claus of Innsbruck cast in bronze for me!
>
> (54–6)

This is the Duke as he sees himself, superhuman tamer of women, and as the reader sees him, a man who, because he is so wholly trapped within his own egotism, and because he can understand no relation other than ownership, has cast his flesh and blood in bronze, becoming not so much a man as a statue of a man. Beauty for the Duke is fixed and dead: for Browning as for the Duchess it is quite otherwise. Browning says so directly in poem after poem, and he says as much in this poem too, in the movement of the verse at once so swift and so decisive. And yet does the poem quite eradicate the suspicion that the pleasure with which Browning uncurtains his Duke for the reader's perusal has an affinity with the pleasure that the Duke takes in displaying to chosen guests the portrait of his Duchess? The dramatic monologue distinguishes poet and speaker and one effect is to make it possible for them to develop unexpected and even uncomfortable relations one with another. The envoy, an emissary from the Count with whose daughter the Duke is negotiating a marriage, remains silent throughout the poem, his responses sometimes signalled ('not the first / Are you to turn and ask thus' (12–3)), but always opaque. The Duke gives the envoy a superb performance of the role that he has spent his life perfecting, the role of himself, but he is offered no clue as to how his performance is received, and in this too his predicament mirrors the poet's. It is, I think, significant that the dramatic monologue should first have been developed in the 1830s, when poets enjoyed such small sales, when publishers were so reluctant to issue their work (Edward Moxon was in that decade the only London publisher prepared to bring out volumes written by a single poet, and he did so usually on the basis that the poet bore the costs) that they can only have suspected that they were talking, like so many speakers of dramatic monologues, to themselves.

'My Last Duchess' is one of the simpler of Browning's dramatic monologues. It is hard, for example, to imagine a reader for whom the Duke's moral character is problematic. The poem's reader is unchallengingly confirmed in his prejudices against foreigners, aristocrats, autocrats, and wife-murderers. It is almost as hard to imagine a reader not charmed by the Duchess even in the Duke's representation of her. But even so the poem has prompted very different readings. The most obvious question that the poem raises is why the Duke should divulge to the emissary of the woman that he plans to marry that he has had his last wife killed. Ina Sessions believes that he is speaking by design, intending that the envoy should pass on to his future bride his view of the behaviour that will be expected of her, and of the consequences of any failure to satisfy those expectations. It may be, on the other hand, as Robert Langbaum supposes, that the Duke is displaying with characteristic flamboyance his utter disregard of how those he considers his inferiors might respond to him. But I suspect that most readers these days will prefer, like Alan Sinfield, to believe that the Duke is in the grip of a compulsion that impels him to rehearse the story of his last marriage no matter how inopportune the occasion.[16] That is my own preference, but my point is that the poem offers very little to support my preferred reading against those I find less persuasive, no more, perhaps, than the suggestion that the Duke may be rehearsing a speech that he has made many times before:

> for never read
> Strangers like you that pictured countenance,

> The depth and passion of its earnest glance
> But to myself they turned ...
>
> (6–9)

Dramatic monologues almost inevitably focus the reader's attention on the act of reading, and on the question of how and with what confidence the reader may arrive at a judgement of a speaker by examining that speaker's words. The speakers of dramatic monologues are always judged in their absence, their voices encountered not directly but in transcript. To read the poem is to listen to the voice of its speaker, but that voice can only ever be reconstructed by the reader from its printed trace. Every dramatic monologue offers a lesson in responsible reading.

That is the burden of Browning's weightiest exercise in the dramatic monologue, a Roman murder mystery, in which the case against Guido Franceschini, executed on February 22, 1698, for the murder of his wife and her parents (although the wife's parentage is disputed) is addressed in a series of monologues by representatives of the various factions into which the case divided the Roman public. Monologues are also given to Guido, who speaks twice, both at his trial and just before his execution; by Browning' red-cross knight, the priest Giuseppe Caponsacchi, who assists Guido's wife in her flight from her husband, and is believed by some to be her lover; by the dying wife, Pompilia; by the defence and prosecuting counsel in Guido's trial, and by Pope Innocent XII, whose responsibility it is to rule on Guido's appeal. *The Ring and the Book* engages an interest that stayed with Browning throughout his career, a concern with the ethics of reading. In the poem's first and final books, in which Browning speaks in his own person, the matter is addressed directly. In the first book Browning relates how he came to purchase from a Florentine bookstall the 'old yellow book' in which he found a collection of documents relating to the case. He picked it out, attracted by its 'lettered back', untempted by the novel by Dumas, the anthology, and the hagiography that flanked it: 'And "Stall" cried I: a *lira* made it mine.' (83) Browning insists on the materiality of that book, 'Print three-fifths, written supplement the rest' (119):

> Do you see this square old yellow Book, I toss
> I'the air, and catch again, and twirl about
> By the crumpled vellum covers?
>
> (33–5)

He needs to give the book weight and texture so that it remains a thing to be read, as Browning claims to have read it, read it all on the short walk back from the Piazza San Lorenzo where he bought the book to Casa Guidi, his house. He reads engrossed as he treads a perilous path:

> Through fire-irons, tribes of tongs, shovels in sheaves,
> Skeleton bedsteads, wardrobe-drawers agape,
> Rows of tall slim brass lamps with dangling gear, –
> And worse, cast clothes a-sweetening in the sun:
> None of them took my eye from off my prize.
> (1, 105–9)

By the time he 'stood at home again', he assures us (though the feat seems incredible), he had read through all 262 pages of that book, 'mastered the contents, knew the whole truth.' (1, 117) *The Ring and the Book* is the longest English poem that is still commonly read, twice as long as *Paradise Lost* and his wife's *Aurora Leigh*, and in all that length it does not qualify the truth that Browning divines as he walks that short distance, his concentration threatened by all the hubbub and the scattered furniture of the Florentine streets. What does disappear is Browning's jauntiness. The reader who dominates the first book, the poet himself, finds his proper counterpart in Book X, in the figure of Pope Innocent XII, an old man approaching death. The Pope is a reader, too. He reaches his verdict, like Browning, by studying the documents of the case, but his decision is weighted by the chastening knowledge that he too, almost as fast as Guido, is approaching his judgement. The Pope's verdict coincides with Browning's, and he shares some of the readerly confidence that Browning had displayed in Book One:

> All's a clear rede and no more riddle now.
> Truth, nowhere lies, yet everywhere in these –
> Not absolutely in a portion, yet
> Evolvable from the whole: evolved at last
> Painfully, held tenaciously by me.
> (10, 228–32)

What distinguishes him from the Browning of the first book is not just his sobering recognition that for all his confidence he might be mistaken ('Mankind is ignorant, a man am I' (10, 258)), but his painstakingness, the patient tenacity with which he reviews all those documents, and reviews too just as patiently the workings of his own conscience.

Browning often seems an ebullient poet, but it is the tired old Pope of the tenth book rather than the vigorous poet of the first that he offers as his perfect reader. The whole poem centres on the body of the dying Pompilia, a white page on which Guido's dagger has inscribed its ghastly message, and Pompilia can neither read nor write. She remains, as it were, a pretext, but she becomes the pretext for an extraordinary surge of textual production by others, from the speeches of the prosecutor and the defence attorney (speeches that are not spoken but presented to the court as manuscripts) to the 'rattling ballad rhyme' 'bawled / At tavern doors' (V, 1452–3) in which, Guido imagines, Caponsacchi might commemorate his cuckolding of Guido. Browning's monologues present their readers with what Eric Griffiths has called printed voices. Browning is a poet as convinced as any lawyer of the 'puissance of the tongue' (I, 1118), but for him, as for the lawyers in *The Ring and the Book*, the power really belongs to the pen 'which simulated tongue' (1, 1118–9). His blank verse repeatedly challenges his reader to work out how it might be voiced, as when the Pope imagines how Guido had suborned the young men who were his accomplices. What proposal did Guido make, he wonders, 'To these stout tall rough bright-eyed black-haired boys' (10, 933)? Young men such as this ought to have resisted him as robustly as the line resists scansion. Guido, in the condemned cell, feels the weight of public opinion against him:

> The mob's in love, I'll wager to a man,
> With my poor young good beauteous murdered wife:
> For hearts require instruction how to beat.
> (11, 1825–7)

But Browning leaves no clear instruction of where in the central line the stresses ought to fall. In his metres, in the clottedness of his syntax, in his densely figurative language, Browning presents his readers with formidable challenges, but they are challenges that compel his readers to own their responsibilities. Browning's is an ethical poetry, but a poetry that engages most closely with the ethics of reading.

To some of his contemporaries, even perhaps on occasion to his own wife, that would have seemed too narrow an acknowledgement of the poet's ethical responsibilities. Elizabeth Barrett Browning wrote 'The Runaway Slave at Pilgrim's Point' (1848) in the months immediately after her marriage, in response to an invitation to contribute a poem to William Garrison's *The Liberty Bell*, a Boston abolitionist annual. The poem is a monologue spoken by the runaway slave, and it has prompted critics to question whether the slave is allowed a voice or whether her voice is appropriated, but that may not be the most pressing question that the poem raises. The poem reveals, or it may even be that it stages, a contest between the formal requirements of the dramatic monologue and the moral imperative to condemn as forcefully as possible the institution of slavery. In the poem's first three stanzas it is the moral imperative that seems to be dominant. The slave kneels on the very mark on which the Pilgrim Fathers had knelt to give thanks when they first set foot on American soil. It seems far too neat a rhetorical gesture to be dramatically credible, an impression only underlined by the impossibility that the runaway could have fled from a slave-owning state to Plymouth Rock in a single night. The seven-line, tetrameter stanza, deftly mingling iambs and anapaests, serves in itself to obtrude the poet on the reader's attention, and so does much of the phrasing:

> I stand on the mark beside the shore
>   Of the first white pilgrim's bended knee,
> Where exile turned to ancestor,
>   And God was thanked for liberty.
> I have run through the night, my skin is as dark,
> I bend my knee down on this mark:
>   I look on the sky and the sea.
>
> (1–7)

That line, 'Where exile turned to ancestor', for example, has a sharper eye for Bostonian snobberies than seems likely in the supposed speaker. It is a poem, one might suppose, that assumes the first person just for rhetorical effect, a poem like 'The Fugitive Slave's Apostrophe to the North Star' (1839) by another poet associated with William Garrison, John Pierpont. But even this first stanza is not quite univocal. In the line, 'I have run through the night, my skin is as dark', three anapaests make a chant of the kind that EBB often allows her more impassioned speakers, and the stanza's final line, repeated as the first line of the thirteenth and the twenty-ninth stanzas, syncopates the stanza's movement: it is the poem's only trimeter. Even in the poem's first stanza two voices are audible, the voice of the imagined speaker and the voice of the British poet who imagines her. Robert Browning, predictably, wanted to mute the second voice. When Elizabeth furnishes her runaway slave with a shawl, he commented in the margin, 'Does this <u>sound</u> like a slave's article of clothing?' But in Barrett Browning's poem the formal obligation to impersonate the speaker is always under threat from the ethical need adequately to express her own indignation.

The threat is never fully realised, because the stanza that seems at first so clearly to signal the presence of the poet can also offer itself as the proper medium for a speaker who often represents herself as singing rather than speaking, as when she makes a song of the name of her lover:

> I sang his name instead of a song,
> Over and over I sang his name,
> Upward and downward I drew it along
> My various notes, – the same, the same!
> (78–81)

It may be this same song that she sings to her dead baby after she has buried him and can make her peace with him at last, because now that he is 'changed to black earth' his face does not put her in mind of the white men who, after they had killed her lover, raped her. She insists, 'I am not mad: I am black', but as the title of one of the poem's manuscripts, 'Black and Mad at Pilgrim's Point', acknowledges, hers is a mad song:

> I am black, I am black!
> I wore a child upon my breast,
> An amulet that hung too slack.
> (106–8)

The child should itself be a charm effective against his mother's violence, her black magic, but this child 'hung too slack', its hold on its mother loosened by a whiteness that lends the child the '*master's* look'. She recalls how she killed her son in lines that bring to mind Porphyria's lover's account of how he had strangled her, but only to point the difference:

> And he moaned and trembled from foot to head,
> He shivered from head to foot;
> Till after a time, he lay instead
> Too suddenly still and mute.
> (148–51)

Porphyria's lover is a madman overheard by an appalled reader: Barrett Browning's speaker inhabits a world to which madness is the only sane response, in which only mad songs are sane.

Her speaker is a Christian, and, from the opening address to the Pilgrim Fathers, the poem butts angrily at the anomaly that slavery might be institutionalized in a supposedly Christian society. The English poet seems more likely than the runaway slave to point the finger at 'the ladies who scorned to pray / Beside me at church but yesterday' (117–8) (the speaker is clearly not a domestic slave and it seems wholly unlikely that a plantation slave would ever have had the opportunity to share a pew with white women), but the account of the child's death is at once more disturbed and more disturbing. The mother compares her child's dead body to a mango:

> But *my* fruit ... ha, ha! – there had been
>   (I laugh to think on't at this hour!)
> Your fine white angels (who have seen
>   Nearest the secret of God's power)
> And plucked my fruit to make them wine,
> And sucked the soul of that child of mine
>   As the humming-bird sucks the soul of the flower.
>
> (155–61)

The white angels seem much too closely akin to the white women in the church and their husbands, the rapists, and their delicacy, sipping the soul as a humming bird sips its nectar, sorts horribly with the grotesque reversal of the natural order. They suck the soul of the child who should be given suck, and they do it to 'make them wine', in a ghastly parody of the eucharist. The poem climaxes in its boldest reversal (the poet's or the speaker's?) in which American slaves are hailed as antichrists, their suffering not an instrument of atonement but of retribution:

> *We* who bleed
> (Stand off!) we help not in our loss!
> *We* are too heavy for our cross,
>   And fall and crush you and your seed.
>
> (242–5)

It is a challengingly forthright conclusion, rather too challenging perhaps, because Barrett Browning adds another stanza in which the poem's speaker is suddenly transformed into a visionary poet, before, in the name of her dead child, she releases the white men from her curse:

> I fall, I swoon! I look at the sky.
>   The clouds are breaking on my brain;

I am floated along, as if I should die
  Of liberty's exquisite pain.
(246–9)

The falling, the swooning, the clouds and the waves, the Promethean gesture of forgiveness in which they culminate, and the movement of the lines, all identify this new voice as incongruously Shelley-like. 'I fall, I swoon' is, like its exclamatory counterparts in Shelley, an embarrassing phrase, which usefully reinforces at the last the sense that this is an embarrassing poem. It is a poem in which sharp sophistication ('Where exile turned to ancestor') is brought uncomfortably together with hit-and-miss exoticism (those mangoes and humming-birds) and with attempts to realize an authentically black voice by introducing rhythms that suggest a primitive chant. But, I would want to insist, the poem's power to embarrass its reader is its chief virtue. It is embarrassing for a middle-class white woman to assume the voice of a black slave, and embarrassing for a British poet to point out to an American readership that the Pilgrim Fathers, the 'Washington-race' (221), have given birth to a generation of 'hunter sons'(204), neither of which embarrassments seems particularly embarrassing at all in comparison with the huge embarrassment that it should still, in the middle of the nineteenth century, have been necessary to write such a poem.

The difference between Elizabeth Barrett Browning and a runaway slave is scarcely greater than the difference between Augusta Webster, a 'matron of long standing' as she described herself to Oliver Wendell Holmes,[17] and the prostitute who speaks 'A Castaway', but Webster chooses to minimize it. She allows Eulalie, the prostitute, her own middle-class upbringing, her own sharp analytical intelligence, and, as the prostitute's name suggests, her own command of language (Eulalie, or well-spoken, may simply indicate the speaker's hankering for conversation, but it also establishes the kinship between the speaker and the poet: Eulalia is the appropriately named woman poet in L.E.L.'s 'The History of the Lyre' (1828)). Her closeness to her speaker was formally registered when the poem was first published in Webster's *Portraits* (1870) by the decision not to capitalize the letters beginning a verse line (the decision was reversed in the enlarged 1893 edition). The effect is to mute the difference between Webster's blank verse and recorded speech. The speaker of D.G. Rossetti's 'Jenny' is never more perturbed than when it strikes him that Jenny and his cousin, Nell, might have been fashioned from the same clay: 'It makes a goblin of the sun.' (206) But that is the point on which the whole of Webster's poem is designed to insist. Eulalie knows that it is idle to behave 'As though your schoolgirl sister or your wife / Could let her skirts brush mine or talk of me.' (56–7) Webster responds by fashioning a poem in which she contrives it that all the way through her own skirt brushes against the prostitute's.

The poem begins, as several of Webster's poems do, with the speaker confronting a version of herself that seems scarcely recognizable. The middle-aged speaker of 'Faded' gazes at a portrait of herself in her youthful bloom, the speaker of 'By the Looking-Glass', finds in the mirror an image that pitilessly contradicts the ideal of beauty that she feels to be 'a part and essence' (35) of her own identity: 'Alas! it is I, I, I'. (25) Eulalie looks in a different kind of mirror when she reads her own schoolgirl diary:

> Its good resolves, its 'Studied French an hour,'
> 'Read Modern History,' 'Trimmed up my grey hat,'
> 'Darned stockings,' 'Tatted,' 'Practised my new song,'
> 'Went to the daily service.'
>
> (2–5)

It seems, she concludes, 'a jest to talk of me / As if I could be one with her'(24–5), a thought that at once distinguishes her as a prostitute and identifies her with her sex, whose common lot it is, as 'Faded' and 'By the Looking-Glass' remind us, to feel alienated from their former selves. Eulalie, too, looks in the mirror and sees gaze back at her a face that does not quite seem her own, but that is because it has a quite unexpected kind of beauty: 'What word will fit the sense but modesty?' (46). She offers the thought as 'a jest', but if it is a joke it is a revealing one. It reveals, for example, that Eulalie owes the earnings that secure her a home 'All velvet and marqueterie and pastilles' (79) to her ability to simulate the appearance of her customers' wives and sisters, and, still more subversively, the joke prompts the question whether modesty ought to be valued as a womanly virtue or whether it should rather be recognized as a particular kind of costume, a matter decided by the choice of fabric for the dress and styling for the hair.

Eulalie complains that she is spurned by other women, but her situation is complicated because she also spurns herself. She mocks a world that will call her 'half a dozen dainty names' to hide the 'one coarse English worst that lurks beneath: / Just that, no worse, no better' (63–6) (the verbal play suggests that the word she has in mind is whore), but it is a word that she cannot herself repeat when it is flung at her by her unforgiving brother, a man ironically named Clement:

> And it was true – *that* killed me: and I felt
> A hideous hopeless shame burn out my heart,
> And knew myself for ever that he said
> That which I was – Oh it was true, true, true.
> (521–4)

The word whore is prohibited entry to the poem, and, for all that she may claim to be 'no sweet slaver-tongue' (83), the prohibition issues from Eulalie herself. But even in her pudeur she is the proper representative of her sex. Eulalie may despise the wives who are unable to 'pin an idiot' to their apron-strings' (114), but she speaks for all women, wives amongst them, when she notes the educational disadvantages that sisters suffer in comparison with their brothers. The sisters must be 'Content with stinted fare and shabby clothes, / And cloistered silent life to save expense' (522–3), while their brothers spend 'in a month' what would have given their sisters 'teachers for a year' (527–8). And she speaks for her whole sex too when she notes the absence outside marriage of any but the most dispiriting career opportunities. There is the life of the governess of which Eulalie has direct experience:

> Tease children with dull questions half the day
> Then con dull answers in my room at night
> Ready for next day's questions.
> (355–7)

Outside that, there is little enough, and nothing for those, like Eulalie, with a middle-class upbringing:

> But where's the work? More sempstresses than shirts;
> And defter hands at white work than are mine
> Drop starved at last.
> (282–4)

Her profession, it seems, although it separates her from the respectable of her own sex, gives her the position from which she can look at her society from the outside, the satirist's position. Although the wives do not escape, her attack is directed primarily at their husbands, as when she denies that her profession is any more disreputable than theirs:

> Our preachers, gloating on your future hell
> For not believing what they doubt themselves:
> Our doctors, who sort poisons out by chance,
> And wonder how they'll answer, and grow rich:
> Our journalists, whose business is to fib
> And juggle truths and falsehoods to and fro:
> Our tradesmen, who must keep unspotted names
> And cheat the least like stealing that they can.
> (86–91)

The lines may not rhyme but they still contrive to mimic the couplets of eighteenth-century satire.

'A Castaway' was admired by contemporary readers – it was 'her masterpiece', according to Theodore Watts-Dunton – but it also perturbed: 'Were it not for the tender pity which inspires this poem as a whole' Mackenzie Bell observed, 'some of the bitter things that fall from the lips of the lost girl would be too terrible and daring for poetic art.'[18] The bitter things would include no doubt the mockery of the 'shrill carping virtues' of women who maintain a respectability from which 'not a soul / Has ever thought of tempting them' (113, 121–2), and of the religious tract posted through Eulalie's letterbox that serves at least to make 'a good leaping blaze' (170). Eulalie's response to the death of her child, 'the baby thing that woke / And wailed an hour or two, and then was dead' (422–3) is bitterer still: "twas well he died: / I could have been no mother' (425–6). But even at such moments Eulalie's voice is not decisively distinguished from Webster's. That happens only at the poem's very end when Eulalie welcomes the visit of a 'cackling goose' in the bleak knowledge that any company is better than none: 'Oh, is it you? / Most welcome, dear: one gets so moped alone.' (629–30) As she gains one companion, she loses another. When she chooses the word 'moped', Webster, to whom 'ennuyée' would have come more naturally, withdraws from Eulalie to become her impersonator, but her withdrawal serves only to confirm the complicity that they have shared through almost the whole of the poem.

Amy Levy, like Barrett Browning and Webster, likes to find herself in speakers who seem at first impossibly remote. She was only seventeen, still a schoolgirl, when she wrote 'Xantippe' (1880) in which she speaks as the wife of Sokrates, the woman whose name had become a common noun for a shrew, 'this Xantippe' as Henry Fielding describes the schoolmaster's wife in Chapter 3 of *Tom Jones*. Sokrates in Plato's *Phaedo* famously excludes Xantippe from his deathbed, fearing that her tears would disturb his conversation with his male friends:

> But Sokrates, looking towards Crito, said, 'Crito, let some one take her home.' Upon which some of Crito's attendants led her away, wailing and beating herself.

Xantippe speaks her monologue as a dawn breaks that she had 'never thought / To see', when the lamp of her life 'burns low' (4). But her husband, condemned to death, spent the hours before he drank the hemlock, demonstrating the immortality into which he believes himself about to pass. Xantippe spends her last hours bitterly reviewing the course of her life, a narrative that does not bring her to a serene acceptance of death but to the sensation that ends the poem, a sense of being stifled:

> Throw it wide,
> The casement, quick; why tarry? – give me air –
> O fling it wide, I say, and give me light.
> (284–6)

Sokrates is supported in his last hours by his adoring male friends. As he lies on his couch he strokes Phaedo's head and plays with his hair, and as he drinks the hemlock his friends can no longer restrain their tears. Xantippe's maids, when she begins to speak, are still fast asleep: 'too soundly have ye slept / That should have watched me' (8–9). Her maids, like Sokrates's friends, weep at the last, but, Xantippe suspects, they weep not in fellow-feeling for her, nor like Phaedo, who weeps for his own misfortune 'in being deprived of such a friend'. Theirs are the comfortable tears of young women irrationally confident that their own lives will prove very different from hers.

Like 'A Castaway', 'Xantippe' is a poem about women's education. It was first published in the *University Magazine* in 1880. Levy herself had joined Newnham College, Cambridge in 1879, just eight years after its foundation, and left in 1881, the year in which women were first allowed to sit university examinations, although it was not until 1921 that the university awarded degrees to women, and they were recognised as full members of the university only in 1947. It is a poem in which Levy traces the exclusion of women from the life of the mind to the point at which Victorians believed that life was born, in Athens in the fifth century B.C. The 'Phaedo' is the poem's chief pre-text, because it is the dialogue in which Sokrates insists most strenuously that the life of the intellect is independent of the life of the body, and yet persists, despite the self-contradiction, in holding that it is a life from which women's bodies exclude them: 'woman's frail – / Her body rarely stands the test of soul' (172–3). Sokrates identifies Aspasia as a rare exception to this rule, but she is a Milesian. Like the British, Sokrates finds it easier to acknowledge intellectual women if, like Germaine de Staël or George Sand, they are foreign. In the marriage of Sokrates and Xantippe it is, in an irony of which Sokrates is wholly unaware, Xantippe rather than Sokrates whose ability to distinguish soul from body has been put to the test. When her father informed her that she was to marry Sokrates, she had to abandon her dream of 'a future love / Where perfect body matched the perfect soul' (77–8), and set herself to the task of recognizing the beauty of a soul hidden in 'flesh / Which half repelled our senses' (67–8):

> So did I reach and strain, until at last
> I caught the soul athwart the grosser flesh.
> (86–7)

It is an effort that goes quite unrecognized by her husband.

Xantippe's climactic memory is of the one occasion when she challenged her husband, 'Lit by a fury' when she hears him claim that woman, if she is offered knowledge, becomes drunk with it, throwing the 'laws of custom, order, 'neath her feet'. (175) She protests at the implication that women are failed experiments, 'half-completed work' (187), fit only

> 'To bleed and quiver, and to weep and weep,
> To beat its soul against the marble walls
> Of men's cold hearts, and then at last to sin!'
> (189–91)

Sokrates's disciples, the beautiful Alkibiades, and Plato with his 'narrow eyes and niggard mouth' (197), respond mockingly to her interruption, and so, far more woundingly, does Sokrates himself: 'I thank thee for the wisdom which thy lips / Have thus let fall among us.' (211–2) Xantippe flings the wineskin that she is carrying 'upon the marble, where it lay / Spouting red rills and fountains on the white'. (220–1) The gesture rather precisely re-enacts her speech, the outburst of words mimicked in the wine that bursts out of the skin and stains the marble floor, as red as her heart's blood.

Xantippe reacts to her husband's contempt by deciding to become the woman he takes her for. She orders out the looms, calls her maidservants about her, and sets about spinning her life away: 'I spun until, methinks, I spun away / The soul from out my body'. (250–1) The monotony of the task is relieved only by gossip, 'aimless talking' (255), and captiousness: she finds she has 'a tongue to cut / With quick incision, 'thwart the merry word / Of idle maidens'(256–8). But the poem is an elegy for the woman she might have been, the woman that, in her jewel-like girlhood memories, she seemed ready to become, as when,

> leaning from the lattice, I have caught
> The fair-far glimpses of a shining sea;
> And, nearer, of tall ships which throng'd the bay,
> And stood out blackly from a tender sky
> All flecked with sulphur, azure, and bright gold.
> (21–5)

Like Barrett Browning in 'The Runaway Slave at Pilgrim's Point' and Augusta Webster in 'A Castaway', Amy Levy is intent on giving a voice to the voiceless. Karen Weisman intriguingly links Levy's poem with an 1866 essay by James Thomson (a poet that Levy was interested in, and the model supposedly for her fine poem, 'A Minor Poet'), 'A Word for Xantippe', in which Thomson recommends it as a proper task to redeem Xantippe from Plato's representation of her, and grimly observes that Sokrates is never more akin to Christ than in his contempt for the domestic affections.[19] In assuming the voice of Xantippe Levy finds a way to express the outrage, an outrage that her experience at Cambridge seems only to have accentuated, at the exclusion of women from the intellectual life, and it may more indirectly indicate, if she thought like James Thomson about Sokrates's affinity with Jesus, her sense that as a Jew (only the second Jewish woman to be admitted to the university, and the first to Newnham) she was excluded additionally from an exclusively Christian intellectual tradition. For Victorian women poets, as Glennis Byron points out, much more clearly than for their male contemporaries the dramatic monologue offered a form that allowed them to engage with the most urgent public controversies of the age.

Endnotes

1. John Keats, *The Letters, 1814–1821*, ed. Hyder Edward Rollins, 2 vols (Cambridge: Cambridge University Press, 1958), 1, p. 387.
2. 'Notes on Poems and Reviews' (1866), Algernon Charles Swinburne, *Major Poems and Selected Prose*, ed. Jerome McGann and Charles L. Sligh (New Haven and London: Yale University Press, 2004), p. 349.
3. H.A. Page (1867) 'The Morality of Literary Art' *Contemporary Review*, **5** (June), 161–89, 187.
4. Isobel Armstrong, *Victorian Poetry: Poetry, Poetics and Politics* (London and New York: Routledge, 1993), especially pp. 13–7.
5. Augusta Webster, *Portraits and other poems*, ed. Christine Sutphin (Peterborough, Ontario: Broadview Press, 2000), p. 370.
6. *Blackwood's Edinburgh Magazine*, **79** (February, 1856), 133.
7. *The Brownings' Correspondence*, 10, ed. Philip Kelly and Scott Lewis (Winfield, Kansas: Wedgestone Press, 1992), p. 22.
8. Elizabeth Barrett Browning, *Aurora Leigh*, ed. Margaret Reynolds (New York and London: W.W. Norton, 1996), pp. 330–1.
9. Hallam Tennyson: *Alfred Lord Tennyson; A Memoir*, 2 vols (London: Macmillan, 1897), 1, p. 305.
10. *Works of Dante Gabriel Rossetti*, ed. W.M. Rossetti (London: Ellis, 1911), p. 649.
11. *Contemporary Review*, **18** (August, 1871), 334–50.
12. D.G. Rossetti, "The *Contemporary Review* and the Stealthy School of Criticism: A Letter to Robert Buchanan, Esq. (Alias Thomas Maitland, Esq.)." London, 1871, reprinted in *Victorian Poetry* 41: 2 (2003), pp. 207–27.
13. Quoted in W.G. Collingwood, *Life of John Ruskin* (Boston: Houghton Mifflin, 1902), pp. 164–5.
14. Ina Beth Sessions (1947) 'The Dramatic Monologue', *PMLA*, **62**(2) (June), 503–16.
15. Hallam Tennyson, *Alfred Lord Tennyson: A Memoir*, 1, p. 193, footnote.
16. Ina Beth Sessions, 'The Dramatic Monologue', p. 510; Robert Langbaum, *The Poetry of Experience: The Dramatic Monologue in Modern Literary Tradition* (London: Chatto and Windus, 1957), pp. 82–5; Alan Sinfield, *Dramatic Monologue* (London: Methuen, 1977), p. 5.
17. In a letter quoted by Christine Sutphin (2000) 'Human Tigresses, Fractious Angels, and Nursery Saints: Augusta Webster's *A Castaway* and Victorian

Discourses on Prostitution and Women's sexuality', *Victorian Poetry*, **38**(4), 511–32, 512.

18. Quoted by Christine Sutphin (2000) 'Human Tigresses, Fractious Angels, and Nursery Saints: Augusta Webster's *A Castaway* and Victorian Discourses on Prostitution and Women's Sexuality', *Victorian Poetry*, **38**(4), 511–31, 514.
19. Karen Weisman (2001) 'Playing with Figures: Amy Levy and the Forms of Cancellation', *Criticism: A Quarterly for Literature and the Arts*, **43** (Winter), 59–79.

3

Victorian Metrics

George Saintsbury's is still the most comprehensive survey of Victorian metrical practice. Noting the 'great multiplication of metres' used by Victorian poets, he speaks of 'the *polymetric* character' of nineteenth-century verse.[1] It was a century in which the leading poets were metrists in a different sense from the poets of preceding centuries. They had a theoretical interest in metre. It was a tendency that culminated in the work of Thomas Hardy, often identified as the very last of the Victorians, who, by Dennis Taylor's extraordinary calculation, used in the 1093 poems that he wrote during his career 'well over 790 different metrical forms'.[2] But for Saintsbury it was Tennyson who first established metrical variety as a distinctive characteristic of Victorian verse, and he did so even before Victoria had come to the throne, in his volumes of 1830 and 1833.

Coleridge defended the metrical irregularity of 'Christabel' (1816 but written much earlier) in his preface to the poem by insisting that it had not been 'introduced wantonly, or for the mere ends of convenience, but in correspondence with some transition, in the nature of the imagery or passion'. The metre, he claimed, was subsumed within the poem's organic unity. Victorian poets might make similar claims still more extravagantly, as when Barrett Browning's Aurora Leigh recalls the moment

> when the rhythmic turbulence
> Of blood and brain swept outward upon words,
> As wind upon the alders, blanching them
> By turning up their under-natures till
> They trembled in dilation.
>
> (1, 897–901)

Reading Victorian Poetry, First Edition. Richard Cronin.

Metre here has its origin in the pulse. It is an all but unconscious register of the poet's passionate inward life. But more often Victorian poets acknowledged a division between the metre of a poem and its sense. In this they took their stand alongside Wordsworth, who argues in his preface to *Lyrical Ballads* (1800) that metre works to temper and restrain the passion of poetry rather than, as Coleridge suggests, to express it.[3] Hopkins told Robert Bridges that he used in his verse 'sprung rhythm' because it was the 'nearest to the rhythm of prose', to 'the native and natural rhythm of speech'. But he recognized too that his rhythms might strike the reader, as he feared the rhythms of 'Harry Ploughman' would strike Bridges, as 'intolerably violent and artificial'.[4] Coventry Patmore wrote one of the most interesting essays on metre in the period, and Hopkins admired it, but Patmore argued that 'Language should always be seen to *feel*, though not to *suffer from* the bonds of verse'.[5] Other commentators were still more ready to accept that 'moving in' bonds and 'manifesting' them might be conflicting rather than complementary responses to the need to conform to a chosen metre. Robert Louis Stevenson preferred, like several others, to borrow the musical term, counterpoint, to describe the relationship between the metre and the sense of the poem.[6] Sir Henry Newbolt located in poetry 'an antagonism, a balance, a compromise, between the metrical ictus, the drum-beat … and the common speech-rhythm of the language',[7] even though in his own best-known poem the compromise may seem rather too easily achieved:

> There's a breathless hush in the Close to-night –
> Ten to make and the match to win –
> A bumping pitch and a blinding light,
> An hour to play and the last man in.
> And it's not for the sake of a ribboned coat,
> Or the selfish hope of a season's fame,
> But his Captain's hand on his shoulder smote
> "Play up! play up! and play the game!"
> ('Vitaï Lampada'(1897), 1–8)

Tennyson begins *In Memoriam* (1850) dreaming of a time when 'mind and soul according well, / May make one music as before' ('Prologue', 27–8), but for the time being he prefers that the sound of poetry remain divided from the sense, if only so that the reader is left free to register how cunningly Tennyson has brought them into concord. Tennyson was almost from the first famous for the skill with which he could manufacture onomatopoeic effects, as, to give just one celebrated example, in the song from *The Princess* (1847), 'Come down, O maid':

> The moan of doves in immemorial elms,
> And murmuring of innumerable bees.
> (*The Princess*, VII, 206–7)

The murmuring of the second line is achieved not just phonetically, but by allowing only three stresses in a hypermetric line in which the other eight syllables come together in a scarcely differentiated buzz. But Tennyson is just as ready to present metre as an unbearable drumbeat, an insistent tune that cannot be got out of the head, as when the speaker of *Maud* (1855) in his madness believes himself dead, but still conscious of the intolerable tramp of passing feet. The dead are buried too shallow:

> Only a yard beneath the street,
> And the roofs of the horses beat, beat,
> The hoofs of the horses beat,
> Beat into my scalp and brain,
> With never an end to the stream of passing feet,
> Driving, hurrying, marrying, burying,
> Clamour and rumble, and ringing and clatter ...
> (*Maud*, Part II, 245–51)

The beat is intolerable because it is at once emphatic and irregular, but the incursion of an external mechanical rhythm into the body's rhythms of breath and pulse might on another occasion be enjoyable, as when Browning admits that the rollicking, doggerel rhythm of *Christmas-Day* (1850) was suggested by the rhythm of the Manchester train:

> A tune was born in my head last week,
> Out of the thump-thump and shriek-shriek
> Of the train, as I came by it, up from Manchester;
> And when, next week, I take it back again,
> My head will sing to the engine's clack again,
> While it only makes my neighbour's haunches stir,
> – Finding no dormant musical sprout
> In him, as in me, to be jolted out.
> (*Christmas-Eve*, 249–56)

The instances from Tennyson and Browning are both of them extreme, but it is characteristic of much Victorian poetry that the metre seems self-conscious, as if imposed on the poem. One result of this is, as Eric Griffiths observes, that in Victorian poems 'even the most lyrical utterance, utterance that might be thought to spring from the fullness of an "I"' seems 'dramatically self-conscious, watched by a "he"'.[8] The division that the reader registers between the poem's sense and its metre is one more device by which Victorian poets produce the 'double consciousness within the poem' so characteristic of Victorian poetry, and which, as Griffiths goes on to point out, is most fully expressed in the most characteristic of all Victorian poetic kinds, the dramatic monologue. In the dramatic monologue the speaker fashions a self in happy ignorance that he or she is all the while being exposed to inspection by a poet who cuts the speech into lines, and imposes on it a metre to which the reader is invited to respond behind the speaker's back.

For Matthew Campbell metre organizes the poem's wayward impulses, bringing them under the discipline of the will, a procedure he traces through a metrical analysis of the lyric to which Tennyson gave the title 'Will' (1855).[9] Tennyson begins the poem by offering a tribute to strength of will that leans heavily on a Horatian ode (III, iii) and his own schoolboy translation of it, but he differs from Horace in suggesting that the triumph that the strong-willed man enjoys is metrical. He is

a promontory of rock,
That, compassed round with turbulent sound,
In middle-ocean meets the surging shock,
Tempest-buffeted, citadel crowned.
('Will', 6–9)

The last line triumphantly rebuffs the poem's iambic beat, substituting for its turbulence an unusual, but unusually emphatic, metre of its own. Still more intriguing is the metre of the second stanza, devoted to the man whose will has been weakened 'through acted crime', or, in an alternative that the smoothly sickening internal rhyme makes far more insidiously threatening, some

seeming-genial venial fault,
Recurring and suggesting still!
(13–4)

Such a man loses all sense of purpose:

> He seems as one whose footsteps halt,
> Toiling in immeasurable sand.
>
> (15–6)

Because the word 'halt' is placed at the end of the line the footsteps seems at once to limp and to come to a standstill. In the following line the iambic beat is abandoned, and the metre, like the traveller, seems baffled, suspended between possibilities. The feet of Tennyson's poem, like the footsteps of the weak-willed man, lose their way. The poem ends surprisingly by granting this traveller, lost in the desert, a strange vision:

> And o'er a weary sultry land,
> Far beneath a blazing vault,
> Sown in a wrinkle of the monstrous hill,
> The city sparkles like a grain of salt.
>
> (17–20)

Life is a pilgrimage, and it is presumably the Celestial City that the pilgrim sees sparkling like a grain of salt. Its diminution marks how far he is from it, and yet the glimpse of it that he is allowed remains oddly compelling. The strong-willed man was 'a promontory of rock', too hard to take any impression. The 'monstrous hill', like the faltering traveller's will, softens in the second stanza, melting into earth in which a seed can be sown, into flesh that can fold into a wrinkle. The weak-willed man may not be 'citadel-crowned' like the promontory, but the city that he is allowed to glimpse, reduced to a grain that sparkles within the hill's fleshly fold, seems far more magical. 'O well for him', the poem begins, heartily commending strength of will. The second stanza points how different the fate of the weak-willed is, 'But ill for him', and yet the poem strangely complicates the contrast. If, as Campbell suggests, the metrical control that Tennyson exerts over the poem figures the strength of will that he seems to be commending, the possibility remains open of reading the poem as a sly tribute to what can be glimpsed only at odd moments, when the sovereignty of the will is in abeyance, and an avenue is left open, as it so often is in Tennyson's handling of his metres, for something wholly unexpected.

Yopie Prins shows how it is possible to reverse Matthew Campbell's argument by associating metre not with the will, and the entire culture of self-discipline that Tennyson's strong-willed man exemplifies, but with all that threatens it.[10] Prins is one of Swinburne's most compelling modern readers. Many of the first readers of the volume with which Swinburne established his reputation, *Atalanta in Calydon* (1863), and of the volume that confirmed it, *Poems and Ballads* (1866), found Swinburne's verse shocking, but they were not threatened by the laxity of the metrical control that he exerted over his materials: they were dismayed by its power. The first chorus of *Atalanta in Calydon* was famously compelling, but the power that the metre exerted over the reader might, just because it was so compelling, be experienced as dangerously seductive:

> When the hounds of spring are on winter's traces,
>   The mother of months in meadow or plain
> Fills the shadows and windy places,
>   With lisps of leaves and ripple of rain.
>
> (65–8)

The incantatory power of the verse works to subjugate the sense of the lines to their music so emphatically that language almost dissolves into an unmeaning natural melody, like the sounds made by lisping leaves and rippling rain. The effect is exacerbated in *Poems and Ballads* when the challenge to the reader's aesthetic principles, the challenge, for example, to the principle that in verse sound should remain the servant of sense, is coupled with an attack on ethical conventions. In 'Dolores' (1866) Swinburne offers a courtesan dominatrix as his counterpart to the Christian Virgin:

> O garment not golden but gilded,
>   O garden where all men may dwell,
> O tower not of ivory, but builded
>   By hands that reach heaven from hell;
> O mystical rose of the mire,
>   O house not of gold but of gain,
> O house of unquenchable fire,
>   Our Lady of Pain!
>
> ('Dolores', 17–24)

But it is less material to Victorian poetry whether metre is associated with the will or with what threatens it than that the poem preserve, by one route or the other, a distinction between its metre and its sense.

For George Saintsbury, Tennyson and Swinburne are the two master metrists of Victorian poetry, but he allows that their achievement is all but matched by a third poet, Christina Rossetti. Her metrical 'tour de force' is *Goblin Market* (1862), a '*fatrasie* or *macédoine* of measures', according to Saintsbury, in which iambic, trochaic, dactylic and anapaestic feet jostle against one another in lines that may shrink to as few as four or expand to as many as ten syllables, and a poem in which the rhyme scheme is as irregular as the rhythm. The metre, according to Sainstsbury, might best be described as 'a dedoggerelised Skeltonic'.[11] Skelton himself had been happy enough to acknowledge that his was a 'bastard ryme, after the dogrell gyse' (*Magnyfycence*, 408). He thought of his poems in Skeltonics as the illegitimate half-brother of his regular verse, demotic rather than courtly, grotesque rather than smooth:

> For though my ryme be ragged,
> Tattered and jagged,
> Rudely rayne-beaten,
> Rusty and mothe-eaten,
> If ye take well therwith,
> It hath in it some pyth.
> (*Colin Clout*, 53–8)

For George Puttenham in his *Arte of Poesie* (1589) Skeltonics or 'ryme doggrel' is the verse form chosen by a poet who will 'be tyed to no rules at all, but range as he list',[12] and the metre kept that character into the nineteenth century. Edwin Guest in his *History of English Rhythms* (1832) speaks disapprovingly of 'the impudent licence of the tumbling metre',[13] but its reputation for licentiousness is precisely what recommends it to Rossetti.

Goblin Market tells the story of how Laura, poisoned by the fruit of the goblin men, is saved by her sister, Lizzie, who heroically secures for Laura the poison's only antidote, a second portion of the very same juices that had poisoned her. *Goblin Market* is a poem about addiction, Laura's addiction to the goblin fruit, but its addictive quality is most powerfully represented metrically, by sound rather than by taste, by the poem's 'iterated jingle / Of sugar-baited words' (234–5). The jingle is established in the poem's first paragraph by the tumbling two-beat line of the goblin chant. It is a jingle so addictive that the very first line is enough to establish the habit:

> Morning and evening
> Maids heard the goblins cry.
> (1–2)

The voice struggles against the stresses that the two verbs of the second line would ordinarily demand. When the goblins begin to list their wares, the jingle quickly becomes strong enough to impose itself even on lines that struggle still harder to resist it, lines such as the last in the following sequence:

> Apples and quinces,
> Lemons and oranges,
> Plump unpecked cherries,
> Melons and raspberries,
> Bloom-down-cheeked peaches.
> (5–9)

When they hear the chant, the sisters know that they should not look. Laura rehearses the rule in two lines of common measure (common sense in this poem expresses itself in common metres):

> 'We must not look at goblin men,
> We must not buy their fruits.'
> (42–3)

But she cannot follow her own advice. Lizzie covers her eyes, but Laura peeps, and as she does so her voice becomes infected by the goblin jingle:

> 'One hauls a basket,
> One bears a plate.'
> (56–7)

After she takes her fill of goblin fruit, paying with a lock of her golden hair, the infection takes hold:

> 'You cannot think what figs
> My teeth have met in.'
> (173–4)

The poem enacts the contest between the sisters and the goblins as a struggle between the 'bastard ryme' of the goblin chant and the more legitimate metres that attempt to repel it, a struggle between the syllabic metres that most Victorian poets continued to use and the accentual metres with which innovative poets such as Hopkins were beginning to challenge them. But in this poem identity and difference have an odd way of changing places. The goblins are as various as the fruit they purvey:

> One had a cat's face,
> One whisked a tail,
> One tramped at a rat's pace,
> One crawled like a snail.
> One like a wombat prowled obtuse and furry,
> One like a ratel tumbled hurry skurry
> (71–6)

The sisters by contrast are identical:

> Like two blossoms on one stem,
> Like two flakes of new-fall'n snow.
> (188–9)

But differences, when there are enough of them and when they are sufficiently extravagant, no longer serve to differentiate. The goblins are so grotesquely individuated that they become scarcely distinguishable one from another:

> Leering at each other,
> Brother with sly brother;
> Signalling each other,
> Brother with sly brother.
> (91–4)

Conversely, the fact that the sisters are indistinguishable only serves to underline their difference: Laura's fails to resist the goblins but Lizzie resists them successfully. The chaste in this poem is not so much the antithesis of the licentious as its rhyme. It is a rhyme of the kind that pairs 'noon' with 'moon', which happens not to be a rhyme that Rossetti quite uses in the poem, although when 'noon' appears in the middle of a line, the moon appears two lines later, and it is the noon that 'waxed bright' (276) quite as if it had been the moon, and the moon that is said to 'burn' in an oddly sun-like manner (279). When Laura cranes her neck the better to see the goblin men, a series of similes seem to establish her as the type of the virginal:

> Like a rush-imbedded swan,
> Like a lily from the beck,

Like a moonlit poplar branch,
Like a vessel at the launch
When its last restraint is gone.
(81–6)

The swan, the lily and the moonlit poplar branch (borrowed, it may be, from Tennyson's 'Mariana') seem types of purity until in the unexpected climax of the passage they become figures for the loss of all restraint. The sisters repeatedly, as in these lines, are figured in lists of similes (compare 184–90, 408–21, and 514–20), and the lists of similes echo the lists so closely associated with the goblins, the lists of the goblins themselves and the lists of their fruit. Both sisters and goblins are associated with the paratactic syntax that dominates the poem, a syntax that, because it never comes to a necessary end and can only be interrupted, is closely implicated with the goblin aesthetic of excess and opposed to the self-restraint that Lizzie practises in order to save her sister. But Lizzie's self-restraint is itself paradoxical. She

Would not open lip from lip
Lest they should cram a mouthful in:
But laughed in heart to feel the drip
Of juice that syrupped all her face,
And lodged in dimples of her chin,
And streaked her neck which quaked like curd.
(432–6)

Lizzie's self-discipline seems somehow far more shameless than the greed that Laura displayed when she sucked the goblin fruit 'until her lips were sore' (136). Exactly the same might be said of the passage in which she cures her sister, saving her from the fate of their neighbour Jeanie who had fallen sick and 'died / In her gay prime' (315–6) after tasting the fruit. Lizzie returns home in triumph and invites her sister to lick the juices from her face:

Hug me, kiss me, suck my juices
Squeezed from goblin fruits for you,
Goblin pulp and goblin dew.
Eat me, drink me, love me.
(468–71)

It is Holy Communion rewritten as a downmarket Valentine in yet another of the disconcerting collisions that the poem manufactures, all of which echo the rencontres between the goblins and the two sisters on which its plot pivots.

Even after Laura has tasted the fruit, the two sisters continue to keep a tidy house. They are early out of bed: 'Fetched in honey, milked the cows, / Aired and set to rights the house' (203–4). But as Laura sickens she begins to fail in her housewifely duties:

> She no more swept the house,
> Tended the fowls or cows,
> Fetched honey, kneaded cakes of wheat,
> Brought water from the brook:
> But sat down listless in the chimney-nook
> And would not eat.
>
> (293–8)

The verse line expands to ten syllables, and then, like Laura, pines away. It is a quiet reminder of how distant the poem's metrical wildness, its aesthetics of disorder, remains from the tidy, domestic virtues that it seems to celebrate. The poem's conclusion takes place 'Days, weeks, months, years / Afterward' ((543–4), when Lizzie and Laura have both become wives and mothers. Laura calls the children about her, and talks 'about the haunted glen, / The wicked, quaint, fruit-merchant men' (552–3). Her tale carries an entirely proper moral, that 'there is no friend like a sister' (562), and yet it seems to carry too the suggestion that the goblins continue to exercise their charm over her. Although the sisters are wives their husbands remain absent from the poem, as if they have been ousted, at least in the imagination, by their competitors, 'The wicked, quaint, fruit-merchant men'. That is an octosyllabic line, scanned most neatly as an iambic tetrameter, but behind that sounding of the line a goblin trimeter remains audible. Metre in *Goblin Market* is used at once to uphold the moral will and to undermine it. It is the poem's metre that most powerfully stages the moral contest that the poem records, but the metrical conflict and the narrative conflict may not reach quite the same conclusion.

George Saintsbury imagines that *Goblin Market* would have been denounced by reviewers earlier in the century as a 'Bedlam of discord', acknowledging the connection that many Victorian readers made between metrical regularity and mental health. It was an association that had been confirmed a decade before with Tennyson's publication of *Maud* (1855), a poem that in its first edition had a subtitle, *Maud or the Madness.* Saintsbury describes how its early readers felt themselves 'jolted and jarred by perpetual changes', like the poem's speaker when he imagines himself dead and buried with the London traffic maddeningly rumbling overhead. In *Maud* as in *Goblin Market*, metrics become thematic. R.J. Mann (whose account of *Maud* had Tennyson's approval) praised the poem for revealing the 'power of language to symbolise in sound mental states and perceptions.'[14] The speaker's struggle to win or to retain his sanity is acted out within the verse line. I doubt that any poem in English keeps its finger so attentively on its own metrical pulse. The speaker claims that he will never rid himself of Maud's scream when she sees her brother dying, shot by the man she loves – 'It will ring in my heart and my ears, till I die, till I die' – but in the very next line of the poem, the scream has been drowned out, or at any rate incorporated into the poem's metre: 'Is it gone? my pulses beat' (Part II, 35–6). When Maud's eyes meet his in church, she 'suddenly, sweetly, strangely blushed', and he responds not by blushing himself but rhythmically. His heart beats a drum roll:

> And suddenly, sweetly, my heart beat stronger
> And thicker until I heard no longer
> The snowy-banded, dilettante,
> Delicate-handed priest intone.
>
> (Part I, 308–11)

Or so he claims, though it seems that his heartbeat is not yet strong enough to drown out his scorn of the clergyman. At the moment when, confident in Maud's love, he seems to have freed himself into happiness, he proves it, as Keats would say, on the pulses, by listening to the rhythms of his body, and finding in them the loose, easy rhythm of long waves:

> Is that enchanted moan only the swell
> Of the long waves that roll in yonder bay?
> And hark the clock within, the silver knell
> Of twelve sweet hours …
>
> (Part I, 660–2)

It is the section of the poem in which Tennyson's lines comes closest to clock-time, to regular iambic pentameters. It is the section in which the feet of the poem seems most closely to approximate Maud's 'light foot'

(Part I, 607), a foot which, even though it has 'so airy a tread', his heart would beat in response to even if it had 'lain for a century dead' (Part I, 917 and 921). But when he imagines himself dead and buried too shallowly, he surrenders to the power of a very different rhythm, a maddening, cacophonous tattoo:

> Only a yard beneath the street.
> And the hoofs of the horses beat, beat,
> The hoofs of the horses beat,
> Beat into my scalp and brain …
> (Part II, 245–8)

He claims at the very end to have subdued the rhythms of his own life to the martial drum of a nation at war, so that he feels his heart and the hearts of his countrymen 'beat with one desire' (Part III, 49), but the lines in which he makes the claim serve to undermine it: their rhythm remain tremulous, their metre uncertain. The poem's conclusion recalls the rhythm of the 'passionate ballad' that Maud sang in the meadow, the song of men marching 'with banner and bugle and fife / To the death, for their native land' (Part I, 171–2), but the recollection is prompted by difference rather than by similarity. Even in its last lines the poem retains its metrical eccentricity, putting in doubt the speaker's assertion that he has become 'one with [his] kind'.

As I have already pointed out, in most but not all dramatic poems the formal characteristics of the poem are ascribed to the poet, although the content is credited to the speaker. In 'My Last Duchess', the Duke is responsible for the account that he offers of his late wife, but it is Browning who delivers the account in ten-syllable couplets. Eric Griffiths, who has written the most suggestive study of the relationship in Victorian poetry between the voice and the printed page, insists firmly that it is exactly the same with *Maud*: 'the fiction of this dramatic monologue [like other dramatic monologues] is that the speaker is not trying to produce poetry'.[15] But in *Maud* the fiction is not continuously maintained. Many of the poem's lyrics all but eradicate the possibility of any distinction between speech and the verse in which it is recorded:

> There has fallen a splendid tear
>   From the passion-flower at the gate.
> She is coming, my dove, my dear;
>   She is coming, my life, my fate;

> The red rose cries, 'She is near, she is near;'
> And the white rose weeps, 'She is late;'
> The larkspur listens, 'I hear, I hear;'
> And the lily whispers, 'I wait.'
> (Part I, 908–15)

It would scarcely be possible to offer a version of what the speaker was saying or thinking to himself that Tennyson has translated into this eight-line stanza, because it is not easy to determine what the stanza's content, when separated from its form, might be. It is, as Ruskin remarked, an 'exquisite' instance of the pathetic fallacy: the speaker attributes his own feelings to the garden flowers. But it seems unlikely that he is suffering from a hallucination in which he believes himself to hear flowers talking. It may be that we should think of the lyric as an aria, a song in which the speaker signals in joyous tetrameters that by falling in love he has brought his disordered emotional life under control. He has left the uncultivated landscape of the 'dreadful hollow' for a garden, and the difference between the two marks the difference between two of the 'different phases of passion' that the speaker passes through. Tennyson claimed that in *Maud* such phases took the place of the different characters that are more commonly found in dramatic poems. [16] But it is just as easy to read the lyric as signalling that the speaker is entertaining himself as he waits for the woman he loves by weaving the poetic fictions that best express his mood of delighted erotic expectancy. Like Keats in 'Ode to Psyche' and just as self-consciously he is dressing a 'rosy sanctuary' with the 'wreathed trellis' of a 'working brain'. Read like this, the lyric reveals that this is a speaker who, even when he is in love, remains as self-enclosed as he had been when he was brooding on his wrongs. The garden walls intimate as much, and so do the stanzas, the rooms of eight lines, into which he partitions his song. R.J. Mann was alert to the unusual difficulty in *Maud* of distinguishing between poet and speaker when he described the poem as 'so many impulsive utterances called forth from a mind strung to the pitch of keen poetic sensibility'.[17] Tennyson recited the poem so frequently, despite the fact that reading aloud so long a poem put his listeners' patience to a rather stern test, in part no doubt because he was aware that its metres puzzled many of the poem's readers, but also surely because in his own recitation he could register his intimacy with the poem's speaker. 'My father's voice would break down', Hallam Tennyson remembers, 'when he came to "I have led her home, my love, my only friend."'[18]

This is not just a technical matter. The difficulty in *Maud* of distinguishing between the private thoughts of the speaker and the verse that Tennyson writes becomes of crucial importance in a poem so concerned with the fraught, puzzling relationship between the public and the private. It is a world the character of which may be wholly determined for the speaker by whether Maud's smile is all that it seemed, or 'a glassy smile' offered only to win for her brother a 'wretched vote' at the 'rotten hustings' (I, 229–45), a world in which the speaker might reach the conclusion that the proper reparation for killing Maud's brother in a duel, the 'red life spilt for a private blow' (II, 331), might be to engage in public violence, embracing the 'blood-red blossom of war' (III, 53), in this case the Crimean War. Bleeding is the poem's central figure for the process by which the inner life spills out of the self, staining the world as it does so. The poem opens abruptly with the 'ghastly pit' (I, 5) into which the speaker's father plunged to his death, a landscape in which his father's blood is still freshly and wetly visible in the 'blood-red' heather that stains its lips:

> I hate the dreadful hollow behind the little wood,
> Its lips in the field above are dabbled with blood-red heath,
> The red-ribbed ledges drip with a silent horror of blood,
> And Echo there, whatever is asked her answers 'Death'.
>
> (I, 1–4)

Dramatic monologues often begin abruptly, but when Browning's Duke casually announces, 'That's my last duchess hanging on the wall', readers are invited to imagine that they have interrupted the Duke as he takes the envoy on a leisurely tour of his palace. In *Maud* there is no such assurance. It is easier to understand the abruptness as registering the speaker's disturbed state of mind. In much the same way, the driving six-beat line functions ambiguously, as at once the means by which the speaker imposes a precarious order on his thoughts, and as the signature tune of the dark obsessions that have usurped his consciousness. It is as if the same metre functioned at once as the accentual goblin chant and the more decorous syllabic metres with which Lizzie tries to resist it. The poem's opening lines describe a perverse echo, an echo that, whatever is said, responds with the same one word. It is a perversity that the verse at once refuses and repeats, refuses by rhyming, and repeats because the rhymes so perfect to the eye, wood and blood, heath and Death, fail to satisfy the ear. There are metrical effects that work similarly. The thought of the father's shattered body prompts a line in which outrage is signalled in an unusually emphatic rhythm, 'Mangled, and flattened, and crushed, and dinted into the ground', but this is followed by a line metrically so uncertain that most readers would stumble over it, 'There yet lies the rock that fell with him when he fell' (I, 6–7). My point is that by accommodating lines that work so differently Tennyson reinforces the reader's sense of being both admitted to and excluded from the speaker's consciousness.

The speaker rapidly shifts from traumatic private memory to angry public denunciation (in both metre and subject matter the opening sections of *Maud* look back to 'Locksley Hall' (1842)):

> And the vitriol madness flushes up in the ruffian's head,
> Till the filthy by-lane rings to the yell of the trampled wife,
> And chalk and alum and plaster are sold to the poor for bread,
> And the spirit of murder works in the very means of life.
> (I, 37–40)

He assumes the mantle of the Carlylean prophet, but it is impossible to determine how far his vision is simply extrapolated from his own experiences, an England populated by food adulterators and wife-beaters produced out of a suspicion that his father killed himself because he had been swindled by his own brother and the memory of how, when his father died, he had heard the 'shrill-edged shriek of a mother divide the night' (I, 16). The odd substitution of 'a mother' for 'my mother' anticipates the process by which his own trauma masquerades as an analysis of the state of the nation, which does not, of course, serve to show that the analysis is wrong. 'I do not mean that my madman does not speak truths too,' as Tennyson pointed out.[19] The first section of the poem ends, like almost all its sections, in thoughts of Maud:

> What is she now? My dreams are bad. She may bring me a curse.
> No, there is fatter game on the moor; she will let me alone.
> Thanks, for the fiend best knows whether woman or man be the worse.
> I will bury myself in myself, and the Devil may pipe to his own.
> (Part I, 73–6)

That final resolution (horrifically realized in Part II, when he believes himself dead and buried) is recorded in one of the very few lines in the section (the only other clear instance is line 61) made up simply of six anapaests, but the line concludes a stanza the first line of which it seems easiest to read as prose. Metrical uncertainty is one way in which the poem incorporates the difficulty that its readers will find in understanding its speaker, and it is also the way that the poem finds to incorporate the difficulty that the speaker has in understanding himself.

Saintsbury is disturbed that so fine metrist as Tennyson should in the six-beat lines of *Maud* have so closely approached the 'Clough-hewn hexameter'.[20] The attempt by nineteenth-century poets such as Longfellow, Arnold and Clough to transplant classical metres into English verse, what Yopie Prins calls the 'hexameter mania' that overcame poets in mid-century,[21] still seems one of the odder of Victorian poetic experiments. As Saintsbury acknowledges, it was Clough who, by using the metre in *The Bothie of Tobie-na-Vuolich* (the title under which the poem was first published in 1848, *The Bothie of Toper-na-Fuosich*, was modified when Clough realized that the Gaelic admitted an improper double entendre) and in *Amours de Voyage* (1858, but written 1849), most closely associated himself with it. Clough recognizes as much himself. The unfinished *Dipsychus* (written shortly after Clough's visit to Venice in the autumn of 1850, but only published posthumously) is Clough's most metrically various poem. It includes couplets, both eight-syllable and ten-syllable, blank verse, quatrains and various other stanzas, and the prologue and epilogue are written in prose. But it is when Dipsychus breaks into hexameters that his Mephistophelian companion remarks it: 'Hexameters, by all that's odious' (V, 70). Dipsychus breaks into the metre as he contemplates 'life':

> Life it is beautiful wholly, and could we eliminate only
> This interfering, enslaving, o'ermastering demon of craving,
> This wicked tempter inside us to ruin still eager to guide us,
> Life were beatitude, action a possible pure satisfaction.
>
> (V, 66–9)

He looks at life in these lines, but he looks at it from the outside. The heroes of all three of Clough's long poems, Philip Hewson, Claude and Dipsychus, are given the task of deciding their way of life, of making their accommodation with the world by choosing between the 'grievously narrow and limited spheres of action' that are all that is ever available (Clough made the remark in his review of Arnold's poems).[22] The hexameter is Clough's signature metre because it is the metre that he associates with that stage of a young man's life, when he looks at the world, but looks at it as Dipsychus looks at it in the lines I have just quoted, as a *spectator ab extra*. The epilogue to *Dipsychus* records the response of the poet's uncle after the poem has been recited to him. The uncle observes that the public schools of his own day, unlike Dr Arnold's Rugby where his nephew, like Clough himself, had been a pupil, were at least 'in harmony with the world'. Hexameters, for Clough, are the measure for those who remain out of harmony with it. It is a student metre, a metre closely associated with Oxford undergraduates whose education was so firmly centred on the study of the classics. Dipsychus seems, like the poet who devised him, still to be an undergraduate (the uncle speaks of 'the worthy head of your college'), Claude of *Amours de Voyage* seems to be making a European tour immediately after graduating, and Philip Hewson in the *Bothie* is part of a reading party visiting Scotland with their tutor in the long vacation before they take their Finals. It is the metre that Clough seems to have associated with young men confronting the difficulty that most young men feel as their student years come to an end and they are obliged to consider how their theoretical understanding of life might best be put into practice.

In the *Bothie* the hexameters work to place the Oxford undergraduates at a bookish remove from the pressing realities of life as it is lived outside the universities. The metre is particularly appropriate to Philip, the poem's hero, who, as his fellow-student, Hobbes, points out, 'speaks like a book', like an especially weighty book, 'a folio' (II, 142–3). The action of the poem takes place in an interval of three weeks in which the young men are released from their studies to wander through the Scottish Highlands. It is a brief respite from books, from the Greek dictionary, 'Liddell-and-Scott' (II, 222), and from the Greek texts that they are studying, 'Aeschylus, Sophocles, Homer, Herodotus, Pindar, and Plato' (II, 227). These are the weeks during which Philip escapes from a merely theoretical appreciation of the beauty of labour into which he had been inducted when he saw an attractive young woman digging potatoes. He escapes by falling in love with the daughter of David Mackaye, who farms the bothie at Tober-na-Vuolich. The poem ends when Philip emigrates with his bride to New Zealand and the two of them start a farm, but the poem itself, as its sub-title, 'A Long-Vacation Pastoral' indicates, stays within the precincts of the university, and what keeps it there is its metre.

Amours de Voyage takes place in Rome in 1848, in the brief summer of Garibaldi's Roman Republic, but its hero, the Oxford-educated Claude, unlike Philip Hewson, cannot quite find it in him to commit himself to a political cause, to a woman, or even, without misgivings, to a work of art. St Peters, crowned by 'Michael Angelo's dome, that had hung the Pantheon in heaven,' is spoiled for Claude, who cannot forget his disapproval of the 'metallic beliefs and regimental devotions' of the Catholic worshippers (110–3). He finds it just as hard to forget his fellow-tourist, the prosperous but disconcertingly bourgeois Mrs Trevellyn, long enough to fall in love with her daughter. Mrs Trevellyn is an intellectual, and yet, even when she 'adventures on Schiller', she manages still to grate 'the fastidious ear with the slightly mercantile accent.' (209–11) Claude's sensitivity to Mrs Trevellyn's voice trains the reader to be equally sensitive to his own, alert to the callowness that it masks as sophistication, to the facetiousness with which it disguises his fear of making a fool of himself, and to the cynicism in which it cloaks his sentimentality. Claude, even more completely than Philip, is fully revealed in Clough's metre, the hexameters that keep him at a remove from the life that he records by revealing that, even in Italy, so far away from Oxford, he remains enclosed within its cloisters. Claude decides that it is providence rather than farcical coincidence that prevents him from catching up with Mary Trevellyn when he leaves Rome in pursuit of her. The thought prompts a reflection:

> Shall we come out of it all, some day, as one does from a tunnel?
> Will it be all at once, without our doing or asking,
> We shall behold clear day, the trees and meadows about us,
> And the faces of friends, and the eyes we loved looking at us?
> Who knows? Who can say? It will not do to suppose it.
>
> (1199–23)

What gives these lines their poignancy is that Claude imagines emerging into clear day while all the time he remains enclosed within his own metrical tunnel, trapped in a verse movement that keeps him separate from the trees and the meadows. When he walks about Rome he carries his guide book with him, and the Murray under his arm marks him out as a tourist in the city, not a resident. His metre has much the same effect, confirming that he looks at life as he looks at Rome, as a tourist.

As Henry Sidgwick pointed out, 'Clough's line is, and is meant to be, conscious of being a hexameter', which is a sign that he has not '*naturalised* the metre'.[23] It is a failure that in *The Bothie* and in *Amours de Voyage* Clough turns into a virtue. It is not one that he seems likely to share with

Thomas Hardy who has so often been represented as a quintessentially English poet, and yet Hardy, as Dennis Taylor has pointed out, was interested like Clough in introducing classical metres into English verse. Dennis Taylor has suggested that the quatrains of 'Neutral Tones', one of the most celebrated of the poems included in *Wessex Poems and Other Verses* (1898, although 'Neutral Tones' is dated 1867), should be thought of as 'roughened Sapphics'.[24] The poem consists of four quatrains in each of which three tetrameter lines conclude in a trimeter:

> We stood by a pond that winter day,
> And the sun was white, as though chidden of God,
> And a few leaves lay on the starving sod;
>   –They had fallen from an ash, and were gray.
>
> Your eyes on me were as eyes that rove
> Over tedious riddles of years ago;
> And some words played between us to and fro
>   On which lost the more by our love.
>
> The smile on your mouth was the deadest thing
> Alive enough to have strength to die;
> And a grin of bitterness swept thereby
>   Like an ominous bird a-wing… .
>
> Since then, keen lessons that love deceives,
> And wrings with wrong, have shaped to me
> Your face, and the God-curst sun, and a tree,
>   And a pond edged with grayish leaves.

The rhyme scheme is Tennyson's in *In Memoriam*, but the truncated last line signals an eagerness that Tennyson does not share to consign, if it were only possible, the past to the past. As in a Wordsworthian spot of time the poem presents a landscape reduced to a few elements, a pale sun, a pond, some fallen leaves, and then returns to the landscape once again, 'the God-curst sun, and a tree, / And a pond edged with grayish leaves' (15–6). But whereas in Wordsworth the repetition endows the moment with meaning, in Hardy the effect is reversed. The scene is as emptied of human value as the white sun of the opening stanza is bleached of colour. Whatever meaning may once have been attached to it has long been discarded, like a riddle that was not so much too difficult to solve as too dull to be bothered with. The poem charts a movement, but a wholly negative one, from a sun the paleness of which suggests that it is 'chidden of God', the object of a displeasure which savingly assumes a God that continues to feel a parental responsibility for the world that he has created (Matthew Campbell perceptively suggests that Hardy is punning on the phrase, children of God[25]), to a 'God-curst sun', a sun that presides over a universe that God has wholly abandoned.

Much more wholeheartedly than Tennyson in *In Memoriam* Hardy presents the business of versification as a 'dull mechanic exercise' only valuable for its narcotic effect, its power to deaden pain. (*In Memoriam*, V, 5–8) Six of the poem's sixteen lines begin with 'And', as if the primary concern was to muffle sharp feeling in the soothing tedium of repetition. The metre at first works similarly. The final line of the first stanza is peculiarly dispiriting, 'They had fallen from an ash, and were gray', a trimeter made up of three anapaests, the first somewhat tentative, because 'fallen' counts as a single syllable, the second and third deadeningly emphatic. The effect is more marked because in the line before, 'And a few leaves lay on the starving sod', the poem had made at least a gesture towards rhythmic vitality by inviting the voice to supply a stress on 'leaves' that the metre disallows.

William Empson observed that 'Hardy often simply drops his rhythm, as a child stops its rattle and stares straight at the skyline, dribbling slightly.'[26] This seems rude, but it is a habit, as Empson knew, that secures some of Hardy's finest effects. Take, for example, the first three stanzas of 'The Voice' from *Poems 1912–13*:

Woman much missed, how you call to me, call to me,
Saying that now you are not as you were
When you had changed from the one who was all to me,
But as at first, when our day was fair.

Can it be you that I hear? Let me view you, then,
Standing as when I drew near to the town
Where you would wait for me: yes, as I knew you then,
Even to the original air-blue gown!

Or is it only the breeze, in its listlessness
Travelling across the wet mead to me here,
You being ever dissolved to wan wistlessness,
Heard no more again far or near?

(1–12)

The ghostly, haunting voice of the dead woman is realized in the dactylic movement of the verse so emphatically established in the first line ('call to me, call to me'), but in the final lines of the second and third stanzas the rattle stops. In the first instance it is as if Hardy has been shocked out of plangency by the unnerving precision of the memory, 'Even to the original air-blue gown!' In the second, it is as if the rhythm collapses into sobs, 'Heard no more again far or near?' There is nothing quite so mesmerising as this in 'Neutral Tones', but in its second stanza Hardy's grip on his rattle at least loosens:

> And some words played between us to and fro
> On which lost the more by our love.
>
> (7–8)

The verbs in both lines are placed on syllables that are metrically unstressed. The sense as well as the rhythm of the lines is uncertain, though I read them as recalling a conversation in which the lovers, rather than disputing as conventional lovers might as to which of the two is the more fortunate, discuss which has been the more impoverished by their relationship. It is odd to describe the lovers' words as playing between rather than issuing from them, an effort perhaps to preserve the studied neutrality of the poem's tone. But it serves also to call attention to the manner in which the line threatens to escape Hardy's metrical control, and in doing so threatens to disclose the 'keen lesson' that the poem seems anxious to conceal, not the general truth that 'love deceives', but the far bleaker perception that there may be a kind of love from the loss of which there is no recovery. In the third quatrain, Hardy energetically plays between life and death:

> The smile on your mouth was the deadest thing
> Alive enough to have strength to die.
>
> (9–10)

The paradox cuts to the heart of a poem that offers its indifference as the most telling acknowledgement of its passion, but it also serves usefully to indicate that, just as the Impressionist painters found that any colour was vivified when brought together with the colour complementary to it, Victorian poets found that emotions were intensified when brought into neighbourhood with their negative counterparts. Here a smile's deadening quality is affirmed by its vitality, and by the power it retains even now to wound. It is one more reason why the Victorians were so attracted to the double poem, but that attraction is evident too in the manner in which they handled their metres, and by the consistency with which they clung to the principle that the rhythm of a poem is properly established in the conflict between the drive to assert metrical regularity and the contrary impulse to subordinate the metre of the poem to its sense.

Endnotes

1. George Saintsbury, *A History of English Prosody*, 3 vols (London: Macmillan, 1910), 3, p. 317.
2. See the 'Metrical Appendix' in Dennis Taylor's *Hardy's Metre and Victorian Prosody* (Oxford: Clarendon Press, 1988).
3. William Wordsworth, *The Poems*, ed. John O. Hayden (Harmondsworth: Penguin, 1977), 1, p. 885.
4. *The Letters of Gerard Manley Hopkins to Robert Bridges*, ed. Claude Colleer Abbott (London: Oxford University Press, 1935), pp. 46 and 263.
5. *Coventry Patmore's 'Essay on English Metrical Law'*, ed. Mary Augustine Roth(Washington: Catholic University of America Press, 1961), p. 8.
6. In 'On Some Technical Elements of Style', Robert Louis Stevenson, *Essays in the Art of Writing* (London: Chatto and Windus, 1919), pp. 16–7.
7. Henry Newbolt, *A New Study of English Poetry* (London: Constable, 1917), p. 32.
8. Eric Griffiths, *The Printed Voice of Victorian Poetry* (Oxford: Clarendon Press, 1989), p. 74.
9. Matthew Campbell, *Rhythm and Will in Victorian Poetry*, (Cambridge: Cambridge University Press, 1999), pp. 23–32.
10. Yopie Prins, 'Victorian meters' in *The Cambridge Companion to Victorian Poetry*, ed. Joseph Bristow (Cambridge: Cambridge University Press, 2000), pp. 89–113.
11. George Saintsbury, *A History of English Prosody*, 3 vols (London: Macmillan, 1910), 3, pp. 353–4.
12. George Puttenham, *The Art of English Poesie*, ed. Gladys D. Willcock and Alice Walker (Cambridge: Cambridge University Press, 1936), p. 76.
13. Edwin Guest, *A History of English Rhythms* (London: Bell, 1882), p. 172.
14. *Tennyson: The Critical Heritage*, ed. John D. Jump (London: Routledge, 1974), p. 209.
15. Eric Griffiths, *The Printed Voice of Victorian Poetry*, p. 155.
16. See Hallam Tennyson, *Alfred Lord Tennyson: A Memoir*, 1, p. 396.
17. *Tennyson: The Critical Heritage*, p. 199.

18. Hallam Tennyson, *Alfred Lord Tennyson: A Memoir*, 1, p. 599.
19. *The Letters of Alfred Lord Tennyson*, ed. Cecil Y. Lang and Edgar F. Shannon, 3 vols, 2 (Oxford: Clarendon Press, 1987), p. 138.
20. George Saintsbury, *A History of English Prosody*, 3, p. 208.
21. Yopie Prins, 'Victorian meters', pp. 100–6.
22. *Prose Remains of Arthur Hugh Clough*, ed. Blanche Clough (London: Macmillan, 1888), p. 357.
23. *Clough: The Critical Heritage*, ed. Michael Thorpe (London: Routledge and Kegan Paul, 1972), p. 286.
24. Dennis Taylor, *Hardy's Metres and Victorian Prosody*, p. 261.
25. Matthew Campbell, *Rhythm and Will in Victorian Poetry*, p. 59.
26. William Empson, *Argufying: Essays on Literature and Culture*, ed. John Haffenden (London: Hogarth Press, 1988), p. 422.

4

Short Poems, Long Poems and the Victorian Sonnet Sequence

As a young man, ambitious to win a reputation as a poet, Tennyson had a gloomy sense that 'most of the big things except King Arthur had been done'. If he was 'to make any mark at all, it must be by shortness': 'the men before [him] had been so diffuse'. He could make the same point more buoyantly: 'A small vessel, built on fine lines, is likely to float further down the stream of time than a big raft'. But both remarks reveal how Tennyson's creative life was shadowed by the intimidating presence of 'the men before [him]', the men who had done the big things.[1] It was the common lot of the Victorian poet, for whom it was no longer possible to write without hearing, like Browning's Childe Roland (1855), 'names in [their] ears / Of all the lost adventurers [their] peers' (194–5). Arnold was perceptive as well as witty when he claimed that three lines from Tennyson's 'Ulysses' 'by themselves take up nearly as much time as a whole book of the Iliad',[2] but the fact remains that Tennyson's supplement to Homer only occupies seventy lines. Even in a poem that unavoidably invites epic comparison Tennyson spurns the big raft in favour of the small vessel.

In this, Victorian poets seem at a very far remove from their American contemporaries. In 1842, when he lectured in New York, Emerson believed that when he characterized the American poet he was imagining a kind of poet who did not yet exist: 'I look in vain for the poet whom I describe.'[3] He was unaware that sitting amongst his audience was Walt Whitman, who was already beginning to conceive how it might be possible to write a poetry that scrupulously divested itself of all the 'sounded and resounded words – chattering words, echoes, dead words.' ('Not Heaving from My Ribb'd Breast Only' (1860), 12) His project, to find a

Reading Victorian Poetry, First Edition. Richard Cronin.

new language for poetry, was akin to Browning's, but Browning tellingly made no direct claim to it, and chose instead to ascribe the project to Sordello, his thirteenth-century Mantuan troubadour, as if to acknowledge that on his side of the Atlantic there was no escape from history. Whitman seems headily confident that *Leaves of Grass* might be continuous with his nation because 'the United States themselves are essentially the greatest poem.' For him, the poet as representative of the American people fulfils a role just as important as that of the nation's elected President. Whitman seems wholly free from the burden of secondariness that preoccupied his British contemporaries. The rhetoric that he devises, his heady paratactic expansiveness and his figurative richness, work together to generate the astonishing affirmatory energy that characterizes so much of his verse. For Whitman, the United States, like the metre, and the diction, and the content of Whitman's poems, is the embodiment of a new dispensation the purpose of which is to do away with obstructive barriers of gender, class, race and nation. He calls his volume *Leaves of Grass* (1855, but Whitman continued to revise and expand the volume until his death), a title that fuses the pages on which his poems are printed with the broad prairies that they celebrate.

Whitman's poems are 'chants of the prairies,' ('Starting from Paumanock' (1860), 40) poems that very often celebrate the unfenced spaces that Whitman's long lines and the paratactic syntax of his poems reach after. British poets, by contrast, seem often to favour the enclosed space. Matthew Arnold's 'Lines written in Kensington Gardens,' (1852) is typical. Arnold writes from a place that is enclosed by the great city of London and yet secluded from it. He lies on grass that is scarcely less fresh than 'the mountain-sod,' (17) a place that reminds him of how, even in his 'helpless cradle', he was 'breathed on by the rural Pan,' (23–4) and yet all through the poem he registers the facts that his quiet quatrains resist, chief amongst them the traffic noises, the 'girdling city's hum' and 'jar' (6 and 38) that, even as he lies beneath the trees, his ears register. Arnold may entertain the illusion that he writes from a place where the birds, the daisies, and the 'air-stirred forest' enjoy an 'endless, active life' (14–6) that exposes the urgent bustle of the city streets that surround him as no more than an 'impious uproar.' (25) But the poem exposes that illusion as well as entertains it. The only human presence that intrudes on Arnold's solitude, the child carrying his broken toy to his nurse, reveals that the place that Arnold associates with the 'Calm soul of all things,' (37) is, in fact, an urban park, a place that cannot offer a true alternative to metropolitan

London, because the park was planned, planted and is maintained by the city that surrounds it. It is London that grants Arnold and the other visitors to the park the experience that the poem celebrates, the illusion that they have escaped the city. Kensington Gardens is rather like the space occupied by Victorian poetry. As Tennyson put it in 'The Gardener's Daughter' (1842): 'Not wholly in the busy world, nor quite / Beyond it, blooms the garden that I love.' (33–4) In his lectures 'On the Study of Celtic Literature' Arnold identifies the Welsh seaside resort of Llandudno as just such a spot. If he looks eastward he sees the Liverpool steamboats bringing the holiday-makers who will take possession of Llandudno's lodging houses, but if he turns around and looks westward he sees a landscape bathed in 'the eternal softness and mild light of the west; the low line of the mystic Anglesey, and the precipitous Penmaenmawr, and the great group of Carnedd Llewelyn and Carnedd David and their brethren fading away, hill beyond hill, in an aerial haze'.[4]

'Lines Written in Kensington Gardens' seems haunted by the guilt felt by all city-dwellers who spend a working day lying in the park, at leisure while the workaday world goes about its business. The slightness of the poem, just forty-four octosyllabic lines, seems properly modest, acknowledging, it may be, that it would not be quite seemly to attempt a poem that made too large a claim on the time of the poet or of his reader. Arnold's poem, unlike Whitman's, refuses to sprawl, and that seems entirely befitting a poet unsure of how much attention poetry could properly claim in the mid-nineteenth century. When George Eliot heard that Browning's *The Ring and the Book* had reached 20 000 lines she was moved to ask, 'Who will read it all in these busy days?'[5] It was, Tennyson claimed, precisely because his predecessors had been 'so diffuse' that he was obliged himself to explore the virtues of 'littleness', and he speaks, it may seem, not just for himself but for all his British contemporaries. Other poets had noticed the snowdrop, but Tennyson would be the first to note the 'lines of green that streak the white / Of the first's snowdrop's inner leaves' (*The Princess*, 5, 188–9), and he recorded such observations in poems that invite exactly the same minute admiration from the reader that the poems themselves extend to the natural world.

Tennyson helped his friend Francis Palgrave make his selection for *The Golden Treasury* (1861), a volume that promised to bring together 'all the best original Lyrical pieces and Songs in our language, by writers not living'. In the first edition this feat was accomplished in just 332 pages. *The Golden Treasury* rapidly became the most successful anthology ever published, which might seem a decisive confirmation of the Victorian preference for finding beauty in the small-scale, for admiring, as Tennyson put it, the lines of small vessels. But the case was more complex than I have suggested. Those long lines of Whitman, for example, seem to challenge Bentham's dictum that prose differs from poetry because in prose all the lines go on to the edge of the page whereas in poetry they 'fall short of it'. His line seems to claim for poetry the spaciousness of prose, and that taste of Whitman's for long lines was shared by many of his British contemporaries; not just his admirers Swinburne and Hopkins, but Browning in a poem such as *La Saisiaz* and Tennyson in a group of poems, amongst them 'Locksley Hall'. Those long lines are a token that Tennyson himself was not immune to the charms of diffuseness, which is surely one of the distinguishing features of the poetic manner that Hopkins called Parnassian, and exemplified in Tennyson's description of the tropical island in *Enoch Arden*: 'in Parnassian pieces you feel that if you were the poet you could have gone on as he has done, you see yourself doing it.'[6] For Swinburne, as T.S. Eliot somewhat grudgingly acknowledged, 'the diffuseness is essential; had Swinburne practised greater concentration his verse would be, not better in the same kind, but a different thing.'[7] Christina Rossetti cultivates more severely than any Victorian poet an aesthetics of modesty that finds its proper expression in the production of brief lyrics. *Goblin Market* (1862) extends exceptionally to 567 lines, but this is because the poem, like the errant sister, Laura, is infected by the goblins and their masculine aesthetics of excess. The 'fiery antidote' with which Lizzie defeats the infection secures for both sisters an 'Afterwards, when both were wives / With children of their own' (544–5), but the contentment that they go on to enjoy seems inseparable from constraint. It is a state in which their lives are 'bound up' in the lives of their children, and its happiness seems completed only when Laura shares with her children her memories of the 'wicked, quaint fruit-merchant men' after whom she had once stretched her neck, 'Like a vessel at the launch / When its last restraint is gone' (85–6). The goblin men carry at once the threat and the promise of that life free from constraint that the verse too seems to reach after:

> 'You cannot think what figs
> My teeth have met in,
> What melons, icy-cold
> Piled on a dish of gold
> Too huge for me to hold,

> What peaches with a velvet nap,
> Pellucid grapes without one seed:
> Odorous indeed must be the mead
> Whereon they grow, and pure the wave they drink,
> With lilies at the brink,
> And sugar-sweet their sap.'
>
> (173–83)

For much of its length the poem employs a paratactic syntax that seems actively to resist being brought to a pause. It is so long because it contains so many lists and the lists threaten never to end. In *Goblin Market* even Christina Rossetti reveals that nineteenth-century miniaturism counters, and is sometimes ousted by, a quite different aesthetic.

Herbert Tucker has produced in his *Epic: Britain's Heroic Muse, 1790–1910* the first comprehensive study of the Victorian gigantism that delighted in the production of epic poems almost as much as in triple-decker novels.[8] His is at 737 pages an appropriately gigantic study of gigantism. Most of these poems had, until he unearthed them, been utterly forgotten. Who, one wonders, was the last before Tucker to have read *Alfred: A Poem*, an epic in forty-eight books and more than 130 000 lines that John Fitchett had been working on for forty years before finally publishing it in 1841–2? Poets, Aurora Leigh insists, must have the faculty of 'double vision' (5, 184), a vision that enables them at once to see the lines of green that streak the inner petals of the snowdrop, and to plumb infinite space, and she says so in Barrett Browning's own 'unscrupulously epic' (5, 214) poem. *Aurora Leigh*, unlike Fitchett's *Alfred*, finds its proper subject matter in

> this live, throbbing age,
> That brawls, cheats, maddens, calculates, aspires,
> And spends more passion, more heroic heat,
> Betwixt the mirrors of its drawing-rooms,
> Than Roland with his knights at Roncesvalles.
>
> (5, 203–7)

Aurora Leigh was identified by those reviewers least disposed to admire it as Barrett Browning's own Spasmodic poem, and it was the Spasmodics, briefly so popular in mid-century, together with Philip Bailey, the predecessor they most admired, who established the composition of a contemporary epic as the achievement to which the Victorian poet ought to aspire. As George

Gilfillan, who elected himself as the champion of Spasmodic verse, put it, 'Wanted, a tutor to the rising age; he must be a creedless Christian – full of faith, but full of charity – wise in head and large in heart – a poet and a priest – an "eternal child", as well as a thoroughly furnished man.'[9]

As Gilfillan intimates, the Spasmodics, like Carlyle, were fully persuaded that in the modern age the poet must be his own epic subject. As David Masson put it, in an admiring review of Alexander Smith, the most successful of them, 'A true allegory of the state of one's own mind in a representative history is perhaps the highest thing that one can attempt in the way of poetry'. It was a notion that Matthew Arnold found so galling that he chose to repudiate his own most ambitious poem, *Empedocles on Etna*, fearing that it came too close to fulfilling the reviewer's brief.[10] When the poet becomes his own epic subject, the distinction between poet and poem evaporates. The poet's collected works become, to use the title of the poem by Alexander Smith that Masson was reviewing, *A Life-Drama*. It was a notion that Wordsworth had introduced in his preface to *The Excursion* (1814), when he offered the poem as a part of the great work that he was never to complete, 'The Recluse'. He described 'The Recluse' as forming 'the body of a gothic church, to which the unpublished *Prelude* served as 'the ante-chapel'. All of his other poems, he claimed, had 'such connexion with the main Work as may give them claim to be likened to the little cells, oratories, and sepulchral recesses, ordinarily included in these edifices.' Wordsworth was offering as his epic achievement his whole oeuvre. It was a principle taken up across the Atlantic by Walt Whitman, whose *Leaves of Grass* was in its first edition of 1855 a slender volume of just 95 pages, but had become by the deathbed edition of 1891–2 a stout tome 438 pages long. Whitman preserved the title as a way of indicating that it was the whole of his published work that constituted his epic of America. British poets seem less flamboyant, but the major Victorian poets, again following Wordsworth who published the first collected edition of his poems in 1815, began to produce collected editions of their poems from mid-career. The first edition of Robert Browning's *Poetic Works*, for example, appeared in 1863, although he was to continue to write and publish for more than twenty-five years. It was a publishing habit that diverted attention from the individual poem to the poetic career, as if the proper object of the reader's admiration was not this poem or that, but a self-making process that was fully represented by a poet's work in its entirety. 'Only in the whole of my work,' Browning counselled Margaret Keep just two years before he died, 'may be expected to appear a general impression of the truth',[11] as if the successive volumes of his verse ought to be read like the successive books of his own epic poem. Browning did not publish that epic, *The Ring and the Book*, until 1868–9, but by publishing his *Poetic Works* in 1863, he had already presented himself as the author of the epic poem 'Robert Browning'.

It was a cultural development to which the Spasmodic poets were finely attuned. George Gilfillan first recognized Alexander Smith's talent when Smith sent him some poems in manuscript. He encouraged Smith to prepare a volume for publication, and in the interim publicized as widely as he could the advent of an extraordinary new talent. Gilfillan seems to have expected a conventional collection, but instead Smith embedded his poems within a single dramatic poem that traced its hero's pursuit of poetic fame, and his achievement of it by the hasty and fevered composition of just such a poem as *A Life-Drama* (1853). The chief influence on *A Life-Drama* is Philip Bailey's *Festus*, in which Festus recommends that a young poet train himself in his craft by studying a vast, sprawling epic poem that he confesses at last is his own composition, and that seems scarcely distinguishable from *Festus* itself. The epic action becomes the composition of the epic poem, a notion to which Bailey devoted his whole career. In its first edition in 1839 *Festus* was a substantial poem of a little more than 8000 lines. By its seventh edition in 1889 it had swollen to almost 40 000 lines, an expansion assisted by Bailey's decision to subsume within it what had once been independent poems.

Victorian poets, it might seem, were divided between those like Tennyson persuaded of the virtues of littleness, and those like Philip Bailey whose poems were subject to a process of continual expansion that could only be arrested by death. But in fact the poets most representative of the period commonly owned a double allegiance. They acknowledged the claims both of the small and of the large. Tennyson, for example, presented himself in his *Poems* of 1842, as a small-scale poet, a poet who preferred the idyll to the epic. He included within the collection an epic fragment, *Morte d'Arthur*, but its fragmentary status, the eleventh book of twelve preserved in a manuscript saved by an admirer from the flames to which the poet intended to have consigned his whole poem, seems only to underline Tennyson's rejection of the epic enterprise. The poet burnt the poem after deciding that 'those twelve books of mine / Were faint Homeric echoes, nothing worth'. ('The Epic', 38–9) But in the sense that I have already outlined, *Poems*, 1842, was itself an epic enterprise, two substantial volumes, in the first of which Tennyson reissued revised versions of his

Poems 1833, in the second included newly written poems, and in the publication of the whole announced himself as 'Alfred Tennyson', the leading poet of his generation. His publication of *Morte d'Arthur* was in itself a characteristically double-faced gesture, at once disclaiming epic ambitions and serving as an advertisement for an epic poem on a theme, King Arthur, that he had long identified as the one big thing that had not yet been done. Tennyson told William Allingham that he had only been prevented from completing the poem at once by John Sterling's review of it: 'I had it all in my mind, could have done it without any trouble'.[12] The confidence is perhaps too airily expressed to be quite persuasive, but thirty years later in 1872, in the Imperial Library edition of his *Works*, Tennyson did finally publish his Arthurian epic, *Idylls of the King* – except that Tennyson, even in his title, denied his achievement. It is not just that idylls and epics are different kinds of poem, they are antithetical: idylls are short (from the Greek, eidyllion, little picture) and epics long; idylls are descriptive, but in epic description is subordinated to action; idylls are work proper to the apprentice, whereas the epic is work for which only the master is equipped; idylls please by their variety, but the epic is divided into books the more clearly to assert its unity. In 1869 a reviewer in *The Spectator* praised Tennyson for having converted 'a very exquisite series of cabinet pictures' into 'a great tragic epic', but did not explain how the feat had been achieved, and Tennyson might not have accepted the compliment. Late in 1872 he wrote to George Grove complaining of R.H. Hutton having 'called the Idylls an Epic which they are not.'[13] It was another thirteen years before Tennyson yielded so far as to allow his poem an epic number of books. In 1873, he divided 'Enid' into two books, 'The Marriage of Geraint' and 'Geraint and Enid', and in 1885 he finally published 'Balin and Balan', which took its place as the sixth Idyll in what had finally become a sequence of twelve. Tennyson began writing *Morte d'Arthur* in 1833, and his project ended in 1885 with the publication of 'Balin and Balan' (though characteristically in 1873 Tennyson had told R.H. Hutton that he must add not one but 'two more Idylls at the least'[14]). That lapse of more than half a century is not at all a sign of Tennyson's recognition of the scale of the epic project, it is a symptom of his inability to decide whether he was writing a long poem or a sequence of much shorter poems.

It was an indecisiveness that Tennyson displayed throughout his career. His first attempt at a long poem, *The Princess* (1847), is subtitled 'A Medley'. Each of the seven books is supplied by a different undergraduate before the poet of the group is invited to 'dress the tale up poetically'. The poet himself acknowledges that the poem he contrives is divided against itself, torn between the desire of the young men for a 'mock-heroic gigantesque' and the wishes of the women, who 'hated banter, wished for something real'. The poem, he confesses, moves 'as in a strange diagonal', between the comic and the serious, between the tale and the songs supplied by the women that punctuate it, '[l]ike linnets in the pauses of the wind', between sympathy for the women's desire for an education, and sympathy for the men's preference for conventional brides ('Conclusion', 1–28). Elizabeth Barrett Browning detected an incongruity between the poem's epic scale and its romance subject matter: 'Now isn't the world too old & fond of steam, for blank verse poems, in ever so many books, to be written on the fairies?'[15] Tennyson's decision to present his poem as a work that the poet had failed to unify allowed him an easy response to such objections: 'it is, after all, only a medley.'[16]

In Memoriam, the most successful of his long poems, has a still more ambivalent status. The poem, first published anonymously in 1850, consists of a prologue, epilogue and 131 lyrics, the first of which had been written on October 6, 1833, days after Tennyson first learned that his closest Cambridge friend and his sister's fiancé had died of a brain haemorrhage in Venice. Hallam Tennyson reports his father as saying, 'I did not write them with any view of weaving them into a whole, or for publication, until I found that I had written so many'.[17] It seems an eccentric procedure, but the most popular of all nineteenth-century volumes of poetry had a very similar genesis. John Keble wrote the poems that he gathered together in *The Christian Year* piecemeal. The earliest of them were written in 1819, but it was not until much nearer the date of their publication, 1827, that Keble had the thought of linking them so that the poems might together comprise a calendar of the ecclesiastical year as set out in the Book of Common Prayer. It remains unclear exactly when Tennyson made the discovery that he had written a single poem rather than a number of independent lyrics. In 1844 he was still referring to 'those poems', but his brother-in-law Edmund Lushington recalled Tennyson telling him in the summer of 1845, 'I have brought in your marriage at the end of "In Memoriam"', and Edward FitzGerald must have thought of it as a single poem in January, 1845, when he complained that it was far too long: 'Lycidas is the utmost length an elegiac should reach'.[18] Two titles that Tennyson thought of giving his poem lean in quite different directions. 'The Way of the Soul' claims a singleness of design that 'Fragments of an Elegy' insistently refuses.[19] As in *The Princess*, the indecision is allowed to infiltrate the poem. The poem ends by paying to 'the one far-off divine event, / To which the whole creation moves' ('Epilogue', 143–4) a tribute that cannot help but claim for the poem that these lines conclude at least a shadow of God's perfectly unified cosmic narrative. But the poem's last two lines, however they may modify, cannot repudiate the very different suggestions Tennyson has let fall in earlier sections, in which the lyrics that make up *In Memoriam* are described as 'wild and wandering cries' (Prologue, 41), '[s]hort swallow-flights of song' (48, 15), and as owning, like the natural world, a 'fantastic beauty' that can only ever be apprehended by some 'wild Poet, when he works / Without a conscience or an aim'. (34, 7–8)

It is in his indecisions that Tennyson reveals himself most fully as the representative Victorian poet. He makes exalted claims on his own behalf – *In Memoriam* is 'meant to be a kind of *Divina Commedia*'[20] – and disclaimers just as emphatic. 'The general way of its being written,' he said of the same poem, remembering how he had drafted it in one of the 'butcher's books' that served as his notebooks, 'was so queer that if there were a blank space I put in a poem'.[21] He shared that odd compound of high ambition and diffidence with many of his contemporaries, and one way that it reveals itself is in not quite deciding whether to attempt big things or to rely instead on the virtues of shortness. The indecision is most fully revealed in Victorian poets' dealings with the sonnet. Wordsworth, when he spoke of 'the Sonnet's scanty plot of ground', could rely on a long tradition that had established the sonnet as an unusually compact verse form. Its popularity amongst so many Victorian poets is another demonstration, it might seem, of the Victorian preference for the small-scale lyric, except that Victorian poets did not simply favour the individual sonnet. One of the more bizarre Victorian revivals was the sonnet sequence, examples of which were produced by Elizabeth Barrett Browning, George Meredith, D.G. and Christina Rossetti, George Eliot, Augusta Webster, and a large number of poets now less well remembered. In Renaissance Europe the fashion for the sonnet sequence was impelled by an interest in adulterous codes of courtly love and neoplatonic metaphysics, neither of which could be reckoned general in the nineteenth century. The sonnet recommended itself to Victorian poets in part because it was so self-conscious a verse form, as Matthew Russell signalled in 1898 when he produced an anthology of sonnets that took as their subject the sonnet itself, *Sonnets on the Sonnet: An Anthology*. The sonnet was unusually accommodating to the self-consciousness that Victorian poets tended to bring to every verse form that they attempted, and sonnet sequences tended to be still more self-conscious than individual examples. The sequence had the additional advantage of having the double identity that Tennyson claimed for *In Memoriam*. A sonnet, according to William Davis in the *Quarterly Review*, was 'a full, rounded, and complete organism' and Charles Tomlinson added that it should be 'capable of being separated and admired for itself, without reference to its position in a collection,' a description that brings out the full ambivalence of the sonnet sequence which is at once a single poem, and a collection of independent poems.[22]

Victorian sonnet sequences, then, have a double character, which is entirely appropriate because so do their speakers. The same might be said of Renaissance sonnet sequences that typically invoke a private history fully available only to a closed circle of readers. Sir Philip Sidney in *Astrophil and Stella* makes covert reference to his relationship with Penelope Devereux, whose married name, happily for a poet who preferred to veil his personal references in puns, was Rich. But the sequence also explores Sidney's interest in love as a Platonic ideal, the longing of the star-lover for his star. That double character is nicely epitomised by Samuel Daniel whose sequence was addressed to 'Delia', who is at once an individual woman and an anagram of 'Ideal'. Again, *In Memoriam* offers the best guide to Victorian practice. It is an intimate, at times an embarrassingly intimate poem, and yet a poem of which Tennyson might reasonably claim, '"I" is not always the author speaking of himself, but the voice of the human race speaking through him.'[23] The sonnet sequence appealed to Victorian poets because it offered the opportunity at once to cultivate a private, lyric voice, and a voice that spoke on behalf of the human race. It was a verse form, then, that was especially receptive to that divided ambition that most Victorians owned.

The most ambitious of these sequences, D.G. Rossetti's *The House of Life*, is distinctive because Rossetti, as his translations of *The Early Italian Poets* (1861, revised and reissued as *Dante and his Circle* in 1874) indicate, had more interest in the philosophy of courtly love than his contemporaries. He also had more interest than most of them in adulterous liaisons. His sonnet sequence was the product of his relationship with William Morris's wife, Jane. Like a number of long Victorian poems from Bailey's *Festus* to Clough's *Dipsychus*, it exists in a number of forms none of which can be regarded as final. It was first published in the *Fortnightly Review* in 1869 as a group of sixteen sonnets entitled 'Of Life, Love, and Death'. In the *Poems* of 1870 it became a collection of fifty sonnets followed by eleven songs, and was guardedly entitled, 'SONNETS AND

SONGS *Towards a Work to be called* 'THE HOUSE OF LIFE'. In the *Ballads and Sonnets* of 1881 it had become *The House of Life. A Sonnet Sequence*, and consisted of 101 sonnets divided into two groups, 'Youth and Change' and 'Change and Fate', and preceded by an introductory sonnet. The poem is Rossetti's Life-Lyric, and the form it took in 1881 is final only because Rossetti died the following year. The organization is loose and provisional: like the clouds that Rossetti describes in 'Silent Noon', a sonnet that was first included in the sequence in 1881, the poems 'scatter and amass'. In that sonnet the lovers lie silently in a landscape that Rossetti describes as 'visible silence', but by a strange alchemy the two silences together make 'the song of love'. It is a privileged moment, a 'wing'd hour ... dropt to us from above', perfectly imaged in the dragonfly that hangs above the grass 'like a blue thread loosened from the sky', and perfectly imaged too in the sonnet that records it. A sonnet, as the sonnet which in 1881 introduced *The House of Life* puts it, is 'a moment's monument'. The phrase expresses a paradox that is spatial as well as temporal. The sonnet has an 'arduous fulness'. It is at once small and big, as small as the 'blue thread' of the dragonfly and as big as the blue sky. The effect is only heightened when the single sonnet is extended into a sequence. For Rossetti the sonnet is inherently paradoxical, like the 'song' produced in 'Silent Noon' by a 'twofold silence'. The sonnet, a verse form defined by the division between octave and sestet that Rossetti always marked on the page, is constituted, as 'Silent Noon' intimates, by its twofoldedness, or, as the introductory sonnet has it, by its twofacedness:

> A sonnet is a coin, its face reveals
> The soul – its converse, to what Power 'tis due.
> (9–10)

The coins are paid to one of three Powers; to Life, in which case they are a tax, to Love, as a dowry, or to Death, as the coin that the ferryman demands to transport the Soul to the Underworld. But in *The House of Life* the three Powers do not remain distinct: they repeatedly fade into one another.

The first sonnets to be written were a set of four, variously positioned in different versions of the poem, but always grouped under the title 'Willowwood'. The lover gazes into the waters of a woodside well, and his eyes meet those of Love who sits beside him, but as Love begins to play his lute the eyes become those of the beloved, and he stoops to kiss her. In the second sonnet Love sings and the wood is filled with lovers but 'each was I or she'. The lovers are replicated, becoming 'a dumb throng', rather as the poems will multiply until they form a long sequence. The third sonnet gives the burden of Love's song, an elegy for a female figure that might be the beloved or might equally be the soul of the lover who must spend 'one lifelong night' wandering in Willowwood. As the song dies in the last sonnet, the face of the beloved sinks back into the waters of the well, leaving the lover uncertain whether he will ever again gaze into his beloved's eyes, but at that moment he feels Love's face pressed against his neck, until 'both our heads were in his aureole'. Rossetti's brother, William, thought these sonnets 'about the finest thing he has done'.[24] Robert Browning was less impressed. He thought them exemplary of 'the effeminacy of his school': 'then, how I hate "Love" a lubberly naked young man putting his arms here & his wings there, about a pair of lovers – a fellow they would kick away in reality'.[25] Browning recoils from a verse that is as insistently fleshly as his own, perhaps because Rossetti's figures seem to him not to keep a proper distance from each other. Rossetti uses a syntax in which the lover, the beloved and Love change places so sinuously that the distinctions between them all but melt away. So, the lover leans forward as the beloved sinks into the wellwater, her drowning face unnervingly recalling the face of Elizabeth Siddall, Rossetti's first wife. In 1852, nine years before she killed herself, she had posed for his friend, Millais, as the drowned Ophelia:

And as I leaned, I knew I felt Love's face
Pressed on my neck with moan of pity and grace,
Till both our heads were in his aureole.
(Willowwood IV, 12–4)

Love, I take it, pushes forward the head of the lover, so that momentarily, just before he loses her, his head and the beloved's become a double portrait, framed in Love's golden halo. But it might just as well be Love's head that is joined with his, in a strange reversal of that moment in the first Willowwood sonnet, when, as Love strikes his lute, the reflection of the lover's eyes meets with the reflection of Love's, and

that sound came to be
The passionate voice I knew; and my tears fell.
And at their fall, his eyes beneath grew hers.
(7–9)

All identity in *The House of Life* is ductile. Love may be Amor or Cupid, Browning's 'lubberly naked young man', but he may equally well figure the love that the speaker feels or the person who inspires that feeling in him, and the object of his love may be Jane Morris, or Elizabeth Siddall, or Love itself, or his own face reflected back to him in the waters of the well. Rossetti had at one time intended that the first sonnet in the sequence should be the sonnet that in 1881 he placed fifth, an indication, perhaps, that he recognized in it an account of what he hoped to achieve in the whole sequence:

> For lo! in some poor rhythmic period,
> Lady, I fain would tell how evermore
> Thy soul I know not from thy body, nor
> Thee from myself, neither our love from God.
> ('Heart's Hope', 5–8)

The long poem for Rossetti just as much as for Clough and Browning, though to very different effect, is justified because only a long poem can accommodate all this shape-shifting, and in doing so adequately address a reality that is for Rossetti as it was for Clough '[f]lexible, changeable, vague, and multiform, and doubtful' (*Amours de Voyage*, 1120).

Christina Rossetti's sonnet sequences, *Monna Innominata*, a sonnet of sonnets, and *Later Life*, a double sonnet of sonnets, a sequence of twenty-eight, (both sequences were published in 1881) recall, like her brother's sequence, the sonnets of the Italian Renaissance. Their father was, after all, a distinguished if eccentric scholar of Dante. *Monna Innominata*, the first of the sequences, was prompted, she explains in her preface, by her thinking of all those 'unnamed ladies, "donne innominate," sung by a school' of Italian poets 'less conspicuous' than Dante and Petrarch, and wondering what the result would have been 'had such a lady spoken for herself'. The eighth sonnet ends with the hope that her prayer might 'for love's sake by Love be granted', but the ninth marks the turn of the sequence, the moment when the poet accepts that her love will never find fulfilment. It begins:

> Thinking of you, and all that was, and all
> That might have been and now can never be ...

In the sestet of the sequence the speaker finds that the act of renunciation invigorates rather than enfeebles her voice. In the twelfth sonnet the self-abnegating thought that she finds her own happiness in the happiness of her beloved so completely that she would welcome rather than begrudge him marrying another woman is expressed in a sonnet so confidently expansive in its rhythms that its fourteen lines complete a single sentence. In the last sonnet of all Rossetti embraces the loss of her youth and the loss of her voice with a strange, dark exuberance:

> Youth gone, and beauty gone if ever there
> Dwelt beauty in so poor a face as this;
> Youth gone and beauty, what remains of bliss?
> I will not bind fresh roses in my hair,
> To shame a cheek at best but little fair,–
> Leave youth his roses, who can bear a thorn,–
> I will not seek for blossoms anywhere,
> Except such common flowers as blow with corn.
> Youth gone and beauty gone, what doth remain?
> The longing of a heart pent up forlorn,
> A silent heart whose silence loves and longs;
> The silence of a heart which sang its songs
> While youth and beauty made a summer morn,
> Silence of love that cannot sing again.

Her brother in 'Silent Noon' claims that the 'song of love' can be made from two silences. Christina Rossetti, more remarkably, suggests that her fourteen songs resolve at the last into a silence that is the only proper expression of the love that has prompted them. Her love ends in silence, and it begins in silence, too. The first sonnet ends:

> Ah me, but where are now the songs I sang
> When life was sweet because you called them sweet?

More than thirty years before Christina Rossetti published *Monna Innominata*, Elizabeth Barrett Browning had published the most famous of Victorian sonnet sequences, *Sonnets from the Portuguese* (1850). Christina Rossetti offers her own sequence as supplying a portrait of the woman lover like the portrait that 'the Great Poetess of our own day and nation' might have supplied had she been 'unhappy instead of happy' in her love. By 1881 *Sonnets from the Portuguese* were commonly read as a sequence of lyrics in which Barrett Browning traced the progress of her love for Robert Browning, but, as the title under which she published them indicates, she had, like Christina Rossetti, first offered them as a literary exercise, poems translated from the Portuguese. In 1850 the information that she was herself 'the Portuguese' (Robert Browning particularly admired her poem 'Catarina to Camoens') remained private. When in his memoir of his sister William Rossetti revealed that the sonnets of *Monna Innominata* traced the history of her love for Charles Cayley, the translator of Dante, Christina Rossetti's sonnets too were transformed into personal lyrics. But in both cases the effect was to distort the character of the sonnet sequence, one defining feature of which is that it occupies a liminal space in between the public and the private.

Robert Browning recalled that it was not until three years after they had been written, three years after their marriage, that his wife first showed him the sonnets. She had been deterred by hearing Robert 'say something against putting one's love into verses'.[26] It is a revealing anecdote because Barrett Browning displays a similar reticence in the sonnets themselves. In sonnet 28, for example, she leafs through all the letters that Robert had written her, recalling their contents, until she comes to a letter the content of which is too intimate to be communicated: 'O love, thy words have ill-availed / If what this said I dared repeat at last!' (13–4). It is a poem that compares love sonnets and love letters only in the end to insist on their difference. Love letters are addressed to a reader, but love poems, love poems written by a professional poet at least, are written for a readership. Barrett Browning signifies this by maintaining in her sonnets an archaising formality of the kind audible in the lofty ease of the opening line of the nineteenth sonnet, 'The soul's Rialto hath its merchandise'. The formality of expression counters the claim that these are poems written involuntarily, poems that come like tears, 'falling hot and real' (30, 14).

The Victorian poets who revived the sonnet sequence behaved rather like the Victorians who revived Gothic architecture and built not only Gothic churches but Gothic railway stations, Gothic factories, even Gothic public conveniences. *Sonnets from the Portuguese* celebrates married love rather than love either adulterous or ideal. George Eliot's sequence of 1869, 'Brother and Sister', celebrates familial love, though the love shared by a younger sister and her brother is allowed a delicately erotic inflection:

I cannot choose but think upon the time
When our two lives grew like two buds that kiss
At lightest thrill from the bee's swinging chime,
Because the one so near the other is.

(1, 1–4)

Several poets, amongst them John Addington Symonds in *Animi Figura* (1882), his sequence of sonnet sequences, celebrated instead of domestic, heterosexual love which is 'sustained / By hope of children and the world's great need', the love that takes root 'Where'er in brotherhood men lay their heads', a love that 'Settles where it listeth unconstrained', and finds its proper end not in the production of children but of 'thoughts and acts, an immaterial breed' (*Paths of Life*, sonnet 2). In her incomplete sequence, *Mother and Daughter* (1895), Augusta Webster claims for her love of her only child the same obsessive, single-minded intensity that the sonneteers of earlier centuries claimed to feel for their mistresses. But it was George Meredith who most radically enlarged the range of subject matter that the sonnet sequence might accommodate in his *Modern Love* of 1862.

As Tony Tanner points out in his seminal study, *Adultery in the Novel*, adultery is the great theme of nineteenth-century fiction. Tanner's study is European in its range of reference: Rousseau, Goethe and Flaubert provide him with his major examples (*Anna Karenina* is the most surprising omission), and necessarily so, because Tanner can only recall one Victorian novel, George Meredith's own *One of Our Conquerors*, that takes adultery as its central theme. In British novels it is much more usually the case that 'adultery is just, but sedulously, averted', as in *Wuthering Heights*, *Jane Eyre* and *Daniel Deronda*.[27] Tanner is quite right to insist that adultery is a central theme of the Victorian novel, but it is a theme that Victorian novelists were inhibited from addressing directly. Poets were less constrained than novelists – their readership was smaller and it was more exclusive – and this made it possible for Meredith to offer in his sonnet sequence, *Modern Love* (1862) the most powerful Victorian treatment of an adulterous marriage. As R.H. Hutton, one of the poem's reviewers observed, verse form allowed poets to 'say so much under its artistic cover which in common prose they could not say at all.'[28] The daring of Meredith's theme is matched by his formal daring. His sonnets are sixteen lines long, and consist of four Italian quatrains. It is an invention that avoids the asymmetrical relationship of octave and sestet that, G.M. Hopkins insisted, was 'the real characteristic of the sonnet',[29] because it was the characteristic on which the structural unity of the form depended. It was the asymmetry that allowed the two parts of the sonnet to marry. Hopkins was celibate, and Rossetti's passionate life was unconventional, but both took that metaphor seriously, and so did Meredith when he devised his own sonnet stanza. The four quatrains that make up his sonnet achieve at best a fragile union that never seems likely to hold. It is the perfect stanza for Meredith's study of a marriage that failed. In an introductory sonnet, added only in the edition of 1892, Meredith describes the poem's music as a 'jangled strain' made up of 'discords', and the stanza he devises is as necessary to that music as the poem's clotted syntax and its figurative density.

Victorian poets hesitated between long and shorter poems in part because they were unsure whether poems should express private emotions or address public issues. John Stuart Mill had distinguished between eloquence and poetry on the grounds that eloquence was heard, but poetry was only overheard.[30] It followed that the only true poetry was lyric poetry. Similar considerations led Edgar Allan Poe to the view that 'a long poem does not exist' and that 'the phrase, "a long poem," is simply a flat contradiction in terms.'[31] It was a view that most Victorian poets could neither accept nor reject, and one symptom of that indecision is the strange popularity in the period of the sonnet sequence, the long poem fashioned from a sequence of lyric moments. The sonnet sequence was so congenial a form not only because it allowed poets to make a long poem from a sequence of lyrics, but because the sonnet sequence by tradition played on the borderline between the public and the private.

The game Meredith plays in *Modern Love* is more dangerous than most. He published the poem in 1862 just months after the death of his estranged wife, the daughter of Thomas Love Peacock, who had left him for the painter Henry Wallis. His wife did not commit suicide like the wife in the poem, but even that circumstance might recall that Wallis's most famous painting is a painting of a suicide, 'The Death of Chatterton'. Meredith recklessly allows the wife in the poem many of his own wife's characteristics, her wit and intelligence for example. The sequence is held together, like many sonnet sequences, by a narrative so lightly sketched that it can only just be traced. The wife's infidelity prompts the husband to embark on an affair himself by way of retaliation; there is a reconciliation that fails, and then the enigmatic conclusion. The wife calls the husband to her bedside:

> 'Now kiss me, dear! it may be now!' she said.
> Lethe had passed those lips, and he knew all.
> (49, 15–6)

As in *In Memoriam* the poem establishes a shadowy chronology. References to the seasons mark the passing of time, the 'golden foot of May is on the flowers' (11, 7), ''Tis Christmas weather' (23, 1), 'it is the season of the sweet wild rose' (45, 1), the starlings flock before beginning their winter migration (47). In the very first sonnet the wife's sobs are 'like little gaping snakes' (1, 5), and snakes wind through the whole sequence, one amongst several metaphoric chains that link the sequence. The sonnets cluster, rather like the swallows that the husband and wife watch in the forty-seventh sonnet 'gathering in the sky'. But after all, the unity that the sequence achieves is as compromised and paradoxical as the marriage that it traces, the 'union of this ever-diverse pair!' (50, 2).

The sequence begins abruptly, in the bedroom, the most intimate of domestic spaces, where husband and wife are lying side by side, at once together and very far apart:

> By this he knew she wept with waking eyes:
> That, at his hand's light quiver by her head,
> The strange low sobs that shook their common bed,
> Were called into her with a sharp surprise,
> And strangled mute, like little gaping snakes,
> Dreadfully venomous to him.
>
> (1, 1–6)

Those snakes hiss all through the sonnet, which accommodates thirty-five 's' sounds, voiced and unvoiced, with a particular fondness for words that begin with an unvoiced and end with a voiced 's',' sobs', 'surprise', 'snakes', 'severs'. Husband and wife lie motionless, like effigies on a tomb, like chivalric lovers whose chastity is assured by the knight's sword that lies between them. They are as intimately joined as Paolo and Francesca, because both are silently reading the same text, but theirs is a bitterly ironic intimacy. They are 'looking through their dead black years, / By vain regret scrawled over the blank wall' (12–3). The poem repeatedly contrives moments like this of estranged intimacy. In sonnet 15, the husband enters the bedroom and finds his wife asleep: 'it must be sleep, when low / Hangs that abandoned arm towards the floor' (1–2). He brings with him incriminating evidence, aware even before he presents it of the absurdly theatrical figure he cuts, Othello played by Kean: 'The Poet's black-stage lion of wronged love, / Frights not our modern dames' (5–6). Even at such a moment, as he is about to awaken his wife, he notices the curve of her eyelid, 'Full-sloping like the breasts beneath' (8), though it remains quite unclear whether his wife's infidelity has failed to inoculate him against desire, or whether, a darker possibility, it has rekindled it. Her eyes as they start open retain momentarily the innocence of her sleeping face, but the 'waking infant-stare / Grows woman' (10–1) when she sees what her husband is carrying, two love letters, one written soon after she had accepted his proposal, and a second – 'the words are very like: the name is new' (14). It is one of several occasions in the sequence in which the husband reveals himself as a determined sadist, but even as he accomplishes his wife's humiliation, and she 'trembles through; / A Woman's tremble – the whole instrument' (11–2), he remains achingly, and self-torturingly conscious of her body. Another such moment is recorded in sonnet 21, when the two are walking on the lawn with a friend and the friend confesses how he has himself at long last fallen in love. He asks that, as a happy couple, they give him their blessing. The eyes of husband and wife meet and 'grow white', and the next moment the wife faints, a happy symptom, their friend assumes, of her pregnancy:

> When she wakes,
> She looks the star that thro' the cedar shakes:
> Her lost moist hand clings mortally to mine.
> (14–6)

She looks at the star, and she looks like it, and the sonnet ends as husband and wife clasp hands in a line in which almost every word seems to repel its neighbour, 'lost moist hand clings'.

Marriage is at once a public institution and a private relationship, and *Modern Love* seeks out those moments in which its ambivalent status is exposed, as in the dinner party of sonnet 17, at which husband and wife play host and hostess so successfully that, 'like true hypocrites'(a sharply exact expression), they fall in love with each other's acting. They have succeeded in converting the sad need to keep up appearances into a parlour game, 'a most contagious game: / HIDING THE SKELETON, shall be its name.'(7–8) That is grimly comic, but the sonnet ends when the husband identifies the 'Warm-lighted looks' that he exchanges with his wife across the table as 'Love's corpse-light', that is, a light that appears in a churchyard presaging a death. The sonnets are love letters, like *Sonnets from the Portuguese*, but they are perverse love letters written to two different women, just as the love letters of sonnet 15 written by his wife are addressed to two different men. Or they are the 'French novel' of sonnet 25 put into verse, except that in the novel the husband forgives the wife's adultery 'ere the tear is used' (11), whereas the English husband cannot persuade himself that this is a complaisance possible in any language other than French.

Or they are, like the lyrics of *In Memoriam*, elegies for a dead love, but elegies jangled by the husband's inability to insulate his love from hatred.

Tennyson said of *In Memoriam* that it 'was meant to be a kind of *Divina Commedia*', but in comparison with Dante's poem Tennyson's seems fragmentary, and one reason that this is so is that Tennyson, unlike Dante, was not at all sure what he believed. Many of his contemporaries were in a similar plight, which may help to explain why so many of them are at once attracted and resistant to the idea of a long poem. In *Modern Love*, for example, Meredith wonders whether love might not be inconsistent with biology. In sonnet 13 Nature speaks to him as she had spoken to Tennyson in lyric LVI of *In Memoriam*, and her drift is much the same:

> 'I play for Seasons; not Eternities!'
> Says Nature laughing on her way.
> (1–2)

Like a stage actress, whose command of her role lasts only as long as the theatrical season, Nature is scarcely capable of 'retrospection'. Nature drops 'a look of fondness' on a dying rose, but swiftly moves on to the next play, the next theatre. The husband asks,

> This lesson of our only visible friend
> Can we not teach our foolish hearts to learn?
> (11–2)

But he has only to ask the question to feel at once that naturalism of this kind cannot accommodate his own experience of love:

> Lose calmly Love's great bliss,
> When the renewed forever of a kiss
> Whirls life within the shower of loosened hair!
> (14–6)

Nature, unlike Love, allows no possibility of reconciling the momentary with the eternal, no possibility of a forever that can be repeatedly renewed. That is the miracle that, according to D.G. Rossetti, the sonnet itself performs, but Meredith lacks Rossetti's faith in art, and he lacks his faith in love too. He addresses the problem most directly in sonnet 30:

> What are we first? First, animals; and next
> Intelligences at a leap; on whom

Pale lies the distant shadow of the tomb,
And all that draweth on the tomb for text.
Into which state comes Love, the crowning sun:
Beneath whose light the shadow loses form.
We are the lords of life, and life is warm.
Intelligence and instinct now are one.
But nature says: 'My children most they seem
When they least know me: therefore I decree
That they shall suffer.' Swift doth young Love flee,
And we stand wakened, shivering from our dream.
Then if we study Nature we are wise.
Thus do the few who live but with the day:
The scientific animals are they.–
Lady, this is my sonnet to your eyes.

Human beings are compounded of intelligence and instinct, and the sonnet begins by asking which of these has priority. It is an ambiguous question, but the answer assumes that it is a question not of which is the more important but of which came first. Victorian science can establish a chronology, but not a scale of values. Before we were human we were animals, and the crucial distinction between the two categories is that humans bear with them the knowledge that they will die. It is a knowledge from which love redeems us, because in the light of love the shadow of the tomb dissolves. Meredith is offering here a rigorously secular version of the Christian scheme, in which humankind is redeemed from its fall into the knowledge of life and death not by the Son of Man, but by the 'crowning sun' of human love. In the experience of love, intelligence and instinct are reconciled. Love's decision to punish us because only those who lead a fully instinctual life are truly her children seems arbitrarily malign, but in fact Nature is simply pointing out that the belief that lovers share, the belief that because their love is immortal they must be immortal themselves, is only an illusion, and illusions bring suffering upon those who entertain them because they cannot be sustained. It is a dream from which we waken 'shivering' as the heroes of so many Romantic poems had awakened, from the hero of Shelley's *Alastor* (1816) to the knight-at-arms of Keats's 'La Belle Dame sans Merci' (1820). It is an awakening not just from Romance but Romanticism, an awakening into the Darwinian world of Victorian England. In the modern world the wise are 'scientific animals', refusing to look beyond nature not because they cannot conceive of death but on scientific principle. The sonnet ends with one of Meredith's more mordant jokes. Poets have always written sonnets to their mistress's eyes, but Meredith may have in mind one sonnet in particular, Shakespeare's sonnet 130, 'My mistress' eyes are nothing like the sun', in which Shakespeare rejects poetic fictions in favour of a naturalistic acceptance that his mistress 'when she walks treads on the ground'. Love is more real, the sonnet persuades us, when it can dispense with illusions:

> And yet, by heaven, I think my love as rare
> As any she belied by false compare.

Meredith by contrast feels reduced by the Victorian age in which he lives to a variety of naturalism that renders any such declaration absurd.

Meredith's stanza, his distorted sonnet, is wholly appropriate for a poet who can neither abandon nor embrace the code of romantic love. *Modern Love* is a poem divided against itself as so many Victorian poems are. Instinct and intelligence are for Meredith at odds, and he traces the thought most intricately in the shifting pronouns of his poem. In the poem's first line, 'By this he knew she wept with waking eyes', the third persons hold husband and wife at arm's length. They become objects of the poet's clinical gaze, like the 'sculptured effigies' to which he compares them, but even in this sonnet the third-person statements seem to yield to first-person importunities. It comes as no surprise when in the third sonnet, as he wonders at his continuing susceptibility to the wife who has betrayed him, a first person ousts the third: 'See that I am drawn to her even now!' (10) Thereafter first, second and third persons, he, she, they, I, you, thee, thou, we and our, map with chilling precision the death dance of the marriage. Sonnet 9 is typical. It begins in a third-person confession of murderous rages. The husband cannot trust himself to accompany his wife 'through certain dark defiles' (4). The poem continues by recalling a tense conversation in which 'he' asks 'Have you no fear?' (6) This prompts a laughing reply, 'No, surely; am I not with you?' (8) Only in the final lines in which the speaker manages to admit, through a perverse echo of Keats's 'Ode on Melancholy', how closely allied his violence is with erotic desire does the first person supplant the third:

> Here thy shape
> To squeeze like an intoxicating grape –
> I might, and yet thou goest safe, supreme.
> (14–6)

Modern Love, like several of the most important long poems of the Victorian period, is made up of a sequence of short poems. That is an appropriate form for poets so many of whom believed that the only true poems were lyrics and yet who retained in spite of that the ambition to build 'a 'big raft' rather than a 'small vessel'. But that inability either fully to accept or fully to reject the long poem is simply one instance of the self-divisions that characterize so much Victorian poetry.

Endnotes

1. Hallam Tennyson, *Alfred Lord Tennyson: A Memoir*, 2 vols (London: Macmillan, 1897), 1, p. 166, and Tennyson, *Idylls of the King*, ed. Hallam Tennyson (London : Macmillan, 1908), p. 436.
2. Matthew Arnold, 'On Translating Homer', *On the Classical Tradition*, ed. R.H. Super (Ann Arbor: University of Michigan Press, 1960), p. 147.
3. Ralph Waldo Emerson, 'The Poet', *Essays: Second Series, Collected Works of Ralph Waldo Emerson*, 3 (Cambridge, Mass.: Harvard University Press, 1983), p. 21.
4. Matthew Arnold, *On the Study of Celtic Literature and other Essays* (London: Dent, n. d.), p. 13.
5. *The George Eliot Letters*, ed. Gordon S. Haight, 7 vols (London: Oxford University Press, 1956), 4, p. 397.
6. *Further Letters of Gerard Manley Hopkins including his correspondence with Coventry Patmore*, ed. Claude Colleer Abbott, 2nd edn (London: Oxford University Press, 1956), p. 217.
7. T.S. Eliot, *The Sacred Wood: Essays on Poetry and Criticism* (London: Methuen, 1960), p. 145.
8. Herbert F. Tucker, *Epic: Britain's Heroic Muse 1790–1810* (Oxford: Oxford University Press, 2008).
9. George Gilfillan, *A Second Gallery of Literary Portraits* (Edinburgh: James Hogg, 1850), p. 393.
10. David Masson (1853) 'Theories of Poetry, and a New Poet', *North British Review*, **19** (August), 297–344. Arnold takes issue with Masson in the Preface to his *Poems* of 1853.
11. Quoted in *Poetic Works of Robert Browning*, 15, Parleyings *and* Asolando, ed. Stefan Hawlin and Michael Meredith (Oxford: Oxford University Press, 2010), p. 294.
12. *Tennyson: Interviews and Recollections*, ed. Norman Page (Basingstoke: Macmillan, 1983), p. 56.
13. *The Letters of Alfred Lord Tennyson*, ed. Edgar F. Shannon, 3 vols (Oxford: Clarendon Press, 1982–90), 3, p. 44.

14. *Diary of Alfred Domett, 1872–1885*, ed. E.A. Horsman (London: Oxford University Press, 1953), p. 79.
15. *The Brownings' Correspondence*, ed. Philip Kelley and Scott Lewis, 12 (Winfield: Wedgestone Press, 1994), p. 29.
16. Hallam Tennyson, *Alfred Lord Tennyson: A Memoir* (London: Macmillan, 1897), 2, pp. 70–1.
17. Hallam Tennyson, *Alfred Lord Tennyson: A Memoir*, 1, p. 304.
18. *The Letters of Alfred Lord Tennyson*, 1, p. 226; Hallam Tennyson, *Alfred Lord Tennyson: A Memoir*, 1, p. 124; *The Letters of Edward Fitzgerald*, ed. Alfred McKinley Terhune and Annabelle Burdick Terhune, 4 vols (Princeton, N. J.: Princeton University Press, 1980), 1, p. 478.
19. Hallam Tennyson, *Alfred Lord Tennyson: A Memoir*, 1, pp. 293 and 393 (footnote).
20. Hallam Tennyson, *Alfred Lord Tennyson: A Memoir*, 1, p. 304.
21. As remembered by James Knowles, *Tennyson: Interviews and Recollections*, ed. Norman Page (Basingstoke: Macmillan, 1983), p. 96.
22. William Davis (1873) 'The Sonnet', *Quarterly Review*, **134** (January), 186–204, 190, and Charles Tomlinson, *The Sonnet: Its Origin, Structure, and Place in Poetry* (London: John Murray, 1874), p. 77.
23. Hallam Tennyson, *Lord Alfred Tennyson: A Memoir*, 1, p. 305.
24. W.M Rossetti, *Rossetti Papers 1862–1870* (London : Sands and Co, 1903), p. 339.
25. *Dearest Isa: Robert Browning's Correspondence with Isabella Blagden*, ed. Edward C. McAleer (Austin, Texas: University of Texas Press, 1951), p. 337.
26. *Robert Browning and Julia Wedgwood: A Broken Friendship as revealed in their letters*, ed. Richard Curle (London: Murray, 1937), p. 114.
27. Tony Tanner, *Adultery in the Novel: Contract and Transgression* (Baltimore: John Hopkins University Press, 1979), p. 12.
28. *Meredith: The Critical Heritage*, ed. Joan Williams (London: Routledge and Kegan Paul, 1971), p.
29. *The Correspondence of Gerard Manley Hopkins with Richard Watson Dixon*, ed. Claude Colleer Abbott (London: Oxford University Press, 1935), p. 71.
30. In 'What is Poetry?' (1833), *John Stuart Mill: Essays on Poetry*, ed. F. Parvin Sharpless (Columbia, South Carolina: University of South Carolina Press, 1976), p. 12.
31. Edgar Allan Poe, 'The Poetic Principle', *Edgar Allan Poe: Representative Selections*, ed. Margaret Atherton and Hardin Craig (New York; American Book Company, 1935), p. 35.

5

Victorian Poetry and Translation

It was not a great age of poetic translation, but in D.G. Rossetti and Edward FitzGerald it had two great translators, and almost all the most important Victorian poets produced translations of one kind or another. Greek tragedy proved particularly attractive: Barrett Browning translated Aeschylus's *Prometheus Bound* not once but twice (1833 and 1850), and Augusta Webster translated it too, before going on to publish a version of Euripides' *Medea* (1866 and 1868). Robert Browning accommodated within two of his later poems, *Balaustion's Adventure* (1871) and *Aristophanes' Apology* (1875), complete translations of two other plays by Euripides, *Alcestis* and *Heracles*. Edward FitzGerald translated the *Agamemnon* (1865) as well as Omar Khayyám. William Morris was the most prolific translator of them all, producing versions of the *Aeneid* (1875), the *Odyssey* (1887), and *Beowulf* (1895) as well as Icelandic sagas. But the idea of translation informs Victorian poetry still more deeply than its practice. *The Ring and the Book* (1868–9), Robert Browning's forensic epic, begins in an act of translation as Browning struggles through the law Latin of the old yellow book that he has purchased from the Italian market stall:

> '*Romana Homicidiorum*' – nay,
> Better translate – 'A Roman murder-case:
> Position of the entire criminal cause
> Of Guido Franceschini, nobleman,
> With certain Four the cutthroats in his pay,
> Tried, all five, and found guilty and put to death
> By heading or hanging as befitted ranks,

Reading Victorian Poetry, First Edition. Richard Cronin.

> At Rome on February Twenty Two,
> Since our salvation Sixteen Ninety Eight:
> Wherein it is disputed if, and when,
> Husbands may kill adulterous wives, yet 'scape
> The customary forfeit.'
>   Word for word,
> So ran the title-page.
>
> (1, 120–32)

'Word for word', Browning insists, but that begs the question of what word for word translation might be. Browning seems to use the word, 'position', for example, to mean something like statement, a possible sense in English, but his choice of word is dictated by the Italian word that he is translating, 'posizione', just as 'cause' is suggested by 'causa'. Browning chooses the English words that seem closest to the Italian, but do they carry quite the same sense? The poem is put together out of the documents that Browning found collected in the old yellow book so that the whole poem might be thought of as an exercise in translation. The difficulty of moving from one language to another becomes the poem's radical metaphor, signalling the still greater problem that every reader of the poem is made to confront of how far, even if we grant that it is possible to understand another language, it is possible to understand another person. Barrett Browning's most popular poem, *Sonnets from the Portuguese* (1846), masquerades as a translation. Her epic, *Aurora Leigh* (1856), traces the 'twofold life' (5, 381) of its poet heroine, and the doubleness that at once empowers and frustrates her is initially represented as linguistic. Aurora recalls that when she takes up residence in England with her aunt.

> I left off saying my sweet Tuscan words
> Which still at any stirring of the heart
> Came up to float across the English phrase
> As lilies (*Bene* or *Che che*), because
> She liked my father's child to speak his tongue.
>
> (1, 387–91)

Victorian poems take up issues connected with translation more often than might be expected, and this is not really surprising, because a translation is perhaps the most emphatic example of the double poem that the Victorians favoured. A translation, after all, is not a single text but rather a relationship between texts.

In his preface to *The Early Italian Poets* (1861), Rossetti suggests that the double character of translation is a little more complex than this. The translator is at once poet and critic, since translation, properly understood, is 'perhaps the most direct form of commentary'. Rossetti announces the defining characteristic of literary translation when he identifies as the 'life-blood of rhymed translation' the principle that 'a good poem shall not be turned into a bad one', but his metaphor suggests that this involves a blood transfusion from one language to another. Translation, Rossetti claims, is a practice that demands 'self-denial' – his own poetic character must be wholly subordinated to the character of the poet that he is translating – and yet he also offers the collection as a kind of autobiography. In 'relinquishing' it, he feels that he has parted company with his own youth, because his 'first associations' were so closely connected with his father's studies of Dante that the poetry of Dante and his contemporaries became his 'natural element'. Translation offers him at once a release from the self and an unusually intimate form of self-expression.

His fine translation of a 'prolonged sonnet' (a Petrarchan sonnet extended to sixteen lines by a couplet) by Niccolo degli Albizzi seems rather to be an exercise in detachment:

> If you could see, fair brother, how dead beat
> The fellows look who come through Rome to-day, –
> Black yellow smoke-dried visages, – you'd say
> They thought their haste at going all too fleet.
> Their empty victual-waggons up the street
> Over the bridge dreadfully sound and sway;
> Their eyes, as hanged men's, turning the wrong way;
> And nothing on their backs, or heads, or feet.
> One sees the ribs and all the skeletons
> Of their gaunt horses; and a sorry sight
> Are the torn saddles, crammed with straw and stones.
> They are ashamed, and march throughout the night;
> Stumbling, for hunger, on their marrowbones;
> Like barrels rolling, jolting, in this plight.
> Their arms all gone, not even their swords are saved;
> And each as silent as a man being shaved.

The poem looks at the defeated army stumbling back into Rome with a startled exactitude that issues in a tense stand-off between pity and contempt. The address to a 'fair brother' seems an archaism, except that it suggests the problem of what it would take to look at such a spectacle fairly. The sonnet's lurching movement mimics the 'rolling, jolting' tread of the exhausted soldiery and the 'sound and sway' of the empty wagons as they cross the bridge. The diction swerves between contemporary slang, 'dead beat', scrupulously mean precision, those 'torn saddles, crammed with straw and stones', and phrases that are altogether more flamboyant – the 'Black yellow smoke-dried visages' might have come from a Jacobean play like Jonson's *The Alchemist*. The silence of the soldiers, so strangely recorded in the sonnet's final line, is moving because it only just fends off comedy. It is the silence of men who have had a close shave, and also the silence of men in shock, of men who have withdrawn into themselves, as men do when they are sitting in the barber's chair and the barber is wielding a cutthroat razor. Rossetti seems throughout to be looking at the poem that he is translating with the same fascinated and appalled stare that the poem directs at the ramshackle army.

Rossetti's version of the sestina that, as Rossetti believes (although, as he admits, there is little warrant for it), Dante addressed to Lady Pietra degli Scrovigni, is probably the finest of all his translations, and it is quite different. For Rossetti the translator has a duty of 'fidelity' rather than 'literality', but he allows that it is best when the two qualities can be combined, and that is what he achieves here. The translation is marvellously close. Dante's poem, as Dante acknowledges in *De Vulgari Eloquentia*, was itself closely modelled on the poem by Arnaut Daniel that had introduced him to the form of the sestina. It follows that Rossetti, even in his scrupulous fidelity, is following his master. His translation becomes a demonstration of how it is possible to find oneself the more completely the more completely one manages to place that self at the service of another. The poem responds to a woman who is herself quite unresponsive:

> Utterly frozen is this youthful lady,
> Even as the snow that lies within the shade.
> (7–8)

But the poem does not end in complaint. In its final three lines it celebrates the transformative power of her beauty:

> How dark soe'er the hills throw out their shade,
> Under her summer-green the beautiful lady
> Covers it, like a stone cover'd in grass.
> (37–9)

Just as Dante offers his poem as a response to the lady's beauty, Rossetti presents his translation as his tribute to the 'great and peculiar beauty' of Dante's poem. Rossetti is occasionally archaic, as in the phrase, 'I have clomb' (which counts as two syllables, in deference, I take it, to the more radical habits of elision that characterize Dante's verse), but it more often surprises by a sharp, modern unclutteredness, 'A while ago, I saw her dressed in green' (25). Rossetti exactly translates the six exceptionally rich 'rhyme' words with which Dante builds his poem. Ombra, colli, erba, verde, pietra, donna become shade, hills, grass, green, stone and lady. It transforms the movement of the poem that five of Dante's six words become monosyllables in Rossetti's English, and yet Rossetti's poem never loses contact with the poem it translates. It moves with an unhurried grave simplicity that he could only have borrowed from Dante because Victorian verse offered him no model for it. The verse form, the sestina, which, as Empson remarks of the double sestina with which Sidney introduced the form into English, seems 'so curiously foreign to the normal modes or later developments of the language',[1] marks Rossetti's poem as exotic. So, too, does the extravagance of the sentiment:

> Yet shall the streams turn back and climb the hills
> Before Love's flame in this damp wood and green
> Burn, as it burns within a youthful lady,
> For my sake, who would sleep away in stone
> My life, or feed like beasts upon the grass,
> Only to see her garments cast a shade.
>
> (31–6)

And yet the movement of the stanza, and especially of its last line, seems wholly English. It is a happy chance that one of the poem's key words should be 'shade', because the poem explores how accurately one poet or one language or one historical period or one social code can ever shadow another.

FitzGerald's ***Rubáiyát*** is itself, in the metaphor that FitzGerald uses to describe human life, 'a Magic Shadow-show' (XLVI). It is a show during which FitzGerald transmutes himself into the hybrid character that he named FitzOmar. He stresses rather than downplays the hybridity. He wrote to the friend who had taught him Persian, 'I am more & more convinced of the Necessity of keeping as much as possible to the Oriental Forms, & carefully avoiding any that bring one back to Europe and the 19th Century,' and he also made to the same correspondent a very nearly antithetical claim: 'But at all Cost a Thing must live: with a transformation of one's own warm life if one can't retain the Originall's better. Better a live sparrow than a stuffed Eagle.'[2] His translation swithers erratically between these poles. On the one hand FitzGerald maintains 'the Oriental Forms' so determinedly that translation is sometimes reduced to transliteration: in this mood he gives us 'Kaikobád and Kaikhosrú' (IX, all references are to the text of the first edition, 1859), a 'High-piping Pehleví' (VI), entitles the poem's best-known section 'Kúza-Náma', and marks its conclusion with the untranslated phrase, 'Tamám Shud'. On the other, he scatters throughout the poem pointedly English expressions; 'Cash in hand' (XII), 'neither Here nor There' (XXIV), 'This and That' (XXXIX), and an item that is sold 'for a Song' (LXIX). The two habits combine to produce a poetic language that teasingly fails to indicate quite how it should be read.

A typical quatrain reads:

> Look to the Rose that blows about us – 'Lo,
> 'Laughing,' she says, 'into the World I blow:
> 'At once the silken Tassel of my Purse
> 'Tear, and its Treasure on the Garden throw.'
> (XIII)

The rose exhibits a magnificent, spendthrift carelessness that is realized phonetically when the word 'Treasure' takes up the sound of the 'Tear' through which the treasure is disbursed. The 'silken Tassel' seems intent on preserving 'Oriental Forms', as does the blowing Rose, one of the poem's commonest figures. But the rose blows in the first line in the sense that it blossoms and in the fourth its petals and the pollen that they shelter are blown or scattered about the garden by the wind. In the second line a third sense may even be lightly indicated. The American colloquial use of the word 'blow' to signal aimless, unplanned movement was already established. FitzGerald's rose says, 'into the World I blow', as if she were some drifter blowing into town.

It is a poem much given to wordplay, but inclined to leave it in doubt whether the play is ingenious or accidental, a poem in which the fortunate and the fortuitous are unusually hard to distinguish. The poem asserts a fatalism that it figures in a polo ball, the course of which is decided by the rider's mallet not by the ball itself: 'The Ball no Question makes of Ayes and Noes'(L). The Parliamentary expression wittily calls attention to the absurdity of human pretensions, but the pun, 'eyes and nose,' seems impossible to make any sense of and equally impossible to dismiss. When the poem tightens its most often repeated precept into a single couplet, 'Ah, fill the Cup: – what boots it to repeat / How time is slipping underneath our Feet' (XXXVII), the reader is left wondering at the 'slide from "boots" to "feet"'. Whimsical collocations such as this are, as Robert Douglas-Fairhurst points out, 'typical of the muzzy felicities of drunken speech which the *Rubáiyát* reproduces.'[3] Another example might be the floral frocks that the reader can scarcely help glimpsing in the 'Room' that 'Summer dresses in new Bloom'. (XXII) The effect is odd, leaving the reader with a dizzying sense that the poem's language is as shifting as Time itself, neither of them offering anything like a firm foothold. In his Preface FitzGerald describes Khayyám as falling 'back upon TO-DAY (which has outlasted so many To-morrows!) as the only Ground he had got to stand upon, however momentarily slipping from under his Feet.'

Erik Gray refers to the poem's 'constant anachronistic slips by which it forgets its supposed author',[4] referring to the allusions to Shakespeare, the Book of Common Prayer, and a host of other texts that postdate the poem that FitzGerald claims to be translating:

> Ah, my Belovéd, fill the Cup that clears
> TO-DAY of past Regrets and future Fears –
> (XX)

Most of the poem's readers will hear in this an echo of Cowper's 'cups / That cheer but not inebriate' (*The Task*, 4, 39–40), but to what effect? It may be that the echo points the contrast between Omar's drunkenness and Cowper's temperate sobriety, but does Omar's casual dismissal of 'future Fears' also recall the agonizing fear that underlies all of Cowper's poetry that he might be predestined to damnation? Or do the lines paradoxically underline the poem's foreignness by allowing into the poem an intrusive and pointless echo of an over-familiar quotation that any 'English' poet would have avoided? As Douglas Fairhurst puts it, FitzGerald remembers other poems but remembers them 'out of the corner of his ear'.[5] The clichés that FitzGerald admits into the poem often work similarly:

> Alike for those who for TO-DAY prepare,
> And those that after a TO-MORROW stare,
> A Muezzin from the Tower of Darkness cries
> 'Fools! your reward is neither Here nor There!'
> (XXIV)

In common usage the phrase neither here nor there suggests that the matter at issue is irrelevant, of no consequence, but it is used here to distinguish between life on earth, 'Here', and in paradise, 'There', as if the cliché were being used by some foreign speaker who misunderstands it or is unaware of the manner in which it is commonly deployed. And yet it is the memory of that common usage that keeps it in mind that in this poem the distinction between this life and the life to come is itself represented as of very little consequence.

Translation becomes for FitzGerald a way in which he can establish a rather odd relationship with the English language – neither quite within it nor quite outside it – and he establishes a very similar relationship with the English literary tradition. It seems somehow wholly appropriate that a poet such as T.S. Eliot, so committed to that tradition, should have firmly repudiated his youthful enthusiasm for the 'smart and shallow view of life' expressed in the *Rubáiyát*,[6] and yet been unable to bury the poem so deeply as to stop himself from digging it up. 'That corpse you planted last year in you garden / Has it begun to sprout?', Eliot wonders in *The Waste Land*, before asking that 'the Dog' be kept 'far hence', 'Or with his nails he'll dig it up again'. The passage recalls, however unwillingly, Omar Khayyám's smart and shallow assurance that all corpses rot alike, and that none of them is converted into 'such aureate earth … As, buried once, / Men want dug up again.' (XV)

The poem that FitzGerald himself seems most unable to forget is, as his critics seem to have surmised, a poem of the very recent past, Tennysons's *In Memoriam*. It was not a poem that FitzGerald much liked. It seemed to him, despite all its fine things, 'monotonous', carrying with it an 'air of being evolved by a Poetical Machine of the highest order'. 'Lycidas' was 'the utmost length an elegiac should reach', and the excessive length of *In Memoriam* seemed wilful: 'I felt that if Tennyson had got on a horse and ridden twenty miles, instead of moaning over his pipe, he would have been cured of his sorrows in half the time.'[7] Most obviously, FitzGerald recoils from Tennyson's faith in personal immortality. The *Book of Common Prayer*'s 'sure and certain hope of the resurrection to eternal life' may have dwindled in *In Memoriam*:

> I stretch lame hands of faith, and grope,
> And gather dust and chaff, and call
> To what I feel is lord of all,
> And faintly trust the larger hope.
> (lv, 17–20)

But even so faint a faith provokes FitzGerald to a rebuttal that only the supreme authority of Shakespeare can make crushing enough (compare 'Sans teeth, sans eyes, sans taste, sans everything' in *As You Like It*):

> Ah, make the most of what we yet may spend,
> Before we too into the Dust descend;
> Dust into Dust, and under Dust, to lie,
> Sans Wine, sans Song, sans Singer, and – sans End!
> (XXIII)

But the relationship between the two poems is subtler than this would suggest. FitzGerald, for example, follows Tennyson in linking his quatrains chronologically. Three Christmases pass in *In Memoriam*, and the *Rubáiyát* begins at dawn, when 'Morning in the Bowl of Night / Has flung the Stone that puts the Stars to Flight' (I), and ends when the 'Moon of Heav'n is rising once again' (LXXIV). More significantly, FitzGerald takes from Tennyson the idea of a poem that can at once offer a statement of faith (in FitzGerald's case an epicurean agnosticism), and deny any such ambition, insisting that it amounts to no more than the disconnected lyrical outbursts of a mind unhinged by grief or, in FitzGerald's case, by drink. *Tennyson* establishes a complex, but predominantly antithetical relationship between his own poem and the perfect poem that God contrives when he brings time to a perfect close in the 'one far-off divine event / To which the whole creation moves'. ('Epilogue', 143–4). The *Rubáiyát* contrives an even more unqualified antithetical relationship with the divine poem:

> The Moving Finger writes; and, having writ,
> Moves on: nor all thy Piety nor Wit
> Shall lure it back to cancel half a Line,
> Nor all the Tears wash out a Word of it.
> (LI)

This is, as it happens, one of the very few stanzas to remain unchanged in all four of the editions of the poem that FitzGerald published in his lifetime. FitzGerald was almost obsessively willing to rewrite his poem, cancelling lines and washing out words without compunction, in a process of revision during the course of which the poem expanded from seventy-five to 110 quatrains before settling back to 101. FitzGerald spent decades revising his poem, but did so unsupported by any confidence that the poem was being improved. 'I daresay Edn 1 is better in some respects than 2', FitzGerald wrote to his publisher, 'but I think not altogether … As to the relative fidelity of the two Versions, there isn't a pin to choose'.[8] The relationship between *In Memoriam* and the *Rubáiyát* is best defined, perhaps, by the relationship between their quatrains, between Tennyson's *abba*, in which, as Seamus Perry observes, Tennyson's contradictory need at once to move on and to look back is formally embodied,[9] and FitzGerald's *aaba*, in which the final line characteristically refuses a possibility that the third line seems to have opened:

> The Ball no Question makes of Ayes and Noes,
> But Right or Left, as strikes the Player goes;
> And He that toss'd thee down into the Field,
> *He* knows about it all – HE knows – HE knows!
> (L)

In that final line the pronoun becomes ever more emphatic, moving from italics to capitals to still larger capitals, but the effect is only to call attention to 'His' failure to offer humankind any clue at all as to what his knowledge might be. It is a stanza that contemplates change only to decide at the last to go back to exactly the same position from which it started, a procedure that several of the poem's quatrains repeat:

> Myself when young did eagerly frequent
> Doctor and Saint, and heard great Argument
> About it and about: but evermore
> Came out by the same Door as in I went.
> (XXVII)

FitzGerald's quatrain is the perfect formal embodiment of his agnosticism, or what Erik Gray calls his 'indifference', and it is an indifference that he defines most exactly by the difference between his poem and *In Memoriam*, a poem that he both admires and repudiates. One reason for FitzGerald's preoccupation with *In Memoriam* is that, almost as soon as it was published, it was widely recognized as the most perfect expression of the literary culture of the age. Translation, Herbert Tucker observes, is for FitzGerald a way of avoiding so fixed an address by keeping the reader 'indeterminately suspended between two languages, two cultures, two histories',[10] a way of keeping the reader, in FitzGerald's own phrase, 'neither Here nor There' (XXIV). It was a place where a number of Victorian poets chose to take their stance.

Lawrence Venuti has traced a Victorian debate as to whether the translator should domesticate the foreign text or translate it in a way that acknowledges its strangeness, but the alternative paths tend to converge.[11] F.W. Newman (John Henry's brother) promised in his translation of Homer (1856) to 'retain every peculiarity of the original, so far as he is able, *with the greater care the more foreign it may happen to be*', and in 1861 Matthew Arnold suavely took issue with him.[12] But Newman goes about his project paradoxically, by choosing for his translation an English ballad metre, and underlining Homer's archaism by employing an obtrusively Anglo-Saxon diction (Arnold finds the use of 'bragly' to mean 'proudly fine' especially amusing). So, Newman preserves Homer's foreignness by aggressively anglicizing him. Arnold objects that Homer's language is 'natural' rather than odd, and that the special characteristic of language as natural as Homer's is that, however old it may be, 'it surprises us as little as the language of a contemporary.' This might lead one to expect Arnold to recommend that Homer be translated into an easy contemporary English, into the blank verse, say, of Tennyson's *Idylls of the King*. In fact, Arnold suggests that Homer should be translated into hexameters, a metre that, as he knows, a majority of English readers found unassimilably foreign. The choice of verse form is itself a confession that, however much Arnold may baulk at it, he remains, as he acknowledges, 'separated from [Homer] by time, race, and language'.

Translation is important to Victorian poets, perhaps, just because it allowed them to take a stance 'neither Here nor There'. In 'The Ballad of Villon and Fat Madge', for example, (probably composed 1862–3, but published only posthumously in 1910) Swinburne, even before the poem begins, destabilizes the reader by choosing two epigraphs: a text from John's Gospel, 'The night cometh, when no man can work', is paired with Falstaff's defence of theft from *Henry IV Part One*, "Tis no sin for a man to labour in his vocation'. The two epigraphs might not be quite as irreconcilable as they seem. Falstaff makes his remark just after the Prince has wondered at how swift the passage might be 'from praying to purse-taking', and the pairing of the two quotations might prompt the reader to remember that Jesus himself came 'like a thief in the night'. Villon in his dealings with Fat Madge encourages Swinburne's readers, like Yeats's Bishop when he accosts Crazy Jane, to look afresh at the antinomies of their existence. The poem's readers are initiated into a new understanding of the relationship between the sacred and the profane. Madge is a whore, and Villon is at once her lover, her pimp, and the brothel's potboy. Villon spends the evening ingratiating himself with the customers ('Look in again when your flesh troubles you'), he clubs Madge across the nose when she comes 'penniless' to bed, and is soundly pummelled in return, but in the morning he yields, when she wakes from drunken sleep and feels her womb 'stir', to her importunate caresses:

> To save her seed she gets me under her
> Wheezing and whining, flat as planks are laid.
> (27–8)

Villon's mistress is his 'lady', the proper object of his courtly devotion, and she is also Fat Madge, and because she is both Villon can properly claim, 'I love her with my soul and my body' (41). 'The Ballad of Villon and Fat Madge' is at once a satire and a love poem, and by tracing the passionate, abusive intimacy of the relationship between the two lovers, it also has something to say about the relationship forged by translation, which is, according to Swinburne, a violent, coercive relationship in which one poet offers another a bruisingly passionate embrace (all translation is a form of catachresis, a misapplication of words, or, to revert to the literal meaning of the Greek term, a form of abuse). But Swinburne was most importantly a follower of Sappho rather than of Villon. It was Sappho that he claimed to be 'the greatest poet who ever was at all'.[13]

'Anactoria', the most notorious poem from *Poems and Ballads* (1866), is loosely based on the poem by Sappho now known as fragment 31. Swinburne imitates Sappho's words rather than translating them because he would not 'debase and degrade them into a viler form'.[14] The verbs make explicit Swinburne's sado-masochistic understanding of the relationship between the poet and her translator, and so does the poem itself, in which Anactoria's transformation into text by Sappho is figured as a sadistic sexual engagement:

> I feel thy blood against my blood: my pain
> Pains thee, and lips bruise lips, and vein stings vein.
> (11–2)

Singing and stinging merge for Swinburne in the poem's metre. 'More than any other's, [Sappho's] verses strike and sting the memory',[15] and that is a necessary consequence of the metrical brilliance that all commentators, ancient and modern, allowed her. The classical metres had been impressed on Swinburne by the strokes of his schoolmasters' cane with effects that determined his sexual identity ('I can't make him understand that biting's no use', complained Adah Menken, the American circus performer, who had been charged with his sexual initiation), and determined too his understanding of poetry and of translation. Swinburne's Sappho begs Anactoria to 'crush love with thy cruel faultless feet' (18), and Swinburne's lines deploy metrical feet that stamp themselves on the reader's ear just as pitilessly:

> I would find grievous ways to have thee slain,
> Intense device, and superflux of pain;
> Vex thee with amorous agonies, and shake
> Life at thy lips, and leave it there to ache;
> Strain out thy soul with pangs too soft to kill,
> Intolerable interludes, and infinite ill;
> Relapse and reluctation of the breath,
> Dumb tunes and shuddering semitones of death.
> (27–34)

In passages such as this Swinburne searches out a vocabulary in which poetic resources can scarcely be distinguished from instruments of torture; device, strain, intolerable interludes. In the passage's most brilliant line the rhythm of the poem merges with the gasps of the victim. The '[r]elapse and reluctation' of her breath figures the resistance or reluctation of the text to its translator that authorizes Swinburne's representation of the relationship between the two as sadistically erotic. It is one of the more glamorous, at least one of the more lurid, achievements of Victorian poetry. But there were contemporaries who figured the relationship very differently.

Michael Field was the name under which Katherine Bradley and her niece Emma Cooper published the jointly written poems which, they claimed, proved their marriage to be so much closer than the marriage of Robert and Elizabeth Barrett Browning, who rather determinedly developed habits of composition that allowed each to preserve creative independence. In their first collection, *Long Ago* (1889), each poem quotes as an epigraph a fragment of Sappho that the poem translates in its opening line. The relationship between the Sapphic fragment and the English poem is figured in the opening poem of the sequence as a kind of plaiting:

> They plaited garlands in their time;
> They knew the joy of love's sweet prime,

Quick breath and rapture;
Theirs was the violet-weaving bliss,
And theirs the white, wreathed brow to kiss,
Kiss and recapture.

(1–6)

Each of the poem's three stanzas begins with the phrase, 'They plaited garlands'. A garland is, then, a stanza, but it also figures a poetic identity that is established when Bradley and Cooper weave their poems from the Sapphic fragment with which they begin, and that process in its turn figures the poetic identity that they produce when they weave or plait their separate identities into a single poetic persona (they claimed to be unable to identify which of them had written any part of a particular poem). Translation, figured by Swinburne as a bruising relationship, becomes for Bradley and Cooper a plaiting or weaving or wreathing that allows two separate individuals to construct a singular identity. It figures the process by which the two women were able to make themselves into Michael Field.

Toru Dutt, born in Calcutta in 1856, launched her career in 1876 with a volume of translations from the French, *A Sheaf Gleaned in French Fields*, just a year before she died, but it is in 'Our Casuarina Tree', first published in a volume of her remains, *Ancient Ballads and Legends of Hindustan* (1882), that Dutt most searchingly addresses the place between two cultures that she occupied. Dutt's poem acknowledges the British sense that the nation, in its strength, its durability, and the protection it offers is best figured in a tree, particularly 'the British oak' 'beneath the shadow' of which Burke imagined the British people calmly grazing like contented cattle. But the figure could accommodate a more complex sense of national identity, as it did for Cowper, writing two years after Burke in 1792. 'Yardley Oak' is a rotten tree, hollowed out by disease, or, as Cowper puts it 'Embowell'd', despite which its root remains 'sincere':

So stands a Kingdom whose foundations yet
Fail not, in virtue and in wisdom lay'd
Though all the superstructure by the tooth
Pulverised of venality, a shell
Stands now, and semblance only of itself.

(120–4)

Dutt's casuarina tree is similarly grotesque, half strangled by a creeper that winds round its trunk like 'a huge Python', but it is a challengingly exotic version of Cowper's oak, an exoticism most forcefully embodied in the stare of the 'grey baboon' that 'sits statue-like alone' on its topmost branch. Dutt's tree, unlike Cowper's, cannot figure her nation, because she has none: Bengal has been reduced from a nation to a province of the British Empire. The tree's situation, in the family garden of her Calcutta home, and its duration, its reach back into the far past and forward into the distant future, make it the totem not of her country but only of her family. The music of her own poem is figured by the music of the wind in its branches just as clearly as the music of 'Dover Beach' is figured in the drag of the pebbles tugged and thrown by the waves (the allusion seems deliberate):

> What is that dirge-like murmur that I hear
> Like the sea breaking on a shingle-beach?
> It is the tree's lament, an eerie speech,
> That haply to the unknown land may reach.
> (30–3)

The unknown land is the land inhabited by those of her family who have died, especially her brother and sister, but the poem is weighted too by Dutt's sense of her own deracination. She heard the tree's 'wail' even during her European travels, even when 'the waves kissed the classic shore / Of France or Italy' (38–9). She had appropriated the European literary classics by translating them, but into English rather than Bengali. Dutt figures her complex relationship with the English language, perhaps, in the relationship between the tree and the creeper that surrounds it. The creeper threatens to crush the life out of the tree, but the tree responds 'gallantly', by wearing the creeper as if it were a 'scarf', an adornment. The creeper, after all, blooms,

> and flowers are hung
> In crimson clusters all the boughs among,
> Whereon all day are gathered bird and bee.
> (6–8)

But Dutt saves her boldest move for the last, when she claims for her own casuarina the status of the trees commemorated by Wordsworth in his 'Yew-Trees' (1815):

> Mayst thou be numbered when my days are done
> With deathless trees – like those in Borrowdale,

> Under whose awful branches lingered pale
> 'Fear, trembling Hope, and Death, the skeleton,
> And Time the shadow.'
>
> (49–53)

Wordsworth had begun his poem by celebrating a yew, the 'pride of Lorton Vale', as the type of a martial nation, its wood supplying bows for the archers of 'Umfraville or Percy ere they marched / To Scotland's heaths' (5–6), as it may have supplied the material for bows still more ancient borne by the English 'at Azincour, / Perhaps at earlier Crecy, or Poictiers' (7–8). But then Wordsworth turns his attention to the four yews of Borrowdale, and these trees are weighted with a significance that seems far older and much stranger than the history of the nation state. They seem suddenly akin to Dutt's casuarina,

> each particular trunk a growth
> Of intertwisted fibres serpentine
> Up-coiling, and inveterately convolved.
>
> (16–8)

The trees are so closely grouped that their boughs intertwine forming 'a natural temple', 'a pillared shade', but it is the cathedral of a religion that seems to antedate Christianity, to be as old as the hills, tempting anyone who enters

> in mute repose
> To lie, and listen to the mountain flood
> Murmuring from Glaramara's inmost caves.
>
> (31–3)

Wordsworth is aware that English yews often pre-date the churches that they neighbour, relics of Druidic sacred groves, and Dutt, although she was converted to Christianity at the age of six, would have recalled that the Hindu sacred tree, the banyan, may grow into natural cathedrals that dwarf the temple formed by Wordsworth's yews. Her poem finds in the casuarina tree an invitation to reach back into a distant past, both cultural and linguistic, in which English and Bengali merge, each a branch of a tree of languages that has a single root.

Bradley and Cooper chose to launch their career with a volume in which they advertised their poems as derivative, a supplement to Sappho, attempts to restore poems that had survived, almost all of them, only as fragments. It seems an eccentric decision but it was oddly representative. Swinburne's first book, *The Queen-Mother and Rosalind* (1860), was by his own account 'of all still-born books the stillest'.[16] It was his second, *Atalanta in Calydon* (1865), especially its choruses, that persuaded its readers that they were in the presence of a new and surprisingly assured poetic voice, and yet *Atalanta in Calydon* is an exercise in pastiche. It is prefaced by a quotation in Greek from Euripides, and some verses in Greek celebrating Walter Savage Landor written by Swinburne himself. It is a poem in which Swinburne contrives flamboyantly to advertise his arrival as a major new poet in a volume that he presents as if it were just the kind of academic exercise that might be expected of the brilliant Balliol undergraduate that Swinburne had been not so long before. In the play's first and most famous chorus, the present has a predatory relationship with the past that it replaces, 'the hounds of spring are on winter's traces' (65), and lustful gods are in fierce pursuit of 'maidens hid' (112). Swinburne's anapaests strike the ear, trampling the reader into submission, the metrical feet echoing the feet of the satyr, 'And the hoofèd heel of a satyr crushes / The chestnut-husk at the chestnut-root.' (103–4) In such passages Swinburne seems to intimate that his text enjoys the same passionately rough relationship with the Greek texts that he is imitating that I located in 'Anactoria'. The plot he chooses seems to confirm this. Althæa's pride in her son Meleager does not prevent her from killing him when she learns that he has slain her two brothers: the relationship between the generations is murderous. But Meleager's aggression does not secure his independence of the older generation any more than Althæa can free herself from her love of her son by taking his life. In *Atalanta in Calydon* the violence with which Swinburne asserts the individuality of his own voice seems only to bind him more tightly to the Greek texts from which his poem derives. The poem's reviewers divided into those who recognized the emergence of a poet fit to stand alongside Tennyson, and those who regretted that Swinburne should have confined himself to imitation, but the most revealing reviews contrived to assert both positions simultaneously. The *Saturday Review* insisted that 'Mr. Swinburne is wholly a modern' but was still 'struck, every few lines, by some phrase' that seemed 'a direct translation of the Greek'. 'Everywhere are echoes of the ancient drama', noted the *Christian Remembrancer*, 'but they come upon the ear spontaneously'.[17] The secondary character of Victorian poetry is nowhere signalled more neatly than in this sentence, from which it appears that poetic originality can only be registered as a strange paradox, a spontaneous echo.

Matthew Arnold's most elaborate attempt to revive the Greek drama, *Merope* (1858), gave the same reviewer the 'impression of a school exercise, a copy made to order'. Arnold's echoes, it seems, in that particular instance lacked spontaneity, but that was not true of all his imitations. Arnold's reputation was not secured until the publication in 1853 of a new edition of his *Poems*, in which he included a selection of pieces from *The Strayed Reveller, and Other Poems* (1849), and *Empedocles on Etna, and Other Poems* (1852), both of which Arnold had himself withdrawn from circulation. The new volume included two important new poems, 'Sohrab and Rustum' and 'The Scholar-Gipsy', and it was the first of these that seems to have made most impression, even though, as all its readers noted, Arnold's story, despite being taken from the Persian, was told in a manner that closely imitated Homer. Like *Atalanta in Calydon* the poem attracted oddly contradictory responses. J.A. Froude, for example, upbraids Arnold for his classicism – 'But why dwell with such apparent exclusiveness on classic antiquity, [...] as if time were divided into the eras of Greece and Rome and the nineteenth century?' – and yet he identifies 'Sohrab and Rustum', a 'picture of life in Homer's manner', as a poem 'as good as any one of the episodes in the *Æneid*.' For Froude, it is 'Sohrab and Rustum' that settles the lofty position that 'Mr. Arnold has a right to claim as a poet'. [18] The poem itself works to ratify such responses. Sohrab, a Tartar warrior, has lived his whole life in an attempt to win the respect of the Persian father that he has never known. He challenges to single combat the Persian champion and is mortally wounded when he drops his shield in bewilderment hearing the Persian shout out as a battle cry, Rustum, his father's name. The poem ends in mutual recognition. First, Sohrab finds that he has been fighting against his own father, and then Rustum discovers that the young man he has mortally wounded is his son. The poem has often been read as a commentary on Arnold's own relationship with his redoubtable father, Dr Thomas Arnold, headmaster of Rugby School, but it seems more pertinently to figure Arnold's relationship to a classical tradition so powerful that it threatened to overwhelm any claims he might make for his own poetry. It is a plight from which Sohrab is saved by a comforting paradox. He achieves the monument that will preserve his fame not by securing victory but by suffering defeat. His father promises to 'heap a stately mound above [his] bones, / And plant a far-seen pillar over all' so that 'men shall not forget [him] in [his] grave' (803–5). The vow allows the poem to conclude in a grand image of reconciliation when the waters of the river Oxus, by which Sohrab has died, issue into the sea:

> till at last
> The longed-for dash of waves is heard, and wide
> His luminous home of waters opens, bright
> And tranquil, from whose floor the new-bathed stars
> Emerge, and shine upon the Aral Sea.
>
> (888–92)

But for some Victorian critics no such luminous merger between the classical and the modern was possible. W.E. Aytoun agreed that by writing 'on the Homeric principle' Arnold had established his superiority to 'the turgid trash with which we have been, of late years, inundated', but he had done so to little effect, because there remains 'an enormous gap' between 'the blind old man of Scio's rocky isle' and 'Mr. Matthew Arnold, who dates from "Fox How, Ambleside," A.D. 1853.'[19] Aytoun writes as if the modern poet had little choice except between being trashy and being imitative, and there seem to have been times when Arnold was inclined to agree with him. It is a thought that all Victorian poets, who had so exalted a sense of the achievements of the past, found hard wholly to repudiate.

Homer's simplicity, Aytoun argues, is quite different from Arnold's. Homer is simple 'because he was addressing a simple audience', whereas Arnold is simple because he is imitating Homer. His simplicity, unlike Homer's, is literary, and that in itself gives the clue to the difference between the primitive Greek society of the ninth century B.C. out of which Homer was produced and the sophisticated, bookish readership that Arnold was addressing. Somewhere in the back of Aytoun's mind hovers a thought that very few Victorians could quite resist, the thought given classic expression by Thomas Love Peacock in *The Four Ages of Poetry* (1820), that poetry is a mode of expression proper only to primitive societies. When society develops, the most important allegiance is to fact, and the pursuit of poetry becomes the symptom of the 'second childhood' undergone by those who respond to the sophisticated civilization of their own age by cultivating a nostalgia for a more primitive era. Poetry, that had once been the most important means by which a society articulated its own identity, in the nineteenth century was so diminished that it could do no more than offer entertainment to 'a multitude of idle listeners, yawning for amusement, and gaping for novelty'. Few of Peacock's successors would have agreed with him any more than did Shelley, who responded to his friend's squib by writing his own 'Defence of Poetry'. Indeed, it is far from clear how far Peacock agreed with himself, but the charge that he levelled haunted poetry throughout the century.

'Sohrab and Rustum' is a Homeric poem re-written for the nineteenth-century study. Lewis Carroll's 'Jabberwocky' is an Old English poem (the first stanza, when Carroll first published it in a family magazine, was presented as a 'curious fragment' of Anglo-Saxon poetry, and the whole poem might be thought of as a condensed version of the Anglo-Saxon epic, *Beowulf*, re-written for the nursery). But the nursery in the nineteenth century was not very distant from the study. In Chapter 6 of *Through the Looking Glass*, Alice's recitation of the poem prompts Humpty Dumpty to give her a tutorial on the relationship between words and their meaning:

> 'Twas brillig, and the slithy toves
>   Did gyre and gimble in the wabe:
> All mimsy were the borogroves,
>   And the mome raths outgrabe.
> (1–4)

Humpty offers Alice interpretative rules. 'Slithy', for example, is identified as a 'portmanteau – there are two meaning packed up into one word', in this case 'lithe' and 'slimy'. This might lead the reader confidently to suppose that to 'gimble' was to gambol nimbly, until Humpty instructs that it is 'to make holes like a gimblet'. Other meanings seem wholly arbitrary: a 'tove', for example, is not a cross between a toad and a dove, but between a badger, a lizard and a corkscrew. Sound associations are untrustworthy. 'Brillig', a sparkling word that might suggest springtime or morning, or, it may be, a chilly word that suggests a wintry day, according to Humpty 'means four o'clock in the afternoon – the time when you begin *broiling* things for dinner.' Humpty holds to the view that the meaning of words is arbitrary – 'When I use a word … it means just what I choose it to mean – neither more nor less'. Carroll knows that it is the business of the poet to gainsay that principle and to make the word and its meaning seem indivisible: it is just that in the conversation between Humpty and Alice the poetic mystery by which this is achieved is reduced to a parlour game.

The Victorian period is the great age of nonsense poetry, the age of Lewis Carroll and of Edward Lear, the two masters of the genre, and a period when many of the most distinguished poets wrote some nonsense verse (Christina Rossetti, for example, published her own volume of nonsense poetry in 1872, *Sing-Song: A Nursery Rhyme Book*), and it was also the period when the division between serious poetry and nonsense was most permeable. Aytoun, for example, calls attention to the 'jaw-breaking names' included in 'Sohrab and Rustum, as when 'long-neck'd cranes'

> Stream over Casbin, and the southern slopes
> Of Elburz, from the Aralian estuaries.
> (113–4)

Aytoun describes these lines as Miltonic, but he might just as easily have called them nonsensical. As in nonsense, words are chosen the sound of which operates independently of sense. An unusual number of Victorian poems seem to lend themselves to translation into nonsense, and no poems lent themselves so readily as those of the exemplary Victorian poet, Tennyson. Take, for example, a famous stanza from *Maud*:

> There has fallen a splendid tear
>   From the passion-flower at the gate.
> She is coming, my dove, my dear;
>   She is coming, my life, my fate;
> The red rose cries, 'She is near, she is near;'
>   And the white rose weeps, she is late;'
> The larkspur listen, 'I hear, I hear;'
>   And the lily whispers, I wait.
> (Part I, 908–15)

This is a poetry that approaches nonsense so closely that Carroll only has to nudge it to produce 'The Garden of Live Flowers' in Chapter Two of *Through the Looking Glass*: '"She's coming!" cried the Larkspur. "I hear her footstep, thump, thump, along the gravel-walk!"' But Edward Lear, as he was himself the first to recognize, was the Laureate's most exact nonsensical counterpart. He once wrote to a friend, 'I want you to write to Lord Palmerston to ask him to ask the King of Greece to give me a "place"'. He was to have an impressive Greek title, translatable as 'the Lord High Bosh and nonsense maker' with 'permission to wear a fool's cap (or mitre) – 3 pounds of butter yearly and a little pig, – and a small donkey to ride on.'[20] Tennyson admired Lear's musical settings of some of his lyrics, but when Lear performed them Tennyson's words were sometimes superseded by nonsense verses of his own. The very last poem he ever wrote, transcribing it in one of his letters as prose, was a nonsense version of 'Mariana': 'He only said, I'm very weary. The rheumatiz he said. He said, it's awful dull and dreary. I think I'll go to bed.'[21] Lear was immensely proud of the complimentary poem Tennyson addressed to him on the publication of his travel book, 'To E.L., on His Travels in Greece' (1853):

> Illyrian woodlands, echoing falls
>   Of water, sheets of summer glass,
>   The long divine Peneïan pass,
> The vast Akrokeraunian walls,
>
> Tomohrit, Athos, all things fair,
>   With such a pencil, such a pen,
>   You shadow forth to distant men,
> I read and felt that I was there.
> (1–8)

But that did not stop him translating it into nonsense:

> Delirious Bulldogs; – echoing calls
>   My daughter, – green as summer grass; –
>   The long supine Plebeian ass,
> The nasty crockery boring falls; –
>
> Tom-Moory Pathos; – all things bare, –
>   With such a turkey! such a hen!
>   And scrambling forms of distant men,
> O! ain't you glad you were not there!

Lear's parody gently mocks Tennyson's skill in contriving a verbal music that seems all but independent of the world he pretends to refer to. He does not so much make nonsense of Tennyson's poem as release a nonsensicality already implicit in it. In a phrase that comes into unusually close neighbourhood with sense, Tennyson is charged with substituting for Lear's topography 'Tom-Moory Pathos', an east like the east of *Lalla Rookh*, dissolved into a play of words and a shimmer of feelings. Lear knew that travel was a strenuous activity – those scrambling men – but in Tennyson's poem all effort is suspended. Travel is re-cast as a large indolence, as unruffled as the waters of Greece, 'sheets of summer glass'. Lear seems truculently to dwell on the contrast between travel as it was experienced by a 'dirty landscape painter' and by armchair travellers such as Tennyson – 'O! ain't you glad you were not there' – except that Lear knew perfectly well that travel books are designed to be read in armchairs just as nonsense poems, for all their wild imaginings, are designed for the nursery.

It is a perception that feeds into Lear's Nonsense, which takes place somewhere in between a domestic space and the far, far away, in between the crockery and the Acroceraunian mountains, somewhere between the pantry where the nutcrackers and sugar tongs are stored and the great Gromboolian plain. The characters in Lear's songs, like Tennyson's Ulysses, are oppressed by the tedium of their mundane lives. In 'The Duck and the Kangaroo' (1870), the Duck complains, 'My life is a bore in this nasty pond' and so she climbs onto the Kangaroo's tale and hops 'the whole world three times round'. In 'The Nutcrakers and the Sugar-Tongs' (1871) the Nutcrackers wearies of a 'stupid existence … So idle and weary, so full of remorse'. What distinguishes them from Tennysonian heroes is that they succeed in escaping to the 'untravell'd world' that Tennyson's Ulysses only dreams of. The Nutcrackers and the Sugar-tongs ride away 'Till far in the distance their forms disappearing, / They faded away. – And they never came back!' In 'The Daddy Long-legs and the Fly' (1871), Mr Daddy Long-legs and Mr Floppy Fly succeed in reaching the 'great Gromboolian plain' where they 'play for evermore / At battlecock and shuttledore', and after 'a year and a day' the 'Owl and the Pussy-cat' (1870) arrive at 'the land where the Bong-tree grows' and 'hand in hand, on the edge of the sand' they dance to the light of the moon.

Like FitzGerald's *Rubáiyát* quatrains, Lear's limericks have a close relation to the stanzas of Tennyson's *In Memoriam*. William Allingham recalled how Tennyson recited his poems with 'a peculiar *incomplete* cadence at the end',[22] an effect that the *In Memoriam* stanza intensifies. As Charles Kingsley notes, the stanza 'always leads the ear to expect something beyond'.[23] But so too does the limerick as Lear writes it, in which the final line, by repeating the first, avoids the click that completes limericks in which the first and final lines rhyme. Tennyson's stanza is, as Christopher Ricks puts it, 'especially suited to turning round rather than going forward.'[24] The same might be said of Lear's limericks, the characters of which tend at once to be frenetically active and not to go anywhere, like the Old Man of the West whose restlessness is cured when 'they set him to spin on his nose and his chin' (There was an Old Man of the

West'(1846). The characters of the limericks, unlike the songs, rarely succeed in escaping. The Young Lady of Portugal for all her nautical ideas 'declared she would never leave Portugal' (There was a Young Lady of Portugal' (1861), the Young Lady of Dorking buys a walking bonnet, but 'very soon went back to Dorking' ('There was a Young Lady of Dorking', 1846), just as the old person of Dover, stung by bees, 'very soon went back to Dover' ('There was an Old Person of Dover', 1861). The Old Person of Anerley enjoys a wonderful explosion of energy in which he 'rushed down the Strand, with a Pig in each hand', but he 'returned in the evening to Anerley' ('There was an Old Person of Anerley', 1861). The old person of Hyde and his bride who reach the shore, always a magical place for Lear, end by exclaiming, 'Would that we'd never left Hyde!' ('There was an Old Person of Hyde', 1872). Like the mourner in *In Memoriam*, they seem incapable of moving on. Lear's limerick characters are typically autistic, blankly unresponsive to their neighbours, and the speaker of *In Memoriam* displays the similar if milder autism of grief.

Tennyson refused to publish 'Anacaona', a poem probably written in 1830, fearing that it was vulnerable to confutation by 'some Midshipman who had been in Hayti latitudes and knew better about Tropical Vegetable and Animal.'[25] He suspected that he may have been guilty of an Edward Lear-like Nonsense Botany ('Bassia Palealensis', 'Queeriflora Babyöides' (1877)), and indeed he had been. Xaraguay is a land where 'the papao tree' grows rather than the Bong-tree, but the difference between the two trees is slight, because the poem works to melt all its tropical accoutrements into patterns of sound: 'She gave them the yuccaroot, / Maizebread and the yuccaroot' (55–6). Tennyson takes a grim tale from Washington Irving's *Life of Columbus*, the account of how Anacoana, the Queen of Xaraguay, welcomed the Spanish newcomers but was killed by them anyway, and fashions it into a mirror image of one of Lear's Nonsense Songs. The Owl and the Pussycat set sail in their pea-green boat and find the place that they are seeking:

> And hand in hand, on the edge of the sand,
> They danced by the light of the moon,
> The moon,
> The moon,
> They danced by the light of the moon.

In Xaraguay, Anacaona's 'loving childhood' need not be recovered because it has never been lost. None is so happy as she, 'All day long with laughing eyes, / Dancing by a palmy bay' (18–9). She dances '[n]aked, without fear' (61), because she has not yet been initiated into shame. All that ends when the white men come. Tennyson, characteristically, does not say what happens, only that Anacoana's long childhood is 'no more':

> But never more upon the shore
>   Dancing at the break of day,
> In the deep wood no more, –
> By the deep sea no more, –
>   No more in Xaraguay
> Wandered happy Anacaona,
>   The beauty of Espagnola,
>   The golden flower of Hayti!
>
> (77–84)

The lines grieve for a lost innocence and they also seek to preserve it, first by softening 'never more' into 'no more', and then by overriding the negative (Tennyson has a song, 'No More' (1830), in which that very phrase becomes a place where childhood innocence is magically preserved, '[l]owburied fathomdeep' in a place called 'NO MORE'). Tennyson finds a way of at once accepting and flinching from the facts as Irving gives them, preserving the saving possibility that Xaraguay might be a nonsense land, a land where 'no more' is a synonym of 'evermore'.

The close kinship between Tennyson, Victoria's Poet Laureate, and Lear, the Victorian laureate of the nursery, is, I think, revealing. Victorian poets were haunted by a suspicion that they lived in an age of prose, and that in such an age poetry was no more than a childish diversion. All poetry had been reduced to a species of nonsense. Poets used language, but displaced it from its proper function, so that it no longer performed its proper prosaic business as a tool with which to make sense of the world. The word in a poem became an object in itself, like the words in nonsense poems, like, for example, the final epithet in a Lear limerick, 'That omblif-erous person of Crete' (There was a Young Person of Crete' (1861)). In a prosaic age the making of poems may be in itself an act of translation, an act in which prosaic good sense is transmuted into something quite different, something that must sometimes have seemed quite closely akin to nonsense.

Endnotes

1. William Empson, *Seven Types of Ambiguity* (London : Chatto and Windus, 1930), p. 45.
2. Arthur J. Arberry, *FitzGerald's Salaman and Absal: A Study* (Cambridge: Cambridge University Press, 1956), p. 20, and *The Letters of Edward Fitzgerald*, ed. Alfred McKinley Terhune and Annabelle Burdick Terhune, 4 vols (Princeton, N. J.: Princeton University Press, 1980), 2, p. 335.
3. Robert Douglas-Fairhurst, *Victorian Afterlives: The Shaping of Influence in Nineteenth-Century Literature* (Oxford: Oxford University Press, 2002), p. 310.
4. Erik Gray, *The Poetry of Indifference from the Romantics to the Rubáiyát* (Amherst and Boston: University of Massachusetts Press, 2005), p. 110.
5. Robert Douglas-Fairhurst, V*ictorian Afterlives: The Shaping of Influence in Nineteenth-Century Literature*, p. 308.
6. T.S. Eliot, *The Use of Poetry and the Use of Criticism* (London: Faber and Faber, 1964). Eliot is, however, less offended by FitzGerald's variety of atheism than Shelley's.
7. *The Letters of Edward Fitzgerald*, 1, pp. 696 and 486.
8. *The Letters of Edward Fitzgerald*, 3, p. 339.
9. Seamus Perry, *Alfred Tennyson* (London: Northcote, 2005), p. 136.
10. Herbert F. Tucker, 'Metaphor, translation, and autoekphrasis in FitzGerald's *Rubáiyát*', *Victorian Poetry*, 16.1 (2008), 69–85, p. 78.
11. Lawrence Venuti, *The Translator's Invisibility: A History of Translation* (London and New York: Routledge, 1995), pp. 118–47, Matthew Arnold, 'On Translating Homer', *On the Classical Tradition*, ed. R.H. Super (Ann Arbor: University of Michigan Press, 1960).
12. *The Iliad of Homer*, translated by F.W. Newman (London: Walton and Maberly, 1856), p. xvi; Matthew Arnold, 'On Translating Homer', *On the Classical Tradition, The Complete Prose Works of Matthew Arnold*, ed. R.H. Super (Ann Arbor; University of Michigan Press, 1960), pp. 97–216.
13. *The Swinburne Letters*, ed. Cecil Y. Lang, 6 vols (New Haven: Yale University Press, 1959–62), 4, p. 124.
14. *Swinburne: The Critical Heritage*, ed. Clyde K. Hyder (London: Routledge and Kegan Paul, 1970), p. 52.
15. *Swinburne: The Critical Heritage*, ed. Clyde K. Hyder (London: Routledge and Kegan Paul, 1970), p. 52.
16. Quoted in *Swinburne: The Critical Heritage*, p. xv.
17. *Saturday Review*, May 6, 1865, p. 541; *Christian Remembrances*, **55** (January, 1868), p. 46.
18. J.H. Froude, *Essays in Literature and History* (London: Dent, 1906), p. 23.

19. 'The Two Arnolds', *Blackwood's Edinburgh Magazine*, **75** (March, 1854), 303–14, p. 310.
20. *Letters of Edward Lear*, ed. Lady Strachey (London: T. Fisher Unwin, 1907), p. 289.
21. *Later Letters of Edward Lear*, ed. Lady Strachey (London: T. Fisher Unwin, 1911), p. 325.
22. *Tennyson: Interviews and Recollections*, ed. Norman Page (Basingstoke: Macmillan, 1983), p. 58.
23. *Tennyson: The Critical* Heritage, ed. John D. Jump (London: Routledge and Kegan Paul, 1967), p. 153.
24. Christopher Ricks, *Tennyson* (London: Macmillan, 1972), p. 222.
25. As reported by Edward FitzGerald in his copy of the 1842 *Poems*, quoted by Ricks, *The Poems of Tennyson*, 3 vols (Harlow: Longman, 1987), 1, p. 308.

6

Victorian Poetry and Life

Matthew Arnold complained in the Preface to his *Poems* of 1853 that his contemporaries lacked the 'architectonic' skills that characterize the greatest poets, skills that reveal themselves in a concern for 'the spirit of the whole' rather than those 'single thoughts' to which even Shakespeare so often allowed precedence. The representative modern poet is Keats: in a poem such as 'Isabella' (1820) there is almost no stanza without 'one of those vivid and picturesque turns of expression' that 'thrill the reader with a sudden delight', and yet it is a poem the action of which is so feebly conceived that it makes almost no impression on the reader as a whole. Arnold is quick to disclaim any suggestion that his own poems are free from the deficiency that he detects in Keats. Even as a critic Arnold often seems more alert to the beauty of single thoughts than to the 'unity and profoundness of moral impression' achieved by the classical poets that he most admires. 'They regarded the whole; we regard the parts', Arnold observes, and his use of the first-person pronoun is not governed simply by politeness. The genius of English poetry is, Arnold claims elsewhere, Celtic, and displayed most clearly in its command of 'natural magic', as when Titania remembers her meetings with Oberon

> on hill, in dale, forest, or mead,
> By paved fountain, or by rushy brook,
> Or in the beached margent of the sea.
> (*Midsummer Night's Dream*,
> 2, 1, 83–5)

Reading Victorian Poetry, First Edition. Richard Cronin.

Or when Keats's 'magic casements' open on 'the foam / Of perilous seas in fairy lands forlorn' ('Ode to a Nightingale', 69–70). In 'On the Study of Celtic Literature' (1867) Arnold concedes that it is precisely because of this that the Celtic genius is displayed in 'passages, lines, and snatches of long pieces' and lacks 'the architectonicé which shapes great works', an excellence that 'comes only after a steady, deep-searching survey, a firm conception of the facts of human life'.[1] But it is natural magic rather than 'architectonicé' for which Arnold's own poems are remarkable. Arnold is at his best in 'passages, lines, and snatches' as when, to give just one example, the fields are still, the shepherds and their dogs have retired to rest, 'And only the white sheep are sometimes seen / Cross and recross the strips of moon-blanched green' ('The Scholar-Gipsy' (1853), 8–9).

Men, Tennyson's Prince tells his father, are 'piebald', divided against themselves. Women, by contrast, are 'whole and one', like his own mother who is 'pure as lines of green that streak the white / Of the first snowdrop's inner leaves' (*The Princess* (1847), 5, 188–9). The thought fractures the wholeness that it claims to exemplify because the snowdrop is rendered too exactly, too magically, to function simply as a type of womanly purity: it retains its magic because it refuses to stop being a snowdrop. Compare Ruskin on the 'slender, pensive, fragile flower' that pierces the snow of the lower Alps in early May. Ruskin offers its 'small, dark, purple, fringed bell' that 'hangs down and shudders over the icy cleft that it has cloven, as if partly wondering at its own recent grave, and partly dying of very fatigue after its hard-won victory' as 'an image of moral purpose and achievement' (*Modern Painters* II (1846).[2] That flower confirms Ruskin's belief that he can read the natural world like a book, and there were Victorian poets who shared that confidence, John Keble, for one, in *The Christian Year* (1827). 'Nature's beauteous book' lies open before him, he writes in his poem for the 'Fourth Sunday in Advent', and the only question is whether he is worthy to read it. It is a thought that often strikes him:

> The works of God above, below,
>   Within us and around,
> Are pages in that Book to shew
>   How God Himself is found.
>   ('Septuagesima Sunday',
>   5–8)

For Keble, who believed with his fellow Tractarians that the natural and the spiritual worlds were linked by a system of analogy, the lilies that grow 'beside our paths and homes' convey a clear message:

> 'Live for to-day! to-morrow's light
> To-morrow's cares shall bring to sight,
> Go sleep like closing flowers at night,
> And heaven thy morn will bless.'
> ('Fifteenth Sunday after
> Trinity', 53–6).

Nature is important for him because of the 'rich wealth of similes' that it makes available to the 'pious mind'.[3] Christina Rossetti agreed: 'Flowers preach to us if we will hear'. ('Consider the Lilies of the Field' (1875, but written 1863), 1) But not all Keble's contemporaries shared his faith, and, as the century wore on, it became a faith a good deal less easy to sustain. It is, for example, harder to locate consoling Christian truths in the natural world as Darwin describes it.

Ruskin admired Alice Meynell's sonnet 'To a Daisy' (1875),[4] predictably because the poem shares Ruskin's own typological understanding of the natural world. The daisy, 'Like all created things' (2), veils a 'great mystery' (6), but its mystery is revealed in a language that Meynell in her earthly life is unable to read, a language that she will only be able to understand when she reads it sitting at 'God's side' in heaven (14). For Meynell, as for Ruskin, nature is a book, but it is a book written in a language that she has not yet learned. Tennyson, like Keble and Meynell, like most Victorians, would have been fluent in the language of flowers, but it was a language that sometimes left him just as disconcerted as Alice Meynell by the distance separating sign and referent. Tennyson was prompted to write 'Flower in the crannied wall' (1870) when he plucked a plant, love-in-idleness or the wild pansy, out of a wall near Haslemere:

> Flower in the crannied wall,
> I pluck you out of the crannies,
> I hold you here, root and all, in my hand,
> Little flower – but *if* I could understand
> What you are, root and all, and all in all,
> I should know what God and man is.
> (1–6)

Tennyson's friend, Spedding, could not hear the metre, and had to be advised by Tennyson that the fifth line begins with two anapaests, although the metre is 'rough doubtless'.[5] But the rhythmic uncertainty seems to shadow a larger puzzlement. The flower seems fraught with meaning, but the meaning remains somehow ungraspable.

For whatever reason, many Victorian poems hinge on the difficulty of forging a connection between the world of fact and the world of value. In D.G. Rossetti's 'The Woodspurge' (1870) the grief-stricken speaker experiences a state of raw disseverance from the world. In Romantic poems such as Shelley's 'Ode to the West Wind'(1820) the wind merges with the breath of the poet, but Rossetti's wind remains quite alien: 'The wind flapped loose, the wind was still' (1). The noise of everyday life intrudes like an outrage on his 'naked ears.' As he slumps, his head bent over the grass, a single plant impresses itself on his memory, the wood-spurge with its 'three cups in one.' The experience offers no consolation nor is it admonitory: it remains simply arbitrary, a version of the Trinity for a wholly desanctified world. Rossetti, it may be suspected, is making a polemical point of his disenchantment, but in Michael Field's 'Cyclamens' (1893) there seems no such intention. The flowers are 'terribly white' in the poem's first line, the whiteness startling even in a snow-covered landscape in which the snow reflects the white moon. The poem ends when the speaker acknowledges the power of the 'chiselled white' of the flowers to strike her to the heart, but the pang remains quite contentless, delivered by the 'handful of cyclamen' like the stroke of a calmly indifferent sculptor. 'Cyclamens' practises the kind of gaze that Bradley and Cooper define in their preface to their second volume of poems, *Sight and Song* (1892), a gaze 'as pure as the gazer can refine it of theory, fancies, or his mere subjective enjoyment.' 'Cyclamens' might seem an Imagist poem before its time. It would be harder to claim William Barnes as a Modernist forerunner despite his influence on Hardy, but in a poem such as 'A Brisk Wind' (1868) he seems as alert as Michael Field to the way in which the world rebuffs attempts to accommodate it within a human subjectivity:

The burdock leaves beside the ledge,
The leaves upon the poplar's height,
Were blown by windblasts up on edge,
And show'd their undersides of white;
And willow trees beside the rocks,

All bent grey leaves, and swung grey boughs,
As there, on wagging heads, dark locks,
Bespread red cheeks, behung white brows.

The wind blows the burdock leaves and the poplar leaves and the willow leaves, and it blows human hair too, and whatever it blows it blows with the same indifference. The poems by Rossetti and Michael Field and William Barnes share a characteristic Victorian preoccupation with the enigmatic relationship between the world observed with such sharp precision and the feelings of the observer, and it is that relationship that I will explore in this chapter.

In his review of Tennyson's *Poems, Chiefly Lyrical*, Arthur Hallam had not found the relationship either distant or enigmatic. 'Modern poetry' such as Tennyson's was a poetry of 'sensation', and demonstrated the 'powerful tendency of imagination to a life of immediate sympathy with the external universe'. One of Tennyson's 'distinctive excellencies' was his skill in bringing together objects in the landscape with the moods of his own mind, or, as Hallam puts it, 'his vivid, picturesque delineation of objects, and the peculiar skill with which he holds all of them *fused*, to borrow a metaphor from science, in a medium of strong emotion'.[6] Hallam is thinking of poems such as 'Mariana' (1830), in which Mariana's arrested life is so finely expressed through the description of her garden. The movement of the verse is checked by a cluster of 'st' and 'ts' sounds, 'blackest', 'plots', 'crusted', 'rusted', 'knots', that clogs the surface of the verse rather like the 'marish-mosses' that choke the pond in the fourth stanza:

With blackest moss the flower-plots
  Were thickly crusted, one and all:
The rusted nails fell from the knots
  That held the pear to the gable-wall.
(1–4)

Many readers assume that the garden is being described as Mariana sees it, its atrophied state a projection of her own, but in fact Mariana never sees her garden at all. All day she keeps her curtains drawn, opening them only when 'thickest dark did trance the sky' (18). It is the poet rather than Mariana who watches while those rusted nails fall. But readers' impressions are trustworthy for all that, because the poem is written out of a sympathy with Mariana so intimate that the distinction between the world as it seems to the poet and the world as it is seen by his character disappears. The world that the poet and his character cooperate to produce is a world in which the difference between what is imagined and what is real has lapsed:

> All day within the dreamy house,
>   The doors upon their hinges creaked;
> The blue fly sung in the pane; the mouse
>   Behind the mouldering wainscot shrieked,
> Or from the crevice peered about.
>   Old faces glimmered through the doors,
>   Old footsteps trod the upper floors,
> Old voices called her from without.
>
> (61–8)

The animal noises, I assume, are real whereas the human presences are ghostly or remembered, and yet the blue fly's buzz and the mouse's shriek seem just as hallucinatory as the faces and the footsteps. It is as if all the objects of the poem are, to use Hallam's expression, fused with one another. Outside the window there is a single tree, a poplar, and, when the moon is low, 'The shadow of the poplar fell / Upon her bed, across her brow' (55–6), but the tree, like the house, is so dreamy that it hardly seems necessary to distinguish between the tree and its shadow, just as it seems unnecessary to decide whether the spectral crucifixion that Mariana undergoes is painful or erotic. The 'sparrow's chirrup', the 'slow clock ticking' and the sound of the wind in the poplar work together to 'confound' Mariana's sense, (73–7), and the poem has a similar effect on its readers. Mariana closes each stanza with a complaint that she has been deserted:

> She only said, 'The night is dreary,
>   He cometh not,' she said;
> She said, I am aweary, aweary,
>   I would that I were dead!'

And the poem ends when she accepts her fate: 'He cometh not' becomes 'He will not come' (82). But it is Mariana's desertion that has prompted the poet to mingle his life with hers: it is because she is abandoned that he feels able to enter her life so completely. In Millais's painting from the poem Mariana's desolate condition is gainsaid by the rich blue velvet of her dress. She leans back and presses her hands into the small of her back in a gesture that is oddly ambiguous, at once weary and seductively languorous, and it is an ambiguity that seems true to a poem in which the absence of Mariana's lover, Shakespeare's Angelo presumably, seems the necessary condition for the poet's intimate presence. The whole of Mariana's life is dreary, but

> most she loathed the hour
> When the thick-moted sunbeam lay
> Athwart the chambers, and the day
> Was sloping toward his western bower.
> (77–80)

In these lines it is the 'th' sounds in 'loathed', 'thick' and 'Athwart' that slow the verse in a manner that seems at once painful and luxurious, as if the verb 'loathed' could at once retain its proper meaning, and become the form that the verb 'loved' has to take when subjected to the phonetic shift needed to bring it into accord with the peculiar sound patterns of Tennyson's poem.

His skill in fusing mood and landscape identifies Tennyson, Hallam notes, as the descendant of Keats and Shelley, and some of Tennyson's contemporaries, Emily Brontë for example, also seem heirs of the Romantics, though Emily Brontë may seem in a more direct line of descent from Byron and Scott. In 'High waving heather 'neath stormy blasts bending' (written in 1836 but not published until 1902) the stormy landscape of the moors and the workings of the creative imagination are inseparably connected. The 'wild forests' lend to the 'life giving wind' a 'mighty voice' that is indistinguishable from the voice of the poem. The wind's modulations, 'Roaring like thunder like soft music sighing', are fused with the movement of the verse. Whereas the wind in Rossetti's 'The Woodspurge' seemed as it 'flapped loose' to represent a natural world entirely without sympathy for the humans who occupy it, Emily Brontë still, like her Romantic forebears, associates the wind with poetic inspiration. In 'The Night-Wind' (1850, but written 1840) the wind is a seducer that the poet resists:

> I said, 'Go gentle singer,
> Thy wooing voice is kind
> But do not think its music
> Has power to reach my mind.

'Play with the scented flower,
  The young tree's supple bough –
And leave my human feelings
  In their own course to flow.'
(17–24)

But the wind disregards the rebuff – 'its kiss grew warmer still' – and the poem, it seems clear, is itself the proof that its music does after all have the power to reach her mind. Yet the poem ends with a quatrain that seems more sardonic than tuneful. In 'Ode to the West Wind' Shelley grants the wind the power to 'quicken a new birth', but the love that the wind offers Emily Brontë only has its being on this side of the grave. The poem ends when the wind offers the poet a warning:

'And when thy heart is laid at rest
  Beneath the church-yard stone
I shall have time enough to mourn
  And thou to be alone'
(33–6)

It ends in an un-Romantic insistence that poetry, whatever claims might be made for it, has no power over death.

Victorian poets are just as likely to part company with their Romantic predecessors as to join them, and when they do so they tend to insist rather strenuously on the discontinuity between human experience and the natural world. Arnold, for example, has a sonnet in which he delivers a withering retort to 'a preacher': '"In harmony with Nature?" Restless fool' (1849). Arnold's point is that the qualities for which human life is valuable are precisely those for which nature supplies no pattern:

Nature is cruel, man is sick of blood;
Nature is stubborn, man would fain adore;

Nature is fickle, man hath need of rest;
Nature forgives no debt, and fears no grave;
Man would be mild, and with safe conscience blest.
('In Harmony with Nature,
To a Preacher', 7–11)

Arnold is careful to couch his rebuke in terms that do not wantonly outrage the preacher's faith. Thomas Hardy is less scrupulous, as when he pauses in Chapter 3 of *Tess of the D'Urbervilles* (1891) to deliver a sharp rejoinder to Wordsworth's 'Lines Written in Early Spring' (1798): 'Some people would like to know whence the poet whose philosophy is in these days deemed as profound and trustworthy as his verse is pure and breezy, gets his authority for speaking of "Nature's holy plan."' But Victorian verse is characteristically more quizzical than this, questioning rather than assertive in its examination of the relationship between human beings and their physical world.

The Brownings fiercely contested the notion that world and spirit, soul and body, might be opposed. When Fra Lippo Lippi's Prior urges him to 'Give us no more of body than shows soul' (188), the painter responds confidently:

> A fine way to paint soul, by painting body
> So ill, the eye can't stop there, must go further
> And can't fare worse!
> ('Fra Lippo Lippi' (1855), 199–201)

The thought comes recommended by Lippo Lippi's personality, his bouncy vigour, but it also comes qualified by his unapologetic fleshliness (he is after all a monk who has been apprehended slipping away from a brothel). One guesses that Browning is sympathetic when Lippo Lippi asks,

> Why can't a painter lift each foot in turn,
> Left foot and right foot, do a double step,
> Make his flesh liker, and his soul more like,
> Both in their order?
> (205–8)

But how far in lines like these does Lippo Lippi defend the body by materializing the soul (Browning's metaphor brings it to the verge of becoming a sole)? The feet, metrical and corporeal, break into a little dance, a soft shoe shuffle, but the dance seems jaunty, almost a kind of caper. It is, of course, one of the defining features of the dramatic monologue to make the reader wonder how far we should judge an opinion by reference to the character of the person who proffers it, but in the Brownings' verse the problem is more deep-rooted than this. Even in verse in which they are writing, or seem to be, in their own person, the more spiritual the topic addressed the more insistently material the metaphors in which they choose to express it. Take the fortieth of Barrett Browning's *Sonnets from the Portuguese* (1850) in which she contrasts Robert Browning's love with what passes for love in the rest of the world. Browning's love, in a characteristic phrase, 'brings souls to touch'. His love is not subject to abrupt transitions:

> Polypheme's white tooth
> Slips on the nut if, after frequent showers,
> The shell is over-smooth.
>
> (7–9)

Polyphemus, the Cyclops, one-eyed, cannibalistic, is offered as her own lover's antithesis. The kind of mean sensual man best represented by Polyphemus would have been repelled, as Robert Browning was not, by her sadness, by her tears, and his love diverted to hatred. The thought seems conventional enough, and yet it does nothing to alleviate the strangeness of the metaphor that carries it. These lines span the sonnet's volta, so that the turn from octave to sestet is figured in the painful little shock that the tooth suffers as it slips and the pressure on the nut's shell becomes the jarring impact of tooth on tooth. Barrett Browning is celebrating what Shakespeare defines in sonnet 116 as 'a marriage of true minds', a love that is not 'Time's fool, though rosy lips and cheeks / Within his bending sickle's compass come', but she does so in a poem that realizes the body – not lips and cheeks but a much more flagrantly intimate space, the interior of the mouth – with a disconcerting vividness. The sonnet addresses what Barrett Browning calls 'the thing called love', the chief mystery of which, curtly registered in the phrase, is how it manages to accomplish the passage between the body in all its fleshly materiality and the soul, how it manages to 'bring souls to touch'.

J.T. Knowles had Tennyson's blessing when he read *Idylls of the King* as illustrating 'the perpetual warfare between the spirit and the flesh', a warfare in which the most calamitous episode is the adultery of Arthur's Queen, Guinevere, with Lancelot, the noblest of his knights.[7] But Tennyson's Guinevere was first exposed to the Victorian public in 1859, a year after Morris had presented them with a Queen who differs from Tennyson's in much more than the spelling of her name. In 'The Defence of Guenevere' the Queen addresses the court in her own defence. Remarkably she all but accepts the truth of the charge of adultery Gauwaine brings against her, and yet still insists that Gauwaine lies. The one proof she offers is that she does not, like Tennyson's Guinevere, feel guilty: 'A great queen such as I / Having sinn'd this way, straight her conscience sears / And afterwards she liveth hatefully.' (146–8) But Guenevere lives in the warm glow of a self-adoration that she sees unwillingly reflected in the faces of all her male accusers. From the time that she first saw Lancelot, she explains,

> I grew
> Careless of most things, let the clock tick, tick,
> To my unhappy pulse, that beat right through
> My eager body.
>
> (74–7)

She experiences her marriage – 'I was bought / By Arthur's great name and his little love' (82–3) – as threatening that union of body and spirit in which she recognizes her life. She feels her marriage as a subordination of the vital rhythm of her pulse to the mechanical ticking of a clock. Lancelot gives her back herself, and it is that self that she offers to her accusers. Her defence consists of a provocative, theatrical act of self-display. She speaks 'With passionate twisting of her body there' (60), but she speaks only as a way of commanding the gaze of her auditors. She acts out for them her own ravishing physicality:

> If I had
> Held out my long hand up against the blue,
> And, looking on the tenderly darken'd fingers,
> Thought that by rights one ought to see quite through,
>
> There, see you, where the soft still light yet lingers,
> Round by the edges.
>
> (120–5)

She offers that delicate collusion of light and flesh as a wholly sufficient rejoinder to all those who would represent the body as sinful, and virtue as the product of its conquest by the spirit. She holds her hand up to the sun as a more lively demonstration of a truth that she first offers in a parable. An angel asks a man to choose between two cloths, 'one blue / Wavy and long, and one cut short and red / No man could tell the better of the two' (34–6). After 'a shivering half hour' the man chooses 'heaven's colour, the blue', only to be told that he has chosen hell. It is Guenevere's confession of the fatal mistake of her choice of husband, a satire on those who dignify aesthetic preferences by representing them as moral choices, and a rich joke at the expense of all those who believe that arbitrary human conventions, such as the notion that blue rather than red is heaven's colour, are in perfect accord with the divine order. Morris, unlike Tennyson (at any rate in 'Guinevere'), finds the relationship between the bodily and the spiritual life problematic, and so does Robert Browning.

'Caliban on Setebos; or Natural Theology on the Island' (1864) has most often been understood as a satire on the notion that the character of God can be derived from a study of the natural world that he created. Browning chose as his epigraph the warning that God gives in Psalm 50, 'Thou thoughtest that I was altogether such an one as thyself'. The poem is directed, then, at natural theologians such as William Paley and Bishop Butler who were still widely respected in the nineteenth century. It was a satire the more urgent because after Darwin's *Origin of Species* (1859) the natural world no longer seemed to provide any very persuasive evidence of a beneficent Creator. But the poem is at least as dramatic as it is satirical, and as a dramatic poem its interest is in the effort that Caliban, its primitive speaker, makes to deduce from his experience of the world a view of how that world is constituted. Caliban asks himself what values govern the world, and he seeks to derive those values from the facts of the world as he understands them. Some readers of the poem have been repelled by Caliban's failures of imaginative sympathy, as when he playacts being Prospero, furnishing himself with a Caliban of his own by snaring a sea creature and ensuring its dependence by splitting the webbing of its feet and blinding it. Other readers have a more chastened awareness of the limits of their own capacity for sympathy (Does it extend, for example, to the ants that Caliban watches so observantly – he notices that the magpies do not eat them?), and may feel that, however much more sophisticated they may be, they share with Caliban a common enterprise, a desire to understand the world with not much more to go on than their own experience of it.

The poem begins as Caliban prepares to plash in a cool mud bath. The opening paragraph works to suggest a press of sensual experience that converts the whole of Caliban's island into a kind of wallow:

> 'Will sprawl, now that the heat of day is best,
> Flat on his belly in the pit's much mire,
> With elbows wide, fists clenched to prop his chin;

And, while he kicks both feet in the cool slush,
And feels about his spine small eft-things course,
Run in and out each arm, and make him laugh;
And while above his head a pompion-plant,
Coating the cave-top as a brow its eye,
Creeps down to touch and tickle hair and beard,
And now a flower drops with a bee inside,
And now a fruit to snap at, catch and crunch.
(1–11)

This is writing that is unusually intimate with the body, like Barrett Browning's when she thinks of how a tooth might slip on the smooth shell of a nut, but it is a body of a very particular kind, a body that does not fully register its difference from the world that it inhabits. This is signalled in the metaphor that has the pumpkin vine curve over the mouth of the cave 'as a brow its eye', in Caliban's failure to recognize the newts that tickle him as alien creatures from which to flinch in disgust or fear, and, most powerfully of all, in Caliban's use of a third person (though the pronoun is omitted) that seems to admit no distinction between subject and object, between himself and his world. Caliban is an exotic creature, taken from Shakespeare's most exotic play, *The Tempest*, but he is also closely akin to the child, as Wordsworth represents him in *The Prelude*, the 'naked savage' who 'Made one long bathing of a summer's day; / Basked in the sun, and plunged and basked again' (1850, 1, 300, 290–1). The first paragraph establishes Browning's Caliban as someone almost unimaginably strange, and yet for all that someone in whom readers are invited dimly to recognize a version of themselves. It is the divided response that Browning's monologues very often invite. The third person in which Caliban speaks is on occasion interrupted by a first person, as when Caliban imagines what it would be like to be able to fly, 'wishing I were born a bird' (74), or in the grotesque song with which at the very end of the poem he imagines attempting to placate a vengeful Setebos:

'What I hate, be consecrate
To celebrate Thee and Thy state, no mate
For Thee; what see for envy in poor me?'
(276–8)

The inconsistency shows Caliban on the verge of emerging into full self-consciousness (he is already aware of himself as divided: he 'talks to his own self' (15)), but it also strengthens the invitation to the reader at once to register a fellow-feeling with him, and to contemplate him at a remove, in horrified disgust.

What Caliban talks to himself about is Setebos, 'that other, whom his dam called God' (16). He thinks of Setebos as the Creator of the world, who dwells in the cold of the moon that Setebos has himself created:

> 'Thinketh he made it with the sun to match,
> But not the stars; the stars came otherwise.
> (26–7)

Browning's editors suggestively cite in comparison the barrow-boy interviewed by Henry Mayhew in *London Labour and the London Poor*: 'Oh, yes, I've heard of God; he made heaven and earth: I never heard of his making the sea; that's another thing'.[8] But Caliban's caveat seems less arbitrary, as if he dimly apprehends the Ptolemaic distinction between the planetary bodies that move and the fixed stars. Lying in his cool mud bath Caliban is reaching out from the intensely sensual life that is his towards the life of the mind. He addresses, for example, the puzzling question of what might have moved Setebos to create the world, and ventures the haunting suggestion that 'it came of being ill at ease' (31). He remembers seeing a freshwater fish that had been swept out to sea by a mountain stream that thrust its fresh water out into the sea like a 'crystal spike'. Caliban imagines the fish longing to enter the warm sea water, 'green-dense and dim-delicious, bred o' the sun', only to find that the salt water will not support its life. The fish is left 'Hating and loving warmth alike' (33–43). He has arrived at an unexpectedly sophisticated understanding of creativity as an organism's response when it is subjected to contradictory impulses. He arrives at that notion through the intensity of his sensual response to the green-dense, dim-delicious seawater, and also through an exercise of the sympathetic imagination, by imagining how that fish might feel. But sympathy is a capacity that he exercises arbitrarily, capriciously, and he suspects that God might exercise his power similarly:

> 'Am strong myself compared to yonder crabs
> That march now from the mountain to the sea;
> 'Let twenty pass, and stone the twenty-first,
> Loving not, hating not, just choosing so.
> (100–3)

Browning's epigraph from Psalm 50 seems chosen as a comment on passages such as this. But can an epigraph cancel from the reader's mind any suspicion that the God that Caliban intuits, grotesque though he might be, is at least consistent with the facts of the world as Caliban experiences them? Those facts are, after all, more consistent with the world as it was described by nineteenth-century naturalists, Darwin chief amongst them, than the Christian possibility that Browning's Karshish so wonderingly entertains:

> The very God! think, Abib; dost thou think?
> So, the All-Great were the All-Loving too –
> So, through the thunder comes a human voice
> Saying, 'O heart I made, a heart beats here!
> Face, my hands fashioned, see it in myself.'
> ('An Epistle Containing the Strange Medical Experience of Karshish, the Arab Physician' (1855), 304–8)

Karshish imagines a God who asks that we grant him our own best attributes, the very procedure that the Psalmist seems to warn against, though the Psalmist does not explain how it is possible to envisage a personal God without ascribing to him the human personality that is, after all, the only personality of which we have any direct experience. Nor does the Psalmist do anything to meet the objections of those who conclude that God, if he is judged by his creation, differs from human beings precisely by falling so far beneath their own best values. As Darwin himself put it, 'I cannot persuade myself that a beneficent and omnipotent God would have designedly created the Ichneumonid [a parasitic wasp] with the express intention of their feeding within the living bodies of Caterpillars.'[9]

Caliban's greatest feat of imagination is to postulate that there might be some other power that has priority over Setebos, that created Setebos, or that Setebos ousted, as Jupiter ousted Saturn. He refers to this power as 'the Quiet' because he imagines it as without attributes, feeling 'nor joy nor grief, / Since both derive from weakness in some way' (133–4). His dam 'held that the Quiet made all things / Which Setebos vexed only' (170–1), but Caliban dismisses the notion because he can understand creation only as an attempt to supply some lack in the Creator, and the Quiet, unlike Setebos, feels no lack. In any case, 'the Quiet', again unlike Setebos, poses no threat to him and can safely be ignored. And yet, simply by imagining such a being, Caliban reveals his ability to emerge from that intense bodily life in which the poem begins, and that it perversely returns to at the very end: Caliban, believing that he has been overheard, attempts to placate Setebos by inflicting pain upon himself, biting through his upper lip until his teeth meet. As a version of primitive man, Caliban may more often repel than beguile, but, for all that, Browning clearly presents him as a type of the artist; he is a type of the sculptor when he imagines that he might be consoled for not being able to fly if he could 'make a live bird out of clay' (76), a type of the dramatist when he pretends to be Prospero, donning the 'skin of a supple oncelot', and keeping a wildcat as his Miranda, 'for his Ariel, a tall pouch-bill crane', and for his Caliban a sea-beast that he lames and blinds to ensure its dependency (155–67), and he is at the last a type of the poet devising his own wild song, 'What I hate, be consecrate / To celebrate Thee and Thy state' (276–7). Victorian poems very often begin with the life of the body, the sensual life, but they typically move outwards in an attempt to make sense of the world. Caliban may be a primitive artist, but he is a primitive artist of a distinctively Victorian kind.

On the face of it, Caliban could scarcely be more different from the speaker of Arnold's 'Dover Beach' (1867 but probably written 1851), and yet the two poems have a similar trajectory. Both move from a sensuous apprehension of the natural world towards a more general meditation on the character of that world and of the human place within it. It is the trajectory characteristic of the Victorian lyric. Caliban follows it clumsily, sometimes repelling, sometimes inviting sympathy. Arnold's voice, by contrast, seems even in its sadness as calm as the sea of the poem's first line, quite free from the confused uncertainty that in the poem's conclusion is said to define the human condition, and yet the poem works to reveal its own calmness, like the calmness of the 'tranquil bay', as illusory.

The elaborate, Keatsian stanza with which 'Dover Beach' begins is not replicated. Each of the poem's four stanzas is unique in the number of its lines, in its metre, and in its rhyme scheme, and one effect is to open up the spaces between them. The poem begins limpidly, almost like a weather report:

> The sea is calm tonight.
> The tide is full, the moon lies fair
> Upon the straits.
>
> (1–3)

Its rhythms become more expansive when the appeal to the eye gives way to an appeal to the ear:

> Listen! you hear the grating roar
> Of pebbles which the waves draw back, and fling,
> At their return, up the high strand,
> Begin, and cease, and then again begin,
> With tremulous cadence slow, and bring
> The eternal note of sadness in.
>
> (9–14)

The lines reproduce the regular beat of the waves, but reproduce it tremulously, as they alternate between eight and ten syllables, and allow an almost-anapaest to interrupt the iambs in the phrase 'With tremulous cadence slow'. The 'grating roar' that Arnold is describing is the distinctive sound of the pebble beaches of the English south coast, which makes the sudden jump through space and time that Arnold takes in the second stanza the more startling:

> Sophocles long ago
> Heard it on the Aegean, and it brought
> Into his mind the turbid ebb and flow
> Of human misery.
>
> (15–8)

Like Keats listening to the nightingale, Arnold claims that the sound he is listening to was heard in 'ancient days', but Arnold's claim is puzzling, partly because the Aegean is not remarkable for its pebble beaches, and partly because it is not clear what particular passage from Sophocles he has in mind. The passage most often adduced, from the third chorus in the *Antigone*, describes sand rather than pebbles being cast up by the sea, and the roar that Sophocles refers to seems to be the noise of the wind. Arnold insists that the two sounds are the same to support his claim that the 'note of sadness' that they sound is 'eternal', a note that defines the human condition in all times and places, but the 'thought' that the sound produces when it is heard 'by this distant northern sea' seems tied to a rather particular place and time:

> The Sea of Faith
> Was once, too, at the full, and round earth's shore

Lay like the folds of a bright-girdle furled.
But now I only hear
Its melancholy, long, withdrawing roar,
Retreating, to the breath
Of the night-wind, down the vast edges drear
And naked shingles of the world.

(21–8)

The sense of loss is expressed with rare delicacy when 'Faith', rather later than expected, finds its rhyme, and it proves to be the one half-rhyme in the whole poem, 'breath'. It seems more like a sleight of hand when the island of Britain, and a very particular part of Britain at that, the pebble beach at Dover, comes to figure the entire globe, the 'naked shingles of the world', and it is a similar sleight of hand that offers the melancholy felt by those Englishmen like Arnold, a rather select group made up of those whose intellectual cultivation had proved incompatible with their childhood religious faith, as the emotion that best defines human experience throughout its history.

Only one word in the first three stanzas, 'Listen!', suggests that the poem is addressed to another person, so that it comes as a surprise when the opening lines of the fourth reveal that it is a love poem, a poem that, tradition has it, was written by Arnold on his honeymoon: 'Ah, love, let us be true to one another' (29). Now that religious truth is no longer possible, all that is left is a different kind of truth, a consolation that may depend too heavily on a play on words, because the truth that is lost is the truth that the poem names as 'certitude', whereas the truth that supplies its place is something more like fidelity, the troth that lovers promise to each other. But it is the social awkwardness of the abrupt transition that has struck readers more forcibly. Anthony Hecht, for example, in his witty retort to Arnold, 'Dover Bitch', allows a voice to Arnold's silent beloved:

To have been brought
All the way down from London, and then be addressed
As a sort of mournful cosmic last resort
Is really tough on a girl.

(16–9)

In Arnold's poem, human love seems oddly ineffectual even as a last resort. It does nothing to mitigate the poem's bleak conclusion. Arnold first denies that the beauty of the bay under the stars could, as Wordsworth had suggested, offer some source of value that might compensate for the loss of religious faith:

> for the world, which seems
> To lie before us like a land of dreams,
> So various, so beautiful, so new,
> Hath really neither joy, nor love, nor light,
> Nor certitude, nor peace, nor help for pain.
> (30–4)

Nature, it seems, cannot function as a substitute for God. The poem ends with a bleak summary of the human condition:

> And we are here as on a darkling plain
> Swept with confused alarms of struggle and flight,
> Where ignorant armies clash by night.
> (35–7)

No Victorian poem has a more marmoreal conclusion, and yet these lines, like the whole of the poem, are more partial than they seem. For example, it seems unlikely that Arnold would have thought of human life in quite this way had he not been looking across the Channel to the last glimmering lights on the French coast. France, especially in 1851when these lines were probably written, just three years after the revolution of 1848, functioned as a forcible reminder of how easily human civilization might lapse into anarchy, the 'red fool-fury of the Seine' as Tennyson called it *In Memoriam*, cxxvii, 7). But it was a function that France served for the English rather than for the world. The metaphor, too, that Arnold chooses suggests that he looks on that world from a distinctive perspective. The battle at night is drawn from Thucydides' description of the Battle of Epipolae, a passage frequently chosen as a translation exercise in Arnold's own Rugby (Arnold's father had edited Thucydides), in England's other public schools and in its two ancient universities.

In 'Dover Beach' Arnold aligns himself with Sophocles whose special virtue it was that he 'saw life steadily, and saw it whole'. ('To a Friend' (1849), 12). It is because of this that his poetry offered 'a criticism of life': 'The end and aim of all literature is in truth nothing but that'. But it must be a criticism the truth of which is unconfined by place or time, 'a source of illumination and joy to the whole human race for ever'.[10] In 'Dover

Beach' Arnold contrives a verse movement, a 'tremulous cadence slow', that persuades all but the most disenchanted reader that just such a criticism has been achieved, even if it scarcely seems all that joyful. The charm of its movement disguises the poem's fragmentary quality, so evident in its four stanzas, each quite unlike the other, and in its generic instability as a nature poem that is also a love poem and a poem of philosophical reflection. The poem makes its claim to voice human experience so powerfully that it takes an effort to remember that the view of the world that it presents is so clearly that of a man, a man living in the middle of the nineteenth century, an Englishman, and an Englishman of a particular class and education. The criticism of life that Browning's Caliban achieves seems grotesque because so clearly arrived at by projecting onto the universe his own very particular experience of it. But is 'Dover Beach' really so very different? Whatever conclusion is reached about that, both poems indicate the difficulty that Victorian poets commonly found in forging any very secure connection between facts and values, between the world they lived in and the values they lived by.

As Stephen Gill has pointed out, during the nineteenth century Tennyson's poetry came to be granted by many readers the kind of spiritual authority that had once been claimed by Wordsworth's, but it was an authority very differently founded. According to J.A. Froude, Tennyson's became the voice in poetry, as Carlyle's was in prose, for all those 'determined to have done with insincerity, to find ground under their feet, to let the uncertain remain uncertain, but to learn how much and what we could honestly regard as true, and believe that and live by it'.[11] In 'Tintern Abbey' (1798) Wordsworth had professed himself:

> well pleased to recognize
> In nature and the language of the sense,
> The anchor of my purest thoughts, the nurse,
> The guide, the guardian of my heart, and soul
> Of all my moral being.
>
> (107–11)

Tennyson, though he was just as persuaded as Wordsworth that a proper appreciation of natural beauty was a primary qualification for a poet, did not find so direct a connection between the natural world and the moral life. Even as an undergraduate, when the question was debated 'Whether the existence of an intelligible First Cause is deducible from the phenomena of the universe', Tennyson had voted, 'No',[12] and in *In Memoriam*, the poem on which Tennyson's status as a religious teacher was principally founded, he maintains the position:

> I found Him not in world or sun,
>   Or eagle's wing, or insect's eye.
>
> (cxxiv, 5–6)

Tennyson was alert, as even the older Wordsworth was not, to the higher status in the Victorian period of 'scientific' accounts of the world, 'scientific' signifying here the practice of describing the world as subject to physical laws which are assumed to be independent of human psychology. When he assumes Wordsworthian habits of mind he often does so playfully. In section xcvii, for example, he introduces a comparison between his relationship with Hallam and the relationship of a celebrated intellectual with a wife who 'knows but matters of the house' by apologising for his tendency to read the whole world as if it were a comment on his feelings for his lost friend:

> My love has talked with rocks and trees;
>   He finds on misty mountain-ground
>   His own vast shadow glory-crowned;
> He sees himself in all he sees.
>
> (xcvii, 1–4)

Wordsworth had himself noted the reflecting, magnifying property of mist and found in them a type of the workings of the poet's imagination (see, for example, the *Prelude* (1850), 8, 262–7), but Tennyson seems to find in the same figure only an insight into the pardonable egotism of love and of grief.

Tennyson often in *In Memoriam* writes as a pastoral elegist, and in pastoral elegy Nature may either sympathize with the mourner's grief or respond with unfeeling indifference. In section lxxxiii in which Tennyson summons a spring that has been too long delayed he seems to reconcile the two possibilities:

> Bring orchis, bring the foxglove spire,
>   The little speedwell's darling blue,
>   Deep tulips dashed with fiery dew,
> Laburnums, dropping-wells of fire.

O thou, new year, delaying long,
Delayest the sorrow in my blood,
That longs to burst a frozen bud
And flood a fresher throat with song.
(lxxxiii, 9–16)

Tennyson represents himself as sharing in Nature's renewal, but in a strange paradox what he hopes for is a renewal of grief. Nature may echo human feeling, but when it does so it is likely to be a 'hollow echo' (iii, 11). In the second section, addressed to a yew, the mourner finds at first in the tree's unchanging dark foliage a promise that grief might be just as steadfast only to recoil at last from the thought that his human life might be caught up in a merely vegetable existence:

And gazing on thee, sullen tree,
Sick for thy stubborn hardihood,
I seem to fail from out my blood
And grow incorporate into thee.
(ii, 13–6)

When this lyric is itself echoed in section xxxix, the yew is admitted to be less stubborn than he had claimed. In spring its 'gloom is kindled at the tips', but the only inference to be drawn from this is that Nature speaks with 'lying lips', because, once spring is past, the tree 'passes into gloom again'. (xxxix, 11–2) The poem presents any relationship between human emotion and the natural world as provisional, or perhaps it would be truer to say as rhetorical. The natural world offers the poet figures of speech, and figures of speech cannot provide the anchor to the moral being that Wordsworth had found in Nature.

In the Prologue to *In Memoriam* Tennyson looks forward to a time when 'mind and soul, according well, / May make one music as before' (27–8), but the peculiar music of *In Memoriam* is produced by the refusal of mind and soul happily to accord with one another. The philosopher Henry Sidgwick wrote to Tennyson's son:

> The Nature for which Wordsworth stirred our feelings was Nature as known by simple observation and interpreted by religious and sympathetic intuition. But for your father the physical world is always the world as known to us through physical science: the scientific view of it dominates his thoughts about it.[13]

There are many poems by Tennyson that Sidgwick might have pointed to in support of this contention, but amongst them would certainly have been those sections of *In Memoriam* in which Tennyson struggles to preserve his faith in personal immortality in the face of a geological record that seems to suggest a world quite differently constituted, a world that might more reasonably be understood as the creation of a God such as Caliban's Setebos rather than the loving God of Christian revelation. Hallam's early death threatens Tennyson's faith that all apparent evils are a necessary part of God's providential care for his creation. He must believe that 'not a worm is cloven in vain' (liv, 9), because that is the assurance of the Bible – 'Are not five sparrows sold for two farthings? and one of them shall not fall on the ground without your Father' – and yet in order to do so he must somehow disregard the contrary evidence that seems to be offered by God's creation:

Are God and Nature then at strife,
  That Nature lends such evil dreams?
  So careful of the type she seems,
So careless of the single life.
(lv, 5–8)

Tennyson insists that his faith survives such thoughts but his confidence fails to communicate itself to his rhythms:

Behold we know not anything;
  I can but trust that good shall fall
  At last – far off – at last, to all,
And every winter change to spring.
(liv, 13–6)

The providential assurance that the stanza reaches towards scarcely survives the fractured, syncopated movement of its third line: 'Trust', as Seamus Perry finely observes, 'can seldom have been invoked so doubtfully'.[14] The lyric recovers its confidence, as so many of the lyrics of *In Memoriam* do, only when Tennyson disclaims responsibility for his own speculations:

So runs my dream: but what am I?
  An infant crying in the night,
  An infant crying for the light:
And with no language but a cry.
(liv, 17–20)

It is yet another of the poem's paradoxes that Tennyson recovers his eloquence when he compares himself with an infant, that is, with a child who has not yet learned how to speak. In the following lyric Tennyson admits the conflict between his intuition of immortality derived, as he believes, 'from what we have / The likest God within the soul' (lv, 3–4), and the evidence supplied by the natural world of a creator quite indifferent to the fate of the individual, and arrives at a wonderfully irresolute conclusion:

I falter where I firmly trod,
  And falling with my weight of cares
  Upon the great world's altar-stairs
That slope through darkness up to God,

I stretch lame hands of faith, and grope,
  And gather dust and chaff, and call
  To what I feel is Lord of all,
And faintly trust the larger hope.
(lv, 13–20)

The quatrains intricately knit together faltering and firmness (the thirteenth line is firm if read iambically, but falters if trochees are allowed to intrude), the notion of falling down the stairs is combated only by the 'slope' being said to lead 'up' to God, and in the final line the long alliterative chain that binds the quatrains together ('falter', 'firmly', 'falling', 'faith', 'feel') reaches a finely paradoxical climax in the word 'faintly'. Tennyson's abba quatrain, in which the enclosing rhyme, so much fainter than the central couplet (the stanza is itself, as Christopher Ricks observes, 'the perfect embodiment of the true relationship of faith to faintness in the poem'[15]), ensures that the hope that concludes the lyric does not compromise its irresolution.

In the very next lyric the claim that Nature, though 'careless of the single life', remains 'careful of the type' must itself be abandoned as inconsistent with the fossil record:

'So careful of the type?' but no.
  From scarped cliff and quarried stone
  She cries, 'A thousand types are gone:
I care for nothing, all shall go.

'Thou makest thine appeal to me:
  I bring to life, I bring to death:

The spirit does but mean the breath:
I know no more.'
(lvi, 1–8)

The voice of Nature, jaunty, insouciant, blithely untroubled by its own limitations, is so gratingly discordant because it is the antithesis of the voice that speaks the greater part of the poem.

For J.A. Froude Tennyson's poetry appealed to those impatient with conventional orthodoxy, 'determined to have done with insincerity', but its appeal extended to the whole of that Broad Church majority amongst Tennyson's contemporaries whose faith was a loosely and no doubt illogically maintained composite, a matter of personal faith, a set of beliefs derived from the Bible, and a faith founded on the teachings of the Church. For such people the authority of *In Memoriam* was sustained by an irresolution properly exemplified in these central stanzas which confront the contradiction between God's two scriptures, the Bible and the Book of Nature only to conclude that the problem remains as yet unanswerable:

What hope of answer, or redress?
Behind the veil, behind the veil.
(lvi, 27–8)

Tennyson, like Browning's Caliban, begins with the natural world, though in these sections of the poem that world is apprehended intellectually or scientifically rather than sensuously, and 'grope[s]' his way towards some kind of faith. One might expect that the procedures of Gerard Manley Hopkins, who as a Roman Catholic priest would have been pleased to be characterized as dogmatic, would be very different, and yet Hopkins has more in common than one would expect with Browning's Caliban, the speaker of 'Dover Beach' and the poet of *In Memoriam.*

Hopkins described 'The Windhover' (written 1877) as 'the best thing I ever wrote',[16] but in its argument it is typical of many of his nature poems. In the octave of the sonnet Hopkins describes an ecstatic encounter with some aspect of the natural world, and in the sestet he puts that experience to the service of his God. In 'The Windhover' more particularly he searches out the relationship between the life lived by the bird on the wing and his own priestly life, a life, as he describes it, of 'sheer plod'. The octave celebrates the perfect adaptation of the bird in flight to the element in which it moves. The kestrel rides the 'rolling level underneath him steady air' that supports him as easily as water supports a swimmer or as a knight is supported by his charger. In Shakespeare's *Henry V*, the Dauphin praises his steed:

> I will not change my horse with any that treads but on four pasterns. Ca, ha! He bounds from the earth as if his entrails were hairs; le cheval Volant, the Pegasus, chez les narines de feu! When I bestride him, I soar, I am a hawk: he trots the air; the earth sings when he touches it.
>
> (III, vii, 13–7)

Shakespeare's Dauphin compares his horse to a hawk: Hopkins compares his hawk, his 'king- / dom of daylight's dauphin', to a mounted horseman, a princely cavalier. The octave ends with 'a colossal smile' ('Henry Purcell', written 1879, 13) as Hopkins exclaims at 'the achieve of, the mastery of the thing!', a mastery displayed equally by the bird's control in flight and by the poet's control of his demanding verse form.

The seamless union of the bird with the wind, and the poet with his sonnet is marked in the octave by a rhyme scheme in which the 'a' and the 'b' rhymes are distinguished only because the 'a' rhymes, 'king', 'wing', 'swing' and 'thing', are stressed, whereas the 'b' rhymes, 'riding', 'striding', 'gliding', hiding', are feminine, the second syllable unstressed. But the watcher remains at a far remove from the bird that he is observing. He is earthbound while the bird rides the air, 'in hiding' while the bird accomplishes its little miracle of self-display. The bird's flight is its way of 'selving', of 'going itself', of crying '*What I do is me: for that I came.*' ('As kingfishers catch fire', probably written 1881–2, 7–8). A hide might already signify the place of concealment used by birdwatchers, but the notion of a life spent in hiding had a more urgent significance for Hopkins. It was central to his vocation as a Jesuit priest. To become a Jesuit priest was to embrace a life of obscurity, the kind of life that Ignatius Loyola had himself lived. Hopkins writes in one of his letters that for Jesuits the part of Christ's life that they find most consoling is what he calls 'the hidden life at Nazareth',[17] that is, the life that Jesus lived in between the miraculous childhood and the life he embarked on at the age of thirty, when he began his mission, the long years in which he lived an obscure, humdrum life, as the son of a carpenter. That was the aspect of Christ's life that the Jesuit priest was called most particularly to imitate.

As he watches the bird Hopkins is 'stirred', and he is stirred at least in part because the life of the bird is so different from the life that he is called upon to live himself, a life given over to the practice of self-restraint. Hopkins's delight in the red coats of soldiers, the earnestness of his wish that he might find the soldiers as spick and span in their inner as in their outer lives, 'as sterling all as all is smart, / And scarlet wear the spirit of war there express' ('The Soldier', written 1885, 7–8), is poignant because it is informed by the contrast between their gorgeous uniforms and his own clerical black, and there is a similar poignancy in his delight as he watches from his own life in hiding a bird whose life on the wing seems so wholly given over to self-display.

His task in the sestet is to reclaim for Christ the gasp of delight that the bird has provoked in him, to justify his having been so deeply 'stirred by a bird' (it is hard not to detect in that internal rhyme a rueful admission that there are other things that might more appropriately stir a priest's emotions). It is a task closely connected to the need he feels to reconcile his priestly with his poetic vocation. The theologian most admired by the Jesuits, Hopkins tells his Anglican friend, Canon Dixon, is Francisco Suarez, and one reason for this is that Suarez is 'without originality or brilliancy; he treats everything satisfactorily, but you never remember a phrase of his, the manner is nothing.'[18] The compliment is predictable because it is by eschewing brilliancy so determinedly that Suarez was able to win fame as a theologian without compromising the Jesuit's obligation to practise self-effacement, and yet it remains an odd compliment when it is paid by Hopkins, the most brilliantly original poet of the nineteenth century, the arch phrase-maker, the poet in whom manner is, if not everything, then at the very least a crucial element of his appeal. In 'The Soldier' Hopkins is able to reconcile and to subordinate his admiration for a redcoat to his love of Christ easily enough, for Christ himself 'knows war, served this soldiering through; / He of all can reeve a rope best' ('The Soldier', 9–10), but it is not always so easy to reconcile a love of Christ and a love of the natural world. In a journal entry he may have noted, 'I do not think I have ever seen anything more beautiful than the blue-bell I have been looking at. I know the beauty of our Lord by it.'[19] At such moments 'The world is charged with the grandeur of God' ('God's Grandeur', written 1877, 1), but that is not always how it seemed. At other times nature's 'ruck and reel' seemed only to constitute a temptation ('The Habit of Perfection', written 1866, 11). The 'dapple' of the natural world only threatened to distract its admirer from the impending judgement, the stark division into 'two flocks, two folds – black, white' on which the attention of the good Christian ought properly to be fixed ('Spelt from Sibyl's Leaves', probably written 1885, 12). In 'To What Serves Mortal Beauty' (written 1885) Hopkins allows that such beauty should inspire gratitude, but insists that the gratitude should be tempered:

> What do then? how meet beauty? Merely meet it; own,
> Home at heart, heaven's sweet gift; then leave, let that alone.
> Yea, wish that though, wish all, God's better beauty, grace.
> (12–4)

In the sestet of 'The Windhover' Hopkins finds it hard to 'buckle' the bird's beauty to 'God's better beauty, grace', as he intimates by a rhyme scheme, which alternates masculine and feminine rhymes, as in the octave, but buckles together rhymes that could otherwise scarcely be more different ('-ere', and '-illion' are so very unlike one another).

The sestet begins by dismissing the beauty of the bird in comparison with the beauty of Christ:

> Brute beauty and valour and act, oh, air, pride, plume, here
> Buckle! AND the fire that breaks from thee then, a billion
> Times told lovelier, more dangerous, O my chevalier!
> (9–11)

The beauty of the bird that buckles together air, pride, plume itself buckles, in the sense of crumples, when compared with the beauty of Christ in his crucifixion, a beauty that only burned the brighter when Christ's body buckled on the Cross. The merely 'brute beauty' of the bird is dismissed when brought into neighbourhood with the divine beauty of Jesus. But even as Hopkins distinguishes the two quite different kinds of beauty he brings them together, buckles them one to another, for Christ on the Cross is as princely, as chivalric, as the bird riding the wind, the one a 'dauphin' the other a 'chevalier'. The need to join rather than dissever divine beauty and the beauty of the natural world is expressed typographically, in the capital letters, 'AND', that so emphatically refuse the disjunctive 'but' that might have been expected. The final tercet seems to celebrate a beauty that does not seem to have much in common with the heroic beauty of Christ in his martyrdom and nothing at all in common with the beauty of the bird in flight:

> No wonder of it: sheer plod makes plough down sillion
> Shine, and blue-bleak embers, ah my dear,
> Fall, gall themselves, and gash gold-vermilion.
>
> (12–4)

It is 'sheer plod', the plod of the ploughman and his horse, that scours the ploughshare until it reflects the sunshine in a burst of light, and nothing could be less plodding than the kestrel in its flight. But Hopkins is thinking in these last lines not of the bird's life, but of his own. Hopkins was fond of just-fallen chestnuts, 'Fresh-firecoal chestnut-falls' ('Pied Beauty', written 1877, 4), 'Chestnuts bright as coals or spots of vermilion',[20] when the husk splits and the nut, before its colour is dulled by the air, glows brightly. The flash of colour figures the kind of beauty that even his own humdrum life might claim. As he wrote to Canon Dixon, 'we cultivate the commonplace outwardly and wish the beauty of the king's daughter the soul to be from within',[21] a beauty like the conker's hidden away in its drab green shell. But in this poem it is the firecoal rather than the chestnut that gives him his figure, the coals at the moment that the ash slips and they are revealed glowing 'gold-vermilion'. The figure, supplied by a commonplace household fire, remains in accord with the life of 'sheer plod' that he has chosen, except that the 'gall' and the 'gash' make a quiet claim that this life is in however modest a way an imitation of Christ, its drab constraint a humble counterpart to the suffering of Christ in his passion. So Hopkins at last succeeds in making a connection with the kestrel through the mediation of Christ, who is, like the kestrel princely and heroic, a figure appropriately addressed in the chivalric language that seems proper to the bird, 'O my chevalier!', and yet a figure too with whom the priest walking his dull rounds, living his life of sheer plod, can claim identity. The thought that binds the poem together is the thought made explicit in 'As kingfishers catch fire', when Hopkins points out that 'Christ plays in ten thousand places, / Lovely in limbs, and lovely in eyes, not his' (12–3). Hopkins chooses a Christocentric aesthetics that defines every instance of beauty as constituted by a resemblance to Christ. The beauty of the falcon in flight might seem wholly unlike the inner beauty that the life of a priest might cultivate, but the difference cannot be absolute, must in fact be apparent rather than real, because the beauty of both consists in its likeness to Christ. But Hopkins's argument is not here my principal concern, which is rather to point out that despite his faith Hopkins found the transition from a sensual experience of the world to a spiritual understanding of it fraught. Hopkins has often been described as the heir of the Tractarian poets such as John Keble, but he is also a post-Darwinian poet, and the analogies he finds between the natural and the spiritual world are forged only by an energetic, even a violent, exercise of mental and linguistic agility. Poems such as 'The Windhover' suggest that he found it no easier to buckle the two worlds one to the other than did Browning or Arnold or Tennyson. Victorian poetry characteristically reveals at once a need to ground belief in an intensely realised experience of the world, and a sharp awareness of the difficulty in finding any plausible connection between an understanding of the physical world and a system of metaphysical or of moral belief.

That is one reason why so many Victorian poets found it at once so desirable and so difficult to exchange a private, lyric voice for a public voice. It is a problem that Claude, the Oxford-educated hero of Clough's *Amours de Voyage* encounters with particular urgency when he visits Rome in the Spring of 1849, and finds that he can neither commit himself to the defence of Garibaldi's Roman Republic nor to his love for his fellow tourist, Mary Trevellyn. One day, coming back from St Peter's, the guide book that signifies his spectatorial detachment from the city under his arm, he thinks he sees a man killed, although he can 'hardly be certain.' He sees a crowd massing, swords lifted, fall, and lifted again: 'Is it blood that's on them? Yes, certainly blood!' Stooping, he glimpses 'through the legs of the people the legs of a body,' and is told by a passer-by that a priest suspected of trying to join the besieging forces has been killed. But the execution that he himself witnesses is a less dramatic affair, performed by a National Guardsman not on the priest but on the priest's hat: he sees him break his sword by 'slashing' at it as it lies on the ground covered in dust. (447–82) The episode dramatizes the high principle or, alternatively, the squeamishness that prevents Claude's republican sympathies from finding any outlet in action, but it might also be understood to figure a more general problem. Claude never succeeds in getting a clear view of the dead body. If it is the poet's peculiar business, as Arnold put it in a poem probably addressed to Clough, to see life steadily and to see it whole ('To a Friend'(1853), 12), the body of that dead Italian priest cannot be a fit subject for poetry. Arnold criticized modern poets for subordinating the whole to the part, so that the 'total impression' is sacrificed for the sake of a 'detached expression.' But it may be that the poets he criticized doubted whether the time in which they lived allowed them any 'total impression' to record.

In British poets such thoughts might be prompted by a sense that they were secondary poets, and that poetry itself had become a secondary art. But even American poets seem often to refuse the 'total impression'. Herman Melville began his volume *Battle Pieces and Aspects of the War* (1866) with a short poem called 'The Portent', in which he looks at the body of John Brown, executed after his murderous raid on Harper's Ferry:

Hanging from the beam,
Slowly swaying (such the law),
Gaunt the shadow on your green,
Shenandoah!
The cut is on the crown
(Lo, John Brown),
And the stabs shall heal no more.

Hidden in the cap
Is the anguish none can draw;
So your future veils its face,
Shenandoah!
But the streaming beard is shown
(Weird John Brown),
The meteor of the war.

The poem records the moment immediately after the execution. The focus on John Brown's body is so intense that it is easy not to notice that the body itself is quite absent from the poem. What it is that is suspended, swaying, and casting its shadow on the field in Charlestown where the scaffold had been erected remains unspoken. The body has disappeared, it may be, because it can no longer be seen amongst all the contradictory meanings that have been imposed on it. John Brown in his death is no longer a human being: he has become simply a portent, a comet, an omen of the coming war. His face, concealed by the hood, signifies that the outcome and the consequences of that war are as yet unknown, but it also intimates why the war is inevitable. In leading the absurd raid on Harper's Ferry, Brown ensured that he would be sentenced to death. It was the end proper to a murderer – 'such the law' – and it was the end that, as Brown himself knew, transformed him into a nineteenth-century Christ, his death an act of atonement for the sin of slavery. The cut on the crown, and the stabs that will never heal, float free of the body not just because Brown's execution ensures that the wounds will be transferred from the body of one man to the body politic, but because when one half of the nation looks at the body it sees only the wounds that Brown suffered, whereas the other half of the nation sees only the wounds that Brown inflicted, at Harper's Ferry and before that in Kansas, where Brown and his sons had hacked to death five pro-slavery settlers. In death Brown has become 'weird', a grotesque figure dangling from a rope, a figure that controls the fate of the nation, an uncanny figure who has become less or more than human. Melville's poem takes this figure and restores to it its strangeness, resisting any pressures to flatten it into heroism or to flatten it into villainy. His task in *Battle Pieces* is to undo the polarized rhetoric of civil war and rediscover a language more adequate to represent a truth that for him, as for Clough's Claude is 'flexible, changeable, vague, and multiform, and doubtful,' and cannot for that reason be resolved into a 'total impression'.

Arnold sometimes thought as much himself. 'The Scholar-Gipsy' (1853) treats the legend of a youth who, because he is too poor to support his studies at Oxford, leaves the university and joins the gypsies. This figure, found by Arnold in a little known seventeenth-century text by Joseph Glanvill, enables him to associate the poetic impulse with the pre-industrial past, with youthful potential that can never be fulfilled, and with a disposition so shy that the scholar-gipsy can be seen only 'by rare glimpses', only out of the corner of the eye. The poem ends enigmatically, with an elaborate and unexplained simile. A Tyrian trader escapes the competition of a 'merry Grecian coaster' by searching out new custom amongst 'the dark Iberians,' 'shy traffickers' who will examine his goods only if he leaves them on the shore and retires. Only in transactions so delicate, Arnold seems to imply, can the poet have dealings with the public world.

Endnotes

1. *On the Study of Celtic Literature* (London: Dent, n.d.), pp. 126–7 and 83.
2. *The Complete Works of John* Ruskin, ed. E.T. Cook and Alexander Wedderburn (London: George Allen, 1903), 4, 146.
3. John Keble, *Lectures on Poetry*, trans. E.K. Francis, 2 vols (Oxford: Clarendon Press, 1912), 2, p. 481.
4. See June Badeni, *The Slender Tree: A Life of Alice Meynell* (Padstow: Tabb House, 1981), p. 52.
5. *The Letters of Alfred Lord Tennyson*, ed. Edgar F. Shannon, 3 vols (Oxford: Clarendon Press, 1982–90), 2, p. 540.

6. 'On Some of the Characteristics of Modern Poetry, and on the Lyrical Poems of Alfred Tennyson', *The Writings of Arthur Hallam*, ed. T.H. Vail Motter (London: Oxford University Press, 1943), p. 192.
7. Hallam Tennyson, *Tennyson and his Friends* (London: Macmillan, 1911), p. 498.
8. Robert Browning, *Selected Poems*, ed. John Woolford, Daniel Karlin, and Joseph Phelan (Harlow: Longman, 2010), p. 626.
9. *Life and Letters of Charles Darwin*, ed. Francis Darwin, 3 vols (London: John Murray, 1888), 2, p. 328.
10. Matthew Arnold, *Lectures and Essays in Criticism*, ed. R.H. Super (Ann Arbor: Univrsity of Michigan Press, 1962), p. 209.
11. Stephen Gill, *Wordsworth and the Victorians* (Oxford; Oxford Univrsity Press, 2001), pp. 40–80; J.H. Froude, *Carlyle's Life in London, 1834–1881* (London: Longman, Green and Co, 1885) 1, p. 291.
12. Hallam Tennyson: *Alfred Lord Tennyson: A Memoir* (London: Macmillan, 1897), 1, p. 44, footnote.
13. Hallam Tennyson, *Alfred Lord Tennyson: A Memoir*, 1, pp. 302–3.
14. Seamus Perry, 'Elegy', in *A Companion to Victorian Poetry*, ed. Richard Cronin, Alison Chapman and Antony H. Harrison (Oxford: Blackwell, 2002), p. 120.
15. Christopher Ricks *Tennyson* (London: Macmillan, 1972), p. 216.
16. *The Letters of Gerard Manley Hopkins to Robert Bridges*, ed. Claude Colleer Abbott (London: Oxford University Press, 1935), p. 179.
17. *The Correspondence of Gerard Manley Hopkins and Richard Weston Dixon*, ed. Claude Colleer Abbott (London: Oxford University Press, 1935), p. 96.
18. *The Correspondence of Gerard Manley Hopkins and Richard Weston Dixon*, p. 95.
19. *The Journals and Papers of Gerard Manley Hopkins*, ed. Humphry House and Graham Storey (London: Oxford University Press, 1959), p. 199.
20. *The Journals and Papers of Gerard Manley Hopkins*, p. 120.
21. *The Correspondence of Gerard Manley Hopkins and Richard Weston Dixon*, p. 96.

7

Poetry and Religion

For many Victorians poetry and religion were so closely associated as to be scarcely distinguishable. John Keble may have been unusual in claiming that 'all poetical pleasure' may be traced to 'the awakening of some moral or religious feeling',[1] but Keble was the author of the most popular of all Victorian poems, *The Christian Year*. Between its publication in 1827 and the expiry of its copyright in 1873, the volume sold more than three hundred thousand copies. For Keble, poetry was necessarily religious and Keble's closest associate, John Henry Newman, completed the thought by observing that religion was 'especially poetical', so that for Christians 'a poetical view of things is a duty'.[2] John Keble was Matthew Arnold's godfather but Arnold could scarcely have diverged from him more widely in his religious opinions. In *Literature and Dogma* Arnold concluded that the only way to preserve Christianity was to dispense entirely with its supernatural trappings. But Arnold agreed with Keble at least on the close association between religion and poetry. The word, God, is for Arnold itself a 'literary term', 'a term of poetry', though he marks his distance from Keble and Newman by the audacity of his phrasing, as when he compliments Christ's teaching on being 'a work of the highest originality'.[3]

The most important of Keble's literary heirs was Christina Rossetti, who seems in her late devotional poems, poems with titles such as 'Advent Sunday', 'Septuagesima', 'Rogationtide' and 'Trinity Sunday', intent on writing a *Christian Year* of her own. But a poem that traces a natural rather than an ecclesiastical calendar, 'A Year's Windfalls' (1866), offers a better introduction to her work. The poem's twelve eight-line stanzas

Reading Victorian Poetry, First Edition. Richard Cronin.

each describe a month. It is an exercise that seems, as many of Rossetti's poems do, entirely conventional, except that sometimes an unusually exact piece of observation fixes the attention, as when the March catkins drop 'Curly, caterpillar-like, / Curious green and brown' (19–20). Each stanza is made up of two abcb quatrains, but the metre is flexible. When in May 'The wind lags warm and sweet' (38), the line lags in sympathy. The shortened December day is wittily marked in a line that shrinks to a dimeter, 'Speeds on the shortest day, / Curtails the sun' (91–2); and the fall of the February snowflakes is marked in a line so slow that it seems to suspend them in mid-air, 'On the wind in February, / Snowflakes float still' (9–10). The poem seems impersonal, almost jauntily detached from the feelings that it notes in others. When the strong October winds pile up the waves, 'It's oh! for mothers' sons at sea, / That they were safe at home.' (79–80) It gives away almost nothing of Rossetti's own feelings, except that the calendar structure allows her to begin and end the poem in a frozen landscape when December 'Brings back the snow' that had flitted down in January.

Rossetti is a great poet of snow,[4] as in the carol of 1875 that is still her best known poem:

In the bleak mid-winter
   Frosty wind made moan,
Earth stood hard as iron,
   Water like a stone;
Snow had fallen, snow on snow,
   Snow on snow,
In the bleak mid-winter
   Long ago.

(1–8)

There is the frozen landscape again, but the poem describes how, as Rossetti meditates on Christ's nativity, her own feelings are unlocked. Unable to offer the infant precious gifts like the Magi, or even humble gifts like the shepherds, she offers what she has:

What can I give Him,
   Poor as I am?
If I were a shepherd
   I would bring a lamb,
If I were a wise man

I would do my part, –
Yet what I can I give Him,
Give my heart.
(33–40)

Despite the freezing weather her heart melts. But the heart that she offers the baby Jesus remains a secret gift. Unlike the lamb, and unlike gold, frankincense and myrrh, it cannot be displayed. The transaction remains unknown except to the giver, and, she trusts, the recipient. It leaves no mark, and that is what makes it appropriate to a landscape so blank that it consists only of an accumulation of whiteness, 'Snow had fallen, snow on snow, / Snow on snow'. Rossetti often focuses on similar kinds of blankness as in the late lyric 'They shall be white as snow' (1893), a poem that begins and ends with the phrase, 'Whiteness most white'.

It is as if her poems yearn after the white page that surrounds them, a yearning that becomes more intense over the years as her poems get shorter, as if she were becoming more and more unwilling to defile the blank page. For John Keble poetry is produced when an overpowering desire to find relief by giving expression to the emotions is countered by a determination that all expressions of emotion should be restrained. His doctrine of reserve had its origins in theology, in an acceptance that human language is necessarily inadequate to the task of expressing divine mysteries, in a principled reluctance to claim an easy familiarity with God's ways, and in a belief that divine truths should be offered only to those fit to receive them. Here, too, religion and poetry approached each other, for in poetry the impulse to seek relief in the expression of overpowering emotion is countered by a reluctance to expose intimate feelings to the reader. That is why the language of religion and the language of poetry are similar: both work by indirection, through parable, simile, or metaphor. Keble chose rather emphatically to exemplify his doctrine of reserve when he came to publish his poems. In his lifetime *The Christian Year* was always published anonymously, Keble's authorship signalled with discreet indirection only by the inclusion of the name of his parish, Hursley. Keble's metrical regularity, his decision to restrict himself to a conventional poetic diction, and his use of conventional, though varied, stanzaic forms work together to prevent his own personality from obtruding between the poems and their readers. His is a lyric poetry that contrives to be at the same time an exercise in self-effacement. It was Keble's example, supported by that of fellow Tractarians such as John Newman and Isaac Williams, that seems to have decisively influenced Christina Rossetti.

Rossetti was in sympathy with Tractarian theology, but the doctrine of reserve had an appeal that extended far beyond High Church circles. Matthew Arnold observed in *Literature and Dogma* that he admired in the Old Testament 'a propriety, a reserve, a sense of the inadequacy of language in conveying man's ideas of God',[5] and Tennyson in *In Memoriam* applies a similar doctrine to the expression of grief:

I sometimes hold it half a sin
  To put in words the grief I feel;
  For Words, like Nature, half reveal
And half conceal the Soul within.
(v, 1–4)

But, as Isobel Armstrong suggests, Keble's aesthetic proved especially attractive to women poets.[6] The poet Dora Greenwell, a friend of Rossetti's, was herself inclined to Quakerism. She accepted Keble's doctrine of reserve not as an Anglican but as a woman bound 'no less by the laws of society than by the immutable instincts of her nature, to a certain suppression of all that relates to personal feeling'.[7]

Gerard Manley Hopkins once told Robert Bridges, 'I always knew in my heart Walt Whitman's mind to be more like my own than any other man's living. As he is a very great scoundrel this is not a pleasant confession.'[8] Rossetti, had she known her work, might have admitted the same of Emily Dickinson. Though she was raised as a Presbyterian, it is Dickinson who offers the most concise summary of the doctrine of reserve, 'Tell all the truth but tell it slant'. She took reserve much further than Rossetti. It led to her scarcely publishing at all, a decision she reflects on in a lyric that offers a powerful commentary on the horror of the marketplace that Rossetti registers in a poem such as 'Goblin Market', as well as sharing Rossetti's interest in brevity, and in snow and in its whiteness. Dickinson begins,

Publication – is the Auction
Of the Mind of Man –
(1–2)

The couplet presents publication as a symptom of moral confusion, the reduction of a person to a commodity of the kind evident in slavery or in prostitution. She seems to register here the particular repugnance that the thought of entering the world of commerce provokes in the middle-class nineteenth-century woman in America as in England:

> Poverty – be justifying
> For so foul a thing
>
> Possibly – but We – would rather
> From our Garret go
> White – Unto the White Creator –
> Than invest – Our Snow –
>
> (3–8)

This seems to allow that others may not be able to afford her scruples, except that by naming her own room a garret she comes close to claiming for herself the glamour of the starving poet. God and Dickinson, whose custom it was to wear a white dress, seem fused in the phrase 'the White Creator,' and whiteness here, as in Rossetti's poems, seems at once to connote purity and the blank page, blankness being the most appropriate representation at once of a being without attributes and of an unpublished poet. The phrase 'Our Snow' at once claims for the poems the uniquely perfect form of the snow crystal, and suggests that the purest poems achieve their perfection because they are conceived rather than written, and hence leave no mark. Dickinson's reluctance to 'invest' suggests both her reluctance to allow her poems to be sold for profit, and her reluctance to allow them to be clothed in language. As so often in Dickinson, the thought is not fully articulated, and the effect is to suggest an utterance addressed to herself rather than an auditor, an utterance that occupies a strange, indeterminate space between silence and articulation, or an inscription that reveals in its narrow compass, as so many of Christina Rossetti's poems do, a reluctance to mark the page. The third stanza seems still more stammering:

> Thought belong to him who gave it –
> Then – to Him who bear
> Its Corporeal illustration –
>
> (9–11)

But it is stammering that results, paradoxically, in unusual compression. It allows the word, 'bear,' to signify at once God's role in engendering the poetic thought, and the poet's in returning the poem to the God who had fathered it, bearing it as a gift. The phrase 'Corporeal illustration' may signify either that the written poem can never be more than a grossly material representation of the original thought, or, because the word 'illustration' in its earliest uses signifies spiritual illumination, that in the poem spirit is made flesh, so that every poem repeats the miracle of the Incarnation. The poem ends bitterly denouncing once again the reduction of art to commodity:

> Sell –
> The Royal Air –
>
> In the Parcel – Be the Merchant
> Of the Heavenly Grace –
> But reduce no Human Spirit
> To Disgrace of Price –
>
> (11–16)

The first two injunctions seem simply and angrily ironic until the third offers them as alternatives preferable to setting a price on the human spirit. Again the lines invite multiple readings. For example, does Dickinson realise that in describing her little tune as a 'Royal Air,' she is putting on airs, or is it her point that as soon as a poem is written rather than spoken, and becomes a text rather than a thing of air (and are any poems of the century more *graphic* than Emily Dickinson's?), it can no longer retain its independence of a material world in which everything has a monetary value? Or is the point that Dickinson's protest against publication is realised only in the moment at which it is shown to be unavailing, in the moment at which her poem is read?

Rossetti explores a similar paradox in 'Winter: My Secret' (1862), a poem that seems less an example of the doctrine of reserve than a blue-print for it:

> I tell my secret? No indeed, not I:
> Perhaps some day, who knows?
> But not today; it froze, and blows, and snows,
> And you're too curious: fie!
> You want to hear it? well:
> Only, my secret's mine, and I won't tell.
>
> (1–6)

This is one of a number of Rossetti poems that might be described as anti-lyrics, poems of personal revelation in which the revelation is that nothing will be revealed. It is a poem that rebuffs its reader, but does so flirtatiously, teasingly. When she remarks 'You want to hear it? well', she seems to offer a promise only to withdraw it in the following line. It is the song of a wounded heart, and it is also a nonsense poem: 'Suppose there is no secret after all, / But only just my fun' (8–9) (as her 1872 volume of children's poems, *Sing-Song*, shows, Rossetti was an accomplished nonsense poet). Today 'it froze, and blows, and snows': it is a cold world, but also a nonsense world in which assonance, the triple rhyme, works to call attention to the dissonance of the tenses. It is a day to wrap up warm, a day 'in which one wants a shawl, / A veil, a cloak, and other wraps' (11–2), but these wraps are of quite different kinds. Shawls and cloaks may protect against an icy wind, but veils guard against prying eyes. In 1853 Rossetti had sat to William Holman Hunt for the head of Christ in Hunt's 'The Light of the World', in which Christ is depicted knocking at a wooden door. Hunt took his text from Revelations, 'Behold, I stand at the door, and knock: if any man hear my voice, and open the door I will come unto him'. The same text may lie behind Rossetti's poem, which would lend it gravity:

> I cannot ope to every one who taps,
> And let the draughts come whistling thro' my hall;
> Come bounding and surrounding me,
> Come buffeting, astounding me,
> Nipping and clipping thro' my wraps and all.
> (13–7)

But if so it is a gravity that all those internal rhymes sharply resist. It may be that it is an erotic rather than a divine intrusion that she repels ('clipping' might not just mean cutting but suggest an embrace). Rossetti's early critics, taking their clue from her brother William, tended to read most of her poems in relation to her supposed erotic entanglements, whereas her more recent critics have shown more interest in her theology than her love life. But many of Rossetti's poems do not specify their topic: they investigate the economy of a desire that reticently refuses to specify its object. This poem ends by suggesting that she may reveal her secret in spring, which is 'an expansive time', before ruling out as unsuitable March, April and May, all three of the spring months, and postponing the revelation to 'some languid summer day', but only if the summer day fulfils a set of conditions that seem all but self-contradictory:

> If there's not too much sun nor too much cloud,
> And the warm wind is neither still nor loud.
> (31–2)

Rossetti is similarly reserved in the lyric, 'Shut Out' (1862), in which she secures the poem's indirection not by withholding a secret but by speaking in parables. The speaker is shut out from a garden that was once her 'home', and can only gaze at it wistfully through the iron bars of the gate. Her situation is much like Alice's in the first chapter of *Alice's Adventures in Wonderland* (1865) when she is confronted with a door so small that, even though she has a key for it, she can do no more than peer through it longingly into 'the loveliest garden you ever saw'. In Rossetti's poem the door is guarded:

> A shadowless spirit kept the gate,
> Blank and unchanging like the grave.
> (9–10)

This seems to fix the significance of the narrative: the garden signifies the afterlife from which the soul, during its earthly life, is excluded. The garden is an Eden – 'It had been mine, and it was lost' (8) – to be regained only in heaven. The speaker asks the spirit to give her some 'buds to cheer [her] outcast state', and, when the spirit fails to respond, asks for just 'one small twig', a plea to which the spirit reacts by bricking up the entrance:

> He left no loophole great or small
> Thro' which my straining eyes might look.
> (19–20)

The spirit recalls the Cherubim who guard the gates of Eden with a flaming sword, but displays a rancour that seems all its own, as if he were the villain of a Gothic romance pitilessly walling up in her convent cell the nun who has failed to subdue her desires. The speaker complains that 'nought is left worth looking at' (23), and yet the last stanza reveals that, although the speaker may be shut out from a garden that was once her home, the prison within which she is enclosed is itself a garden:

A violet bed is budding near,
  Wherein a lark has made her nest:
  And good they are, but not the best,
And dear they are, but not so dear.
(25–8)

The poem is written in the *In Memoriam* stanza, which may itself inflect the speaker's grief with a suggestion of some more personal loss, but it preserves its mystery to the last.

'Shut Out' is typical of Rossetti's poems in failing to make it clear whether she is speaking for all of us or just for herself. It is an indecision characteristic of a good deal of Victorian poetry, but it is especially marked in the period's religious verse. Keble deploys in his poems a voice that seems determinedly unindividualized. It is one aspect of his doctrine of reserve, and one reason why a number of his poems could successfully be set as hymns: 'New every morning is the love / Our wakening and uprising prove' ('Morning', 21–2). After his conversion to Rome, Keble's fellow Tractarian, F.W. Faber, chose only to write hymns, judging, it may be, the composition of poems of any other kind inconsistent with his priestly vocation. Hopkins, whose conversion was superintended by Newman himself, seems to take an almost shockingly different path, writing poems remarkable for their idiosyncratic individuality. But it may be that Hopkins addressed the issue in his most intense religious poems, first by insisting that he speaks only for himself, his 'poor Jackself' ('My own heart let me have more pity on' (probably written1885), 9), and second by making the poems out of an experience of God's absence rather than his presence: 'Comforter, where, where is your comforting?' ('No worst there is none' (probably written 1885), 3). Hymns by contrast are communal rather than individual lyrics. They express sentiments in which the whole congregation is invited to join. They signal their communal character most obviously by preserving a strict metrical regularity (it is revealing that Christina Rossetti's hymns, even the best-known of them, 'In the bleak midwinter' and 'Love came down at Christmas', are metrically unusually various). Poems that claim to speak for a congregation ought not to suggest an individual voice. But it was not only in religious verse that Victorian poets dreamed of finding a voice that escaped the merely individual. The extraordinary metrical variety of Tennyson's *Maud* (1855) comes to figure a painfully constricting enclosure within the self from which the poem's speaker dreams of escaping, a dream realised first when he hears Maud singing 'A passionate ballad gallant and gay, / A martial song like a trumpet's call' (1, 165–6), and again at the very end of the poem, when he decides to enlist and the fourteeners of the lines in which he announces his decision fall into common metre and mimic momentarily the regular tramp of marching feet:

> I have felt with my native land, I am one with my kind,
> I embrace the purpose of God, and the doom assigned.
> (3, 58–9)

But it is in religious verse that the cultivation of a collective voice is most marked. In Tennyson's 'Supposed Confessions of a Second-Rate Sensitive Mind' (1830), for example, the speaker's recalcitrance, his inability to subdue himself to the conventional faith in which his mother had raised him, is expressed through the poem's marked formal irregularity, evident both in its tetrameters and its rhyme scheme. It is a poem in which 'were' (68) rhymes with 'prayer' (72), it includes a couplet in which 'pains' rhymes with 'whence' (161–2), and a passage in which 'man' (124) rhymes with 'tarn' (129). Its speaker confesses that he lives his life 'Unpiloted' (96), and his refusal to submit to the authority of a heavenly pilot is as evident in the way that he writes as in the way he behaves. In 'The Two Voices' (1842) the religious crisis represented in the poem is resolved not by any individual effort but when the speaker awakes on a Sunday morning to see the local people walking to church:

> On to God's house the people prest:
> Passing the place where each must rest.
> Each entered like a welcome guest.
> (409–11)

Relief from suicidal thoughts comes not from reflection but from an impulse to join the community of the faithful. Similarly, *In Memoriam* begins with a 'Prologue' that was adapted as a hymn, and ends when the isolated voice that speaks throughout most of the poem is displaced in the final lyric by a communal voice in which Tennyson supplies, even if under protest, the 'marriage lay', the epithalamium, demanded by his sister for her wedding.

Christmas-Eve (1850) was the first major poem Robert Browning wrote after his marriage, and the religious views that it expresses seem closer to his wife's than to his own. It is a poem less concerned with a profession of faith than with the question of which congregation to join. Elizabeth Barrett Browning had advised him that it is an uncomfortable decision: no matter what choice is made, 'there is a little to revolt, & a good deal to bear with'. She chooses herself to worship in a Dissenting chapel for all that the services make you feel 'bigotry & innocence pressing on you on all sides, till you gasp for breath like one strangled'.[9] The speaker of Browning's poem shelters from a squall of rain in the porch of a Congregational chapel. He decides to go in only because he is put out by the way that the lower-class worshippers glare as they push past him. Sanctimoniousness is irritating, especially in one's social inferiors:

> I very soon had had enough of it,
> The hot smell and the human noises,
> And my neighbour's coat, the greasy cuff of it ...
> (139–41)

Worst of all is 'the preaching man's immense stupidity'. He flings out of the stuffy chapel into the cool night air and feels that he has entered 'God's church door', not the 'lath-and-plaster' porch of the chapel with its absurd superscription, 'Mount Zion', but the temple of nature:

> Oh, let men keep their ways
> Of seeking thee in a narrow shrine –
> Be this my way!
> (372–4)

He mimics a Romantic rejection of institutionalized religion for a solitary communion with natural 'immensities', but visionary isolation is no longer the badge of the prophet, it has become the mark of the snob. When Christ appears to him, it seems at first a mark of special distinction, confirmation that he has a dispensation to worship God in his own way. It is only later that he understands it as a sign that he is a lost sheep. Christ first takes him to Rome, where he witnesses in St Peter's a religion reduced to its forms, and then to Germany, to a small town very like Göttingen, where he hears a professor very like David Friedrich Strauss lecture. The exposure to German Higher Criticism warns him of the opposite danger, religion reduced to a rationalist morality. His first thought is that Christ is teaching him a lesson in tolerance. He must learn to recognize beneath all the flummery of the Mass as it is celebrated at St Peter's a love for the Saviour in which he can unite with the Catholic worshippers, and to detect even in the German professor's lecture a vestige of true religious faith: 'If love's dead there, it has left a ghost' (1071). But 'While [he] watched [his] foolish Heart expand / In the lazy glow of benevolence' (1166–7), the hem of Christ's robe slips from his grasp, and he finds himself back in the Chapel, and realises with a start that he had fallen asleep during the sermon. His task, he realizes, is to choose his Church: not to imagine the kind of Church that might perfectly suit him, but to choose the best of what is available, and he chooses the Congregational chapel, its stupid preacher, and his ramshackle flock. The poem ends when he lays down his pencil, and joins in the singing of the last hymn:

> I put up pencil and join chorus
> To Hepzibah tune, without further apology,
> The last five verses of the third section
> Of the seventeenth Hymn of Whitfield's Collection,
> To conclude with the doxology.
>
> (1355–9)

He chooses Whitefield's hymn book, perhaps, because its title, *Hymns for Social Worship*, underlines the progress from solitary reflection to communal singing that the poem traces. The *Athenaeum* complained in its review of the poem (April 6, 1850) that Browning's 'doggrel … is not that in which the mysteries of faith, doubt, and eternity can be consistently treated', and more recent critics have agreed. Ian Jack, for example, contends that 'the free metrical form which Browning has chosen is completely unsuited to his subject-matter'.[10] The Hudibrastic rhyming still has the power to shock; 'enough of it' rhyming with 'cuff of it' (139, 141), 'Manchester' chiming with 'haunches stir' (231, 234). Browning described *Christmas-Eve* as 'a Christmas story *in verse*', which suggests that he thought of it as akin to Dickens's Christmas stories, and especially the most famous of them, *A Christmas Carol* (1843). Browning's Christ takes the poem's speaker on a journey very like the journeys on which the Spirits of Christmas take Scrooge. But it is the difference that strikes. Dickens is fully at one with his material, whereas the 'doggrel' of *Christmas-Eve* seems designed to dramatize Browning's discomfort with his. It is the most forceful expression of the unease he feels at the prospect of 'joining chorus', of fitting his thoughts and feelings to a particular tune:

> A tune was born in my head last week,
> Out of the thump-thump and shriek-shriek
> Of the train, as I came by it, up from Manchester ...
> (249–51)

And this, or something like it, is the tune of his poem. It grates on the reader's ears as it grates on Browning's. It is one of those irritating tunes that he cannot get out of his head, and it is what gives the poem its awkward honesty. It is a poem in which Browning registers the impulse he shared with so many of his contemporaries to escape from the lonely expression of an isolated subjectivity into a communal voice, but it also admits the awkward, comic embarrassment of merging with the crowd by allowing the rhythm of the verse to merge with the rhythm of the dull preacher, and the 'old fat woman', who twirls her thumbs faster and faster, keeping time with the sermon (173–6).

Lack of faith, too, can be registered metrically. Hardy's 'The Impercipient' (1898) is spoken, as its bracketed subtitle '(At a Cathedral Service)' indicates, by a member of the congregation, but it is a member who acknowledges, 'with this bright believing band / I have no claim to be'. (1–2) Hardy's poem is written in common measure, except that the four-line stanza is extended to six. He establishes the metre but cannot quite bring himself to conform to it. Its tune sounds underneath the poem, a token of his nostalgia for a faith the loss of which leaves him feeling like 'a bird deprived of wings' (29), but it is by failing to conform that Hardy arrives at a distinctive music of his own:

> I am like a gazer who should mark
> An inland company
> Standing upfingered, with, 'Hark! hark!
> The glorious distant sea!'
> And feel, 'Alas, 'tis but yon dark
> And wind-swept pine to me!'
> (19–24)

The regular rhythm of the faithful, preserved in the fourth line of the stanza, cannot drown out the tremulous, uncertain movement of the line before, an effect Hardy quietly calls attention to by contrasting the regular rhythm of the waves with the more uncertain, more wistful rhythm of the wind in the trees. The metre plays out Hardy's inability to join in.

Keble framed his doctrine of reserve in part at least to guard against the over-familiarity that he associated with evangelical forms of worship. If in the Dissenting chapel Browning feels a similar repugnance, queasily conscious as he takes his place in a packed pew of the 'hot smell and the human noises / And my neighbour's coat, the greasy cuff of it' (149–50), it is an over-familiarity that he chooses in the end to embrace. But in much of his religious poetry Browning's use of the dramatic monologue ensures the indirection that Keble recommended. In 'An Epistle Containing the Strange Medical Experience of Karshish, the Arab Physician' (1855), 'Cleon (1855)', and 'A Death in the Desert' (1864) Browning finds in the first and second centuries of the Christian era a mirror image of his own epoch. Cleon anticipates the free-thinkers of Browning's own day when he mocks the doctrines preached by 'Paulus' and 'Christus', if they be, as he rather doubts, two separate people, and reaffirms his own staunch Epicurean ethic: 'Live long and happy, and in that thought die / Glad for what was' (336–7). John, as he lies dying, imagines 'unborn people in strange lands', who will ask, 'Was John at all, and did he say he saw?' ('A Death in the Desert', 194, 196), foreknowing in that moment Strauss and all those followers of his who so confidently assigned John's Gospel to a date no earlier than the late second century. In his suspicion of miracles and in his shock at the notion that God might have created the world and then 'came and dwelt in flesh on it awhile!' Karshish too foreshadows the nineteenth century, and Victorian intellectuals such as Matthew Arnold who fastidiously flinched from the vulgarity of 'that favourite doctrine of our theologians, "the blessed truth that the God of the universe is a Person"'.[11]

These poems inevitably engage contemporary theological debates, but that seems not to be their principal concern. In 'Karshish', for example, the centrality of the incarnation to Browning's religious thought is evident enough. The incarnation proclaims the union between the God of power, the creator, and the God of love, the redeemer:

> The very God! think, Abib; dost thou think?
> So, the All-Great, were the All-Loving too –
> So, through the thunder comes a human voice
> Saying, 'O heart I made, a heart beats here!
> Face my hands fashioned, see it in myself.
> ('Karshish', 304–8)

The incarnation promises that what seemed to Browning's favourite, Shelley, an insurmountable impasse, 'the wise want love, and those who love want wisdom' (*Prometheus Unbound*, 1, 627), can be overcome. But the poem offers a more wide-ranging reflection on the relationship between soul and body. Karshish, an Arab physician travelling in the Holy Land at some time around 69 C.E., has a straightforwardly pneumatic view of the soul. It is a 'puff of vapour'. The doctor's business is to keep it from escaping the body to 'rejoin its source' before the due term. (6–14) The body is dependent on the soul for its life, but to the soul the body is wholly repugnant, a prison that it constantly seeks to escape. Karshish's experience of the world rehearses in exaggerated form the experience that I have suggested was characteristic of Victorian poets. He feels no connection at all between the world of material fact and the spiritual world that is the source of value. That is why his meeting with Lazarus is so unsettling for him. He is not puzzled by Lazarus's account of being raised from the dead – 'Such cases are diurnal' (102), they are met with every day, and they yield easily to rational explanation. Rather, he is perturbed by Lazarus's claim that the healer was none other than 'God forgive me – who but God himself' (268), a claim so shocking that Karshish cannot bring himself to repeat it: Lazarus, he reports, insists that his healer 'was ... what I said nor choose repeat'. (274) Karshish refuses to repeat the blasphemous thought in writing, but he cannot let go of it. He cannot dismiss Lazarus's testimony, although what impresses him seems not so much to be Lazarus's account of what happened to him as the way that he lives his life since his resurrection. He lives on in a state of benign stupefaction. Lazarus, alerted to 'some trifling fact' may 'gaze rapt / With stupor at its very littleness' (150–1), and yet 'Should his child sicken unto death' (159–62) he will scarcely register the event. For him, Karshish conjectures in a celebrated simile, mortal life is only a 'thin black thread' that 'runs across some vast distracting orb / Of glory' (180–1). He is stupefied because he is simultaneously aware of the world that we all of us inhabit and of eternity.

That makes him, Karshish insists, 'stark mad' (264), but it also makes him a kind of poet, even if a silent one, for, as Elizabeth Barrett Browning puts it in the poem that she was writing at the time, the gift conferred on poets is rather like the gift that has been conferred on Lazarus: 'O sorrowful great gift / Conferred on poets, of a twofold life'. (*Aurora Leigh* (1856), 5, 380–1) It is a gift that, as he writes his letter, rubs off on Karshish. He begins his letter gracefully punning on his own name which means in Arabic, one who gathers, 'Karshish, the picker-up of learning's crumbs' (1). His modesty is disarming, but it is also justified by much of his letter.

He speaks of what he has learned on his travels as 'the stuffing of my travel-scrip', and that is exactly what it amounts to, disconnected fragments of knowledge very little different from the objects he encloses with his letter, 'Three samples of true snake-stone – rarer still, / One of the other sort, the melon-shaped' (17–8). These for him are the 'things of price' from which he has been distracted by 'trivial matters' such as the tale of Lazarus (278). He makes an effort to recover himself:

> I noticed on the margin of a pool
> Blue-flowering borage, the Aleppo sort,
> Aboundeth, very nitrous. It is strange!
> (280–2)

But his letter ends only when he returns to Lazarus's account of what Jesus had told him:

> 'Thou hast no power, nor may'st conceive of mine,
> But love I gave thee, with Myself to love,
> And thou must love me who have died for thee!'
> The madman said He said so: it is strange.
> (309–12)

Browning clearly offers his 'epistle' as a counterpart to the epistles of Paul – he supplements the Apostle's letters with the letter of an unbeliever – but he is also interested in letters. Letters have their being in the world of contingency. Karshish has to depend for its safe delivery on the 'Syrian run-a-gate' (49) he entrusts it to, and in its content too his letter, like most letters, focuses on contingent matters, snake-stone and borage and the 'gum-tragacanth' they have in Judea that 'Scales off in purer flakes, shines clearer-grained' (55–6). Even Paul's epistles make room for contingencies, as when he passes on to the people of Colossae greetings from Aristarchus and from Marcus, Barnabas's nephew (*Colossians*, 4, 10). Letters are, after all, instrumental: they serve a purpose. But as he writes, Karshish becomes aware that his letter has outrun its purpose, that the story of his meeting with a madman in Bethany conveys no useful information. He confesses that he has continued the letter not because he had something to say, but because 'An itch I had, a sting to write, a tang!' (67). Paul's epistles are redeemed from contingency, they become scripture, because of the message they communicate, the message of the incarnation, the message that Christ is the son of god. Karshish's letter is redeemed from contingency, too, not by becoming scripture but by becoming a poem, something written not to serve any purpose except to relieve an itch in the poet. Browning is quietly intimating that the miracle of the incarnation that alone makes sense of human life is shadowed in the writing of each and every successful poem, because the incarnation and poetry both have the power to convert a world of contingency into a world of meaning.

The thought would have been familiar to Browning from his Romantic predecessors, but he is characteristically Victorian in choosing to explore it through a story, the story of Lazarus, that would have been familiar to his Christian readership from childhood, and he is characteristic, too, in choosing to articulate his own Christian belief in a poem in which he assumes the voice of an unbeliever. Arnold persisted in describing himself as a Christian only by means of what must have seemed to many a sleight of hand. In 'Stanzas from the Grand Chartreuse' (1855) the chief monastery of the Carthusians resembles for Arnold 'some fallen Runic stone' (83) because it commemorates a faith that is no longer comprehensible. The poem ends when Arnold figures his own generation as children 'reared in shade', brought up in a secluded forest glade in the shelter of a ruined abbey and 'its close of graves,' (169–74) who have become far too used to their surroundings to respond to the future when it calls them. Arnold, unable quite to abandon a faith in which he no longer believes, mirrors Karshish, unable to put out of his mind a faith he cannot bring himself to accept. As he reflects on the great Carthusian monastery Arnold forges once again the 'tremulous cadence slow', the 'melancholy, long, withdrawing' music ('Dover Beach'), which, as he well knew, gave his poems their distinctive, Arnoldian character, but it is a music, as he also knows, that he can forge only by mournfully echoing the music of the Christian faith that he has discarded. Keble had recommended that poets should only express religious truths indirectly, but Browning and Arnold practise kinds of indirection that he would scarcely have found congenial. So too does Tennyson, who developed in *In Memoriam* (1850) the expressive devices that so many of his contemporaries thought of as most adequately expressing their faith. It is a poem remarkable for the number of proverbs that it coins, as for example:

> There lives more faith in honest doubt,
> Believe me, than in half the creeds.
> (XCVI, 11–2)

This achieves the appropriate proverbial robustness by ignoring niceties ('*half* the creeds'?), but it does at least register that the newly minted commonplace gives memorable expression to an extreme paradox by immediately following the word 'doubt' with the interjection, 'Believe me'. Doubt is presented as the most convincing authentication of faith. Faith and doubt are often represented as the opposite poles between which Victorian religious poetry swings, but this does not sufficiently recognize in how much of the poetry of the period the two dispositions are so implicated one with another that it becomes very difficult to distinguish them.

One sign of Tennyson's difference from Keble is his indifference to church ceremony. Tennyson did not attend Hallam's funeral, and the funeral service is registered only very slightly in the poem: 'They laid him by the pleasant shore' (XIX, 3). The omission is accentuated by the rather full account of his sister's marriage service with which the poem ends:

The ring is on,
The 'wilt thou' answered, and again
The 'wilt thou' asked, till out of twain
Her sweet 'I will' has made you one.
(CXXXI, 54–6)

The passing of three Christmases is noted, but although Tennyson registers that the day marks 'the birth of Christ' (XXVIII, 1), Christmas remains a seasonal rather than a Christian festival, associated with holly wreaths, 'dance and song and hoodman-blind' (LXXVIII, 12), and a mantling 'bowl of wassail' (CV, 18). For Tennyson it would compromise the authenticity of his grief if it were to be incorporated with any outward ceremony.

It is the unbelieving Swinburne, in his elegy to Baudelaire, 'Ave atque Vale' (1878), who invests death with ceremonial splendour. The poem's eleven-line stanza is itself a gorgeous invention. In its opening line it acknowledges the French poet with an alexandrine, and the stanza closes with a trimeter. Its opening lines rhyme abba, like the stanza of *In Memoriam*, but it is Tennyson's stanza opulently swollen. Hallam had been Tennyson's closest friend, but Swinburne, as he registers in the poem, had never met Baudelaire, 'O hand unclasped of unbeholden friend' (47), a line surely designed to recall how in *In Memoriam* the pain of loss is most intimately realised in Hallam's 'hand that can be clasp'd no more' (VII, 5). Swinburne mourns not the man but the poet, or more precisely he commemorates Baudelaire as a book, what Swinburne calls a 'shut scroll' (102). It is the book that Swinburne can 'clasp', 'As though a hand were in my hand to hold' (108), and the book, unlike the man, is not lost to him. *Les Fleurs du Mal*, from which Swinburne chooses his epigraph retains its vitality, even its ability to reproduce. The 'genoux énormes' of Baudelaire's 'La Géante' become the 'great knees' of Swinburne's 'Titan-woman', and Baudelaire's desire, 'Dormir nonchalamment à l'ombre de ses seins', produces a still more extravagant representation of the female body as landscape:

> Under the shadow of her vast fair head,
> The deep division of prodigious breasts,
> The solemn slope of mighty limbs asleep,
> The weight of awful tresses that still keep
> The savour and the pain of old-world pine-forests
> Where the wet hill-winds weep?
>
> (61–6)

Swinburne wrote his poem in May, 1867, in response to a false report that Baudelaire was dead (he did not in fact die until August), and the mistake has a kind of appropriateness because, since Baudelaire is for Swinburne only a metonym for his poems, he is not really subject to mortality. In these circumstances elegy becomes an exercise in absurdity, as the poem takes some pains to point out. It is an empty charade, an offering made to gods in whose existence Swinburne firmly disbelieves. Hence the poem builds its rich funeral music out of negatives: 'For thee no fruits to pluck, no palms for winning,' (48) 'Thee not Orestes nor Electra mourns.' (129) It is a poem written in full consciousness of its own futility, always aware that it is addressed to someone who is 'far too far for wings of words to follow,'(89) and always fully aware that poetry is helpless in the face of death and just as helpless in the face of life: 'not all our songs, O friend, / Will make death clear or make life durable.' (171–2) 'Ave atque Vale' ends by addressing a corpse for whom 'all winds are quiet as the sun, / All waters as the shore.' (197–8) It ends, that is, in an address that is recognized even as it is spoken to be entirely futile. Tennyson's poem is driven on by his need to believe that the soul survives the body, but in Swinburne's poem the parting of the soul from the body and the rotting of the body, the parting of flesh and bone, are all but synonymous:

> Is it not well where soul from body slips
> And flesh from bone divides without a pang
> As dew from flower-bell drips?
>
> (42–4)

Baudelaire, as far as Swinburne is concerned, is merely a text. Even Sappho, 'the supreme head of song' (18), survives only as a metre, in the rhythm of the waves beneath which her body is irrecoverably lost. All experience in this poem becomes textual. The 'dead yew-leaves' (50) have their only being on the 'leaves of holy poets' pages' (128). Swinburne cannot offer the flowers trod by 'tropic feet' that Baudelaire would prefer, only the 'gleanings of a northern shore', but in a poem in which all flowers are flowers of rhetoric and all feet are metrical the distinction scarcely signifies. *In Memoriam* is a poem chastened by Tennyson's scrupulous doubt. In 'Ave atque Vale' Swinburne's verse achieves an opulence made possible only by the firmness of Swinburne's unbelief. Like 'Karshish', 'Ave atque Vale' explores the relationship between religion and poetry, but for Swinburne they are similar because the language of both is contentless, both perform empty ceremonies. Swinburne had invented long before Wilde imagined it in *De Profundis* (written in 1897) the possibility of a religion for those who cannot believe, a 'Confraternity of the Faithless, one might call it, where on an altar, on which no taper burned, a priest, in whose heart peace had no dwelling, might celebrate with unblessed bread and a chalice empty of wine.'

It is the atheist poetry of the century that cultivates evangelical fervour more impressively than the Christian. In *Dipsychus* Clough's hero represents himself as undergoing a conversion experience: he is reborn as an unbeliever, and he discovers in his unbelief the dynamic emotional range, from joy ('Ting, ting, there is no God; ting ting' (V, 13)) to despair ('Dong, there is no God; Dong' (V, 26)) that earlier poets had found in their faith. Dispychus is methodistical, almost priggish, in comparison with the Mephistophelian 'Spirit' who tempts him to reconcile himself with the world. The Spirit is an orthodox church-going man. Like Tennyson's 'Morte d'Arthur', *Dipsychus* comes with a frame in which the poem is read by its author to his uncle. The uncle thinks that much of what the Spirit says would be sensible enough were it not for his manner, whereas his nephew has been equipped by Dr Arnold at Rugby with too scrupulous a conscience. He is in danger of losing his faith for the paradoxical reason that he, like the whole of his generation, is 'so pious'. The uncle is an urbane, sophisticated relic of the Regency. The mother in John Davidson's 'A Woman and Her Son' (1893) is far more pitiable as her son harangues her on her death-bed, insisting that she renounce her faith in favour of the uncompromising brand of Nietzschean atheism that Davidson's character shares with Davidson himself, but she responds very similarly: 'my son, you seem to me a kind of prig' (58). Clough's 'Easter Day. Naples, 1849' (not published until 1951) is his most rousing hymn to unbelief:

> Eat, drink and die, for we are souls bereaved,
> Of all the creatures under this broad sky
> We are most hopeless, that had hoped most high,
> And most beliefless, that had most believed.
>   Ashes to ashes, dust to dust;
>   As of the unjust, also of the just –
>   Yea, of that Just One too.
>   It is the one sad Gospel that is true,
>   Christ is not risen.
>
> (86–94)

Unlike Tennyson's modest faith, Clough's unbelief demands the grandly assertive rhythms of the ode (Wordsworth's 'Ode: Intimations of Immortality' seems to be Clough's chief model, although it is mortality that his own poem intimates). He represents the poem much as Keble represented all poetry as what results when the repression of an emotion produces a pain that can only be relieved by being allowed expression:

> My heart was hot within me; till at last
> My brain was lightened, when my tongue had said
>   Christ is not risen!
>
> (3–5)

But for Keble, the urge to give vent to emotion is countered by a duty to maintain reserve, and the opposition of the two impulses produces the characteristic indirection of poetry. Clough's poem is shockingly unreserved, bracingly free from indirection. The effect is still more marked in James Thomson's *The City of Dreadful Night* (1874) at the centre of which is a sermon spoken from a 'dark pulpit'. The preacher bids the congregation in 'yearning' tones to rejoice because humanity is the product of impersonal natural laws, because 'this little life is all we must endure,' and because those who find their brief life too long may 'end it' when they will 'without the fear of waking after death.' (710–69) Keble disliked evangelical Christianity in part because its professors seemed to him to lack the reserve that was the proper response to divine mystery. Clough and Thomson write evangelical poetry, but of a paradoxical kind, for they are evangelists of unbelief.

Endnotes

1. John Keble, *Occasional Papers and Reviews* (Oxford: James Parker, 1877), p. 152.
2. John Henry Newman, *Essays*, 1, p. 23.
3. Matthew Arnold, *Literature and Dogma,* in *Dissent and Dogma*, ed. R.H. Super (Ann Arbor: University of Michigan Press, 1968), pp. 170, 171 and 22.
4. On Christina Rossetti as a Tractarian poet and as a poet of snow, see Emma Mason (2002) 'Christina Rossetti and the Doctrine of Reserve', *Journal of Victorian Culture*, 7(2), 196–219.
5. Matthew Arnold, *Literature and Dogma*, p. 187.
6. Isobel Armstrong, *Victorian Poetry: Poetry, Poetics and Politics* (London and New York: Routledge, 1993), pp. 332–67.
7. Dora Greenwell, *Essays* (London and New York: Alexander Strahan, 1866), p. 3.
8. *The Letters of Gerard Manley Hopkins to Robert Bridges*, ed. Claude Colleer Abbott (London: Oxford University Press, 1935), p. 155.
9. *The Brownings' Correspondence*, ed. Philip Kelley and Scott Lewis, 13 (Winfield: Wedgestone Press, 1995, pp. 253–4.
10. *The Athenaeum*, 1171 (April, 1850), p. 370; Ian Jack. *Browning's Major Poetry* (Oxford: Clarendon Press, 1973), p. 127.
11. Matthew Arnold, *Literature and Dogma*, p. 290.

8

Conclusion: The 1890s

The 1890s is the only decade of the Victorian period that regularly functions as a description rather than a date. It is the decade presided over by Wilde, illustrated by Aubrey Beardsley and Charles Ricketts, caricatured by Max Beerbohm, anthologized in *The Yellow Book* and the *Books of the Rhymers' Club*, a decade that ended prematurely in 1895 when Wilde was sentenced to two years imprisonment with hard labour, or belatedly in 1902 when Lionel Johnson died after falling from a bar stool in the Green Dragon in Fleet Street. Almost all commentators on the period begin by protesting against this burlesque version of its literary character, but, like all vigorous burlesques, however often it is demolished it contrives somehow to survive. It is a decade that, it might even be claimed, was inaugurated almost a decade before the due date by a burlesque, by Gilbert and Sullivan's comic opera *Patience*, first performed in April, 1881. It was Gilbert who first defined the representative nineties poet:

> A pallid and thin young man,
> A haggard and lank young man,
> A greenery-yallery, Grosvenor Gallery,
> Foot-in-the-grave young man.
> (Act Two)

Reginald Bunthorne, who sings these lines, can scarcely have been modelled on Wilde who was only two years out of university and had published little when *Patience* was first performed. It is more likely that Wilde modelled himself on Bunthorne. Alerted to the opera's subject matter, Wilde

Reading Victorian Poetry, First Edition. Richard Cronin.

took a three-guinea box for its opening night. The role of Bunthorne was taken by George Grossmith who, as the run proceeded and Wilde's celebrity grew, began more and more to introduce Wildean mannerisms into his performance. Wilde brought out his *Poems* shortly after the opening of *Patience*, no doubt recognizing the time as opportune, and later in the year he agreed a contract with the producer of *Patience*, Reginald D'Oyly Carte, for a lecture tour of the United States. D'Oyly Carte seems to have thought of Wilde's tour, which was timed to coincide with the opera's American opening, as an extended advertisement for *Patience*. It is in *Patience* that Bunthorne threatens to 'walk down Piccadilly with a poppy or a lily in [his] mediæval hand' (Act Two). The Harvard undergraduates who guyed Wilde by attending a lecture clutching a lily or a sunflower were naively unaware that they were caricaturing a caricature. It is an innocence of which Wilde, for whom 'Life imitates art far more than Art imitates life',[1] would not have been capable. He wrote 'Symphony in Yellow' in 1889 in homage to Whistler, who has two paintings entitled 'Symphony in White'. An 'omnibus' crawls across the bridge 'like a yellow butterfly', a barge of yellow hay' moves against a quay shrouded in Whistlerian fog, and the poem ends:

> The yellow leaves begin to fade
>   And flutter from the Temple elms,
> And at my feet the pale green Thames
>   Lies like a rod of rippled jade.
>
> (9–12)

It is hard not to glimpse in the stanza a sly reference to the 'greenery-yallery Grosvenor Gallery'. Gilbert was, after all, marking an association between the Grosvenor Gallery and aestheticism that was sealed in 1878 when it exhibited Whistler's 'Nocturne in Black and Gold', a decision that Ruskin described as 'flinging a pot of paint in the public's face', prompting Whistler to sue for libel. Wilde supplies after the event the poem that prompts Gilbert's epithet, the poem that 'greenery-yallery' burlesques.

The 1890s have from the first enjoyed a double character. On the one hand they mark the end of a period, a decadence, a fin de siècle. On the other, they represent a beginning: it was the decade of art nouveau, of the new woman, the decade in which Wilde's Lord Henry Wotton proclaimed a 'new Hedonism' and W.E. Henley launched the *New Review*. Some poems of the decade, especially Housman's in *A Shropshire Lad* (1896), preserve this double character by finding a way of speaking that is at once youthful and as if spoken from the brink of the grave, an odd perspective that helps to explain why the volume meant so much to soldiers on active service, first in the Second Boer War and then again in World War One. In 'Loveliest of trees, the cherry now', the blossoming of the cherry is celebrated by a speaker who is twenty years old, as young as the year, but the speaker's joy is haunted throughout by the sense of his own death as imminent, even though he imagines that he will live his full three score years and ten. The thought is clinched in the lyric's final word when the springtime blossom is figured as wintry snow:

And since to look at things in bloom
Fifty springs are little room,
About the woodlands I will go
To see the cherry hung with snow.
(9–12)

It is a happy thought that he may have borrowed from an earlier west-country poet, William Barnes, who noticed in 'Be'mi'ster' (1844) how 'flow'rs o' blackberries do blow / Upon the brembles, white as snow' (13–4). If snow and blossom, the sense of an ending and the sense of a new beginning, coincided in the 1890s, so they did all through the Victorian period that the decade brought to an end. It was an inevitable consequence of the impression that so many Victorians had of living in an age of transition, 'between', as Arnold put it with characteristic glumness, 'two worlds, one dead, / The other powerless to be born'. ('Stanzas from the Grande Chartreuse' (1855), 85–6).

Some of the decade's writers represent themselves as in violent reaction against their Victorian predecessors, in reaction most particularly against Victorian earnestness. 'No artist has ethical sympathies. An ethical sympathy in an artist is an unpardonable lapse of style,' wrote Wilde, but he wrote it in a series of epigrams that he prefixed to *A Picture of Dorian Gray* (1891), a story which is, or at least disguises itself as, a moral fable. The hedonism to which Wilde and other nineties writers gave their allegiance had been formulated most authoritatively by Walter Pater in the 'Conclusion' to *Studies in the History of the Renaissance* (1873). As late as 1936 W.B. Yeats acknowledged Pater's crucial role by introducing his *Oxford Book of Modern Verse* with Pater's description of the 'Mona Lisa' set out as verse. But Pater's Conclusion had first been published in 1868 in a piece for the *Westminster Review*:

> Not the fruit of experience, but experience itself, is the end. A counted number of pulses only is given to us of a variegated, dramatic life. How may we see in them all that is to be seen in them by the finest senses? How shall we pass most swiftly from point to point, and be present always at the focus where the greatest number of vital forces unite in their purest energy?
>
> To burn always with this hard, gem-like flame, to maintain this ecstasy, is success in life.

This may have given Lord Henry Wotton the kernel of his philosophy, but Pater first expressed these thoughts in a paper, 'Poems by William Morris', reviewing Morris's first three volumes of verse.[2] 1890s aestheticism had its origin in a review of the poems of Ruskin's most fervent disciple, or it may be that it had a still earlier origin. Another of Pater's disciples, W.B. Yeats, rejected the Victorian notion that poetry should be 'full of thoughts that might have been expressed in prose' for the more 'modern' assumption that it was a poet's job 'to express life at its intense moments'.[3] But as he well knew, his preference for a poetry of sensation over a poetry of reflection had been anticipated by Arthur Hallam in his review of Tennyson's *Poems, Chiefly Lyrical* of 1830, the volume that, a remarkable number of anthologists agree, inaugurated the Victorian period that Yeats claims to be repudiating. Wilde may have thought himself at war with Victorian earnestness, but it was a war in which the battle lines are very hard to draw, because the Victorians were from the first at war with themselves. In 'The Decay of Lying' (1889) Wilde's Vivian insists, 'To us, who live in the nineteenth century, any setting is a suitable subject for art except our own'. But at once he feels that he has talked enough: 'And now let us go out on the terrace, where "droops the milk-white peacock like a ghost," while the evening star "washes the dusk with silver."'[4] Wilde ends his anti-Victorian manifesto with two quotations, one from Blake's 'To the Evening Star' (1783) and one from a song, 'Now sleeps the crimson petal', from what has seemed to many an exemplary Victorian poem, Tennyson's *The Princess* (1847).

W.S. Gilbert was once again prophetic. In *Patience*, the aesthetes, Reginald Bunthorne and Archibald Grosvenor, are opposed by the Officers of the Heavy Dragoons, whose Colonel sets out in a song the recipe for the production of one of their kind:

> Take all the remarkable people in history,
> Rattle them off to a popular tune.

The pluck of Lord Nelson on board of the *Victory* –
  Genius of Bismarck devising a plan –
The humour of Fielding (which sounds contradictory) –
  Coolness of Paget about to trepan –
The science of Jullien, the eminent musico –
  Wit of Macaulay, who wrote of Queen Anne –
The pathos of Paddy, as rendered by Boucicault –
  Style of the Bishop of Sodor and Man –
The dash of a D'Orsay, divested of quackery –
Narrative powers of Dickens and Thackeray –
Victor Emmanuel – peak-haunting Peveril –
Thomas Aquinas, and Doctor Sacheverell –
  Tupper and Tennyson – Daniel Defoe –
  Anthony Trollope and Mister Guizot! Ah!
  Take of these elements all that is fusible,
  Melt them all down in a pipkin or crucible,
  Set them to simmer, and take off the scum,
  And a Heavy Dragoon is the residuum!

(Act One)

The recipe includes together with the eighteenth-century novelists, Fielding and Defoe, who retained their popularity in the nineteenth, a large gallery of Victorian men of letters; Macaulay, the Irish dramatist, Dion Boucicault, Dickens, Thackeray, Walter Scott ('peak-haunting Peveril'), Martin Tupper, author of the phenomenally popular *Proverbial Philosophy*, and Anthony Trollope. This is the literature, Gilbert suggests, against which the aesthetes reacted. But it was a conflict that remained unresolved even in the 1890s, when the poets often described as the Decadents were opposed by a rival group sometimes described as the Hearties.

The heartiest of them all was Rudyard Kipling. In 'The "Mary Gloster"' (1894), Sir Anthony Gloster, a self-made man, who began life as a common seaman, and went on to become a master mariner, an iron master, a ship builder, and at last a shipping magnate, gives instructions for his burial to his only surviving son. The son has been educated at 'Harrer and Trinity College' (71), but, in the father's view, it has only served to spoil him:

For you muddled with books and pictures, an' china, an' etchin's an' fans,
And your rooms at college was beastly – more like a whore's than a man's.

(75–6)

His son has developed the tastes of Whistler, of Gilbert's Bunthorne, who is an authoritative 'judge of blue-and-white and other kinds of pottery', and of Wilde, who once wittily represented himself as 'trying to live up to [his] china'.[5] There seems little doubt as to whether it is the father or son that Kipling finds the more sympathetic character. But even in this poem Kipling is not quite so clearly at odds with the decadents as might be supposed. Sir Anthony's wish is to be buried at sea, in the ship named after his wife, the ship on which she had died, at the precise point, 'by the Little Paternosters, as you come to the Union Bank'(125), at which her body had been committed to the sea. It is a gesture as grand as any late Romantic could have conceived, and it registers his devotion to the wife to whom he credits all his success. Not that, in his widowhood, he has remained faithful to her memory. He leaves 'poor Aggie a hundred' (96) as the best of the various women that since his wife's death he has paid for 'out o'hand' (170), but in spite of such doings he denies that he has at all compromised the single-mindedness of his devotion to his Mary. He can still insist,

I've allus heeded to you,
Excep' – I know – about women; but you are a spirit now;
An' wife, they was only women, and I was a man. That's how.
(166–8)

Kipling's metre, his demotic, anapaest-riddled hexameters, could not be more different from Dowson's in his most famous poem:

Last night, ah, yesternight, betwixt her lips and mine
There fell the shadow, Cynara! thy breath was shed
Upon my soul between the kisses and the wine;
And I was desolate and sick of an old passion,
Yea, I was desolate and bowed my head:
I have been faithful to thee, Cynara! in my fashion.
('Non Sum Qualis Eram Bonae
Sub Regno Cynarae'
(1896), 1–6)

But the sentiment is similar, and some readers may judge that it is Kipling who expresses it more delicately.

In the 1890s English poetry seemed more clearly divided between rival camps than at any time in the Victorian period, but the convergences between the rival groups are in some ways still more remarkable. Two famous poems of the period powerfully express the horror of capital punishment, one by the heartiest of the hearties, the other by the most flamboyant of the aesthetes. In Kipling's 'Danny Deever' (1890) the Colour-Sergeant and 'File-on-Parade' engage in a terse dialogue as Deever is hanged:

> 'What's that so black agin the sun?' said Files-on-Parade.
> 'It's Danny fightin' 'ard for life,' the Colour-Sergeant said.
> 'What's that that whimpers over'ead?' said Files-on-Parade.
> 'It's Danny's soul that's passin' now,' the Colour-Sergeant said.
> (25–8)

In Wilde's 'The Ballad of Reading Gaol' (1898) it is a discharged soldier who is hanged, and his death is imagined rather than witnessed by his fellow inmates:

> And as one sees most fearful things
> In the crystal of a dream,
> We saw the greasy hempen rope
> Hooked to the blackened beam,
> And heard the prayer the hangman's snare
> Strangled into a scream.
> (373–8)

Both executed men are guilty of murder, the one has shot a sleeping comrade, the other has cut his wife's throat, but their guilt only sharpens the pity.

Although all the prisoners imagine the hanged man's death, none imagines it, Wilde claims, as vividly as him, 'For he who lives more lives than one / More deaths than one must die' (383–4). In all his writings Wilde was fascinated with those who live a double life, but my point is that poetry in the 1890s, divided between the Decadents and the Hearties, lived just such a life, and so did the poetry of the century that it brought to a close. It is a trait best exemplified by Victoria's laureate. For Gilbert, Tennyson is one of the ingredients that go to the making of a Heavy Dragoon. It is another instance of his prescience because Tennyson was the very next year in 1882 to supplement his 'Charge of the Light Brigade' (1854) by publishing in *Macmillan's Magazine* 'The Charge of the Heavy Brigade at Balaclava'. Shortly after his appointment as laureate, in 1852, Tennyson published a series of poems in response to the threat of French invasion as bellicose as anything by any of the 1890s Hearties: 'O where is he, the simple fool, / Who says that wars are over?' ('The Penny-Wise', 1–2), 'Rise, Britons, rise, if manhood be not dead' ('Britons, Guard Your Own', 1), 'O speak to Europe through your guns! / They *can* be understood by kings' ('Hands All Round', 51–2). And yet Alfred Austin, who succeeded Tennyson as Poet Laureate in 1896, characterized him very differently: 'If we were to sum up the characteristics of Mr Tennyson's compositions in one word, the word we should employ would be "feminine"', and this is why his poetry is so representative of the age: 'we have, as novelists and poets, only women, or men with womanly deficiencies, steeped in the feminine temper of the times'.[6] Austin had exacting standards of manliness, as he demonstrates in his memorial verses 'Henry Bartle Edward Frere' (1890), in which Frere, the instigator of the Zulu War, is represented as putting the current generation to shame:

> The very fear of Empire strikes us numb,
> Fumbling with pens, who brandished once the blade.
> (24–5)

But Austin's characterization of Tennyson is not perverse. He was responding to poems by Tennyson such as 'Mariana', 'Oenone', 'The Palace of Art', and 'The Lady of Shalott', poems in which Tennyson inhabits the female consciousness of his characters, establishing with them what Austin clearly found a disconcerting intimacy.

Arthur Symons's *The Symbolist Movement in Literature* (1899) in its exclusive focus on French poetry underlines one crucial respect in which poets of the 1890s registered their difference from their predecessors. 'God bless the narrow sea which keeps her off,' the Tory member's son exclaims in Tennyson *The Princess* (1847), when he looks across the Channel and glimpses the coast of France ('Conclusion', 51). He is repudiating French politics, but Tennyson seems to have had a suspicion almost as intense of French poetry. Wilde by contrast made himself into a French poet. His play *Salomé* (1893) was first written in French and first published in Paris. John Gray's *Silverpoints* (1893), perhaps the most exquisitely produced book of poetry of the decade with the elegant willow leaf pattern of its front board, its slimness underlined by the tall, thin page (it was designed by Charles Ricketts), includes poems imitated or translated from Baudelaire, Rimbaud, Verlaine and Mallarmé, but even an original poem such as 'Les Demoiselles de Sauve' has a title that disguises it as a translation from the French. Frenchness in the 1890s signalled modernity and a sensibility liberated from English bourgeois provincialism. Arthur Symons dreams of a world populated by women whose only desire is to be like buttonholes, used just once and then discarded, and the name that he gives to this land of dreams is 'Paris':

> And every woman with beseeching eyes,
>   Or with enticing eyes, or amorous,
>   Offers herself, a rose, and craves of us
> A rose's place among our memories.
> (9–12)

But Symons's posture has a history that predates the 1890s. Swinburne masqueraded as a Frenchman long before Wilde, introducing into his 1867 review of Arnold's poems two lengthy passages in French, supposedly quotations from an imaginary French critic, in which Arnold is advised that ethical questions and questions of religious faith are domestic matters that may be of importance to a poet 'chez lui', but have no place at all in poetry. It was even earlier, in 1862, that Swinburne published his review of Baudelaire's *Les Fleurs du Mal*, a volume in which he finds 'the languid lurid beauty of close and threatening weather – a heavy heated temperature, with dangerous hothouse scents in it', and from which he draws the conclusion that 'the art of poetry has absolutely nothing to do with didactic matter at all.'[7] The review clearly prefigures Swinburne's own *Poems and Ballads*, that first appeared in 1866, and might be thought of as the very first example of 1890s poetry, except that to trace the 1890s to a year in the first half of Victoria's reign seems scarcely tenable. In any case, it was more than twenty years earlier than this, in 1844, that Elizabeth Barrett Browning had signalled her own freedom from English provincial priggishness by addressing sonnets to another scandalous French writer, George Sand.[8] Even Tennyson did not succeed in maintaining his distance from the French. Baudelaire admired him, placing him in his *L'Art Romantique*, 1869, alongside Byron and Poe amongst Romanticism's 'étoiles de première grandeur', and Mallarmé made prose translations of 'Mariana' and 'Lady Godiva', astutely recognizing in Tennyson's work a precedent for his own experiments in the poetry of sound.[9]

Other poets of the 1890s signalled their allegiance to Théophile Gautier, Théodore de Banville and the French Parnassians by introducing into English some of the more demanding French verse forms. Edmund Gosse wrote the movement's manifesto in 1877 when he published in the *Cornhill Magazine* 'A Plea for Certain Exotic Forms of Verse'. He particularly recommended the *rondel*, the *rondeau*, the *triolet*, the *villanelle*, the *ballade* and the *chant royal*, this last a form so intricate and so peculiarly French that the only English example he was able to offer was a specimen that he had written himself.[10] The cultivation of difficulty was a self-consciously anti-democratic stratagem, designed as Austin Dobson, the chief poet of the movement, explained, to guard against the possibility that, 'barred no more by Lack of Skill, / The mob may crowd *Parnassus* Hill' ('The Toyman' (1885), 27–8). As Gosse made clear, it was a reaction against Whitman's 'barbaric yawp' (*Song of Myself* 1860, 1333), or, as Gosse put it, 'the uncouth prose in which a certain American rhapsodist clothes his prophetic utterances'. A typical example of the kind of verse that Gosse was recommending is Wilde's villanelle 'Theocritus' (1881):

> O Singer of Persephone!
>   In the dim meadows desolate
> Dost thou remember Sicily?
>
> Still through the ivy flits the bee
>   Where Amaryllis lies in state;
> O Singer of Persephone!
>
> (1–6)

Such poems aspire to be self-enclosed, the verse equivalent of the Anglo-Japanese blue and white china that was such a prominent feature of aesthetic interior decoration in the 1880s and 1890s. The verse forms ensure that the poems remain exotic, unaccommodated to the English language in which they are written, and serenely indifferent to their readers. Such poems are at an extreme remove from the verse in which a contemporary such as Edward Carpenter, a disciple of Whitman, celebrates the coming of a socialist millennium in *Towards Democracy* (1892, line numbers not marked):

> The writer shall write, the compositor shall set up, the student by his midnight lamp shall read, a word never seen before.
> The railway porter shall open the carriage door and the long expected friend shall descend to meet him.
> The engine-driver shall drive in faith through the night. With one hand on the regulator he shall lean sideways and peer into the darkness – and lo! a new signal not given in the printed instructions shall duly in course appear.

But the extreme formal divergence between Wilde and Carpenter serves usefully to draw attention to the similar, if less extreme divergences that characterize poetry throughout the Victorian period, divergences as apparent within writers as between them. Elizabeth Barrett Browning can be on occasion heartily dismissive of formal constraints, 'Keep up the fire, / And leave the generous flames to shape themselves' (*Aurora Leigh*, 5, 235–6), and yet she is just as likely to write in restrictively intricate verse forms such as the Petrarchan sonnet. Robert Browning and even Tennyson seem also to respond to contradictory tugs. Indeed it may be that the metrical excitement generated by a poem such as *Maud* (1855) is produced by the contradiction.

Some of the printed volumes of the 1890s might be thought of as the material embodiment of a poetic form such as the villanelle. John Gray's *Silverpoints*, as I have already noted, is a case in point, as are Wilde's *Poems* of 1892, also designed by Ricketts, or the English version of *Salome* (1894) illustrated by Aubrey Beardsley. Volumes such as these were offered as aesthetic objects in themselves, as were the volumes that William Morris produced for the Kelmscott Press. Such books were produced in tiny print runs (the fine paper edition of the Kelmscott Chaucer, for example, was limited to 425 copies), which served a rhetorical purpose, signalling a rejection of the techniques of mass production that made possible the Victorian best-seller, but also had an economic function, safeguarding the investment of the purchaser. The books of the 1890s that supplemented their appeal to the mind with a direct appeal to the eye mirror at the end of the Victorian period the Annuals that had dominated the market for poetry at its beginning. The Annuals succeeded by subordinating the verses to the lavish steel engravings that illustrated them in what Wordsworth termed a 'vile abuse of pictured page' ('Illustrated Books and Newspapers' (1849), 12). It might seem a reverse image of the 1890s practice, because the appeal of the Annuals was not at all exclusive. In fact the Annuals were commonly regarded with intellectual condescension. In Chapter 27 of *Middlemarch* (1871–2, but the scene is set in the early 1830s), it is Ned Plymdale rather than Rosamond Vincy's intellectual suitor, Lydgate, who tries to ingratiate himself by showing her a copy of *The Keepsake*, 'the gorgeous watered-silk publication which marked modern progress at that time; and he considered himself very fortunate that he could be the first to look over it with her, dwelling on the ladies and gentlemen with shiny copper-plate cheeks and copper-plate smiles, and pointing to comic verses as capital and sentimental stories as interesting.' But in fact decorative books of both kinds had the same origin. They were both responses to the collapse of the market for poetry in the 1820s, the effects of which were still apparent at the end of the century. Despite the extraordinary sales of *The Christian Year*, and the very substantial sales of Tennyson's volumes after the publication of *In Memoriam*, very few poets of the Victorian period manages to support themselves from their writing. The publishers of the Annuals produced decorative texts in order to compensate for the limited appeal of verse: the publishers of the decorative books of the 1890s produced books that would appeal to bibliophiles, a very small group but a group prepared to buy volumes at a price that would secure a profit on even a very small print run.

Several 1890s poets based their claim to originality on writing urban poetry, a claim that the titles of their volumes often underline, as in Amy Levy's *A London Plane-Tree and Other Poems* (1889), W.E. Henley's *London Voluntaries and Other Verses* (1893), and Arthur Symons's *London Nights* (1894). But other poets of the decade continued to assert the rural, provincial character of their inspiration, as in A.E. Housman's *A Shropshire Lad* (1896), and Thomas Hardy's *Wessex Poems and Other Verses* (1898). In fact, the rival postures support each other. Amy Levy chooses the plane-tree as her emblem because, unlike other species, the plane flourishes in the city. But the plane's distinction is only secured because of all the other trees that 'hold the town in scorn' ('A London Plane-Tree', 14). In much the same way, Housman's Shropshire and Hardy's Wessex assertively claim a provincialism that by the nineteenth century could only be defined in relation to the metropolitanism that it repudiated. Housman and Hardy may find in the natural world a sense of belonging that city dwellers never know, but both recognize the experience as illusory. Housman can contrive entrancing moments of natural magic:

> On russet floors, by waters idle,
> The pine lets fall its cone;
> The cuckoo shouts all day at nothing
> In leafy dells alone.
> ('Tell me not here, it needs not saying', 7–10)

But it is the poet, not nature, who is the magician, using his skill to hide momentarily the bleak truth that 'nature, heartless, witless nature / Will neither care nor know' (25–6). Housman and Hardy can remain defiantly provincial poets in part because they are able to find in rural England the lonely sense of alienation that many of their contemporaries needed to migrate to the city to experience. Much, and perhaps the most characteristic, Victorian poetry is neither urban nor rural but takes place in between the countryside and the city, which makes it appropriate that in *In Memoriam* (1850), Arthur Hallam should be allotted two memorial sites. One of them is the isolated village church overlooking the Bristol Channel of lyric LXVII. The other is the door of 67 Wimpole Street, the 'long unlovely' London street where Tennyson stands in lyric VII, as 'ghastly through the drizzling rain / On the bald street breaks the blank day' (11–2). It is why Arnold's 'Lines written in Kensington Gardens' (1852) is so representative a poem. Nature offers a peace that 'Man did not make, and cannot mar' (40), but it is a peace experienced in a city park, within hearing of the London traffic.

The poets of the Celtic revival, at least in so far as they are fairly represented by Yeats, might be thought of as exponents of a provincialism less ambivalent than Housman's or Hardy's, retreating not only from the cities to the rural fastnesses of Scotland and Ireland, but retreating also from the broad day of nineteenth-century rationalism into an occult twilight. In *Idylls of the King*, the battle in which Arthur's reign is ended and the Round Table finally destroyed takes place in the far west of the kingdom,

> Where fragments of forgotten peoples dwelt,
> And the long mountains ended in a coast
> Of ever-shifting sand, and far away
> The phantom circle of a moaning sea.
> ('The Passing of Arthur'
> (1869), 84–7)

Arthur's was an imperial project, and Victoria, to whom Tennyson dedicated the poem, was Queen of a world-wide empire. But the forging of the United Kingdom, completed only in 1801 in the Act of Union with Ireland, was itself an imperial venture and the national unity that it secured was most precarious on the peripheries of the kingdom, at those margins where 'fragments of forgotten peoples dwelt'. Arnold's 'On the Study of Celtic Literature' (1867) was one response to that threat. Arnold was prompted by a notion that the Union might be strengthened if the English could learn to look more benignly on the difference of their Celtic compatriots. The Celtic revival had, as Arnold knew, started early, in 1761, when James Macpherson published his first translations from Ossian, but

Macpherson's is an elegiac epic, the warriors that it celebrates magnified in the mists of time, their greatness most evident in defeat rather than in victory, which is why Ossian could so easily be incorporated into a centralized, Anglo-Saxon national mythology. Thomas Moore's 'Irish Melodies', Irish folk tunes set by Moore to English words, continued to be sung throughout the century. Amongst the most popular was Moore's elegy for the Irish revolutionary Robert Emmet:

Oh! breathe not his name, let it sleep in the shade,
Where cold and unhonour'd his relics are laid:
Sad, silent, and dark, be the tears that we shed,
As the night-dew that falls on the grass o'er his head.

But the night-dew that falls, though in silence it weeps,
Shall brighten with verdure the grave where he sleeps;
And the tear that we shed, though in secret it rolls,
Shall long keep his memory green in our souls.
(1808)

Emmet was reputed, after being sentenced to death, to have delivered a speech from the dock in which he urged, 'Let no man write[his] epitaph' before Ireland had secured its independence. It must have amused Moore when the song became a drawing-room favourite, but it is hard to see how its revolutionary burden could have survived the transformation. James Clarence Mangan's 'My Dark Rosaleen' (1846), a loose translation from the Gaelic that Mangan presents as an allegorical address to the nation, is more resistant to appropriation:

Over hills and thro' dales
Have I roamed for your sake;
All yesterday I sailed with sails
On river and on lake.
The Erne at its highest flood
I dashed across unseen,
For there was lightning in my blood,
My Dark Rosaleen!
My own Rosaleen!
O there was lightning in my blood,
Red lightning lightened thro' my blood,
My Dark Rosaleen!
(13–24)

The repetitions ('sailed with sails') remain foreign, and the rhythm sometimes resists English metrics, but if Rosaleen figures the nation, it is as a young woman in need of a male protector, and a woman who seems in danger, like Edgar Allan Poe's 'Annabel Lee' (1849), of losing all materiality until she is reduced to the merely phonetic existence of a woman who survives only in the chant of her name. The result is that even when her champion vows to rescue her with 'redundance of blood' (74) the effect remains oddly unthreatening. In the 1890s the poetry of the Celtic revival maintained the ambivalent relationship with the centre that the English poets of the 1890s shared with their predecessors. Yeats hears the summons to 'The Lake Isle of Innisfree', in 'the deep heart's core' (12). Only by retreating to an uninhabited island on Lough Gill can he rediscover the centre of his being, but he hears the lake waters lapping as he stands in London, 'on the roadway, or on the pavements grey' (11). Just as much as Arnold's Kensington Gardens, Yeats's Lake Isle is defined by the city from which it offers refuge, which makes it a little less of a surprise that the poem should be echoed by an imperialist poet such as Kipling. 'Chant-Pagan' is spoken by a veteran of the Boer War, who, riding over the veldt at night, has known 'the silence, the shine an' the size / Of the 'igh, unexpressible skies' (29–30), and finds it hard to adjust to England where there are ''ouses both sides of the street', and he is expected to touch his hat to 'the parson and gentry' (6–8). He plans like Yeats to escape, to go back to the Cape, where, he is confident, the Boer farmer that he has fought will have a job for him. Kipling's old soldier simply repeats Yeats' 'I will arise and go now' in a cockney accent[11]:

I will arise an' get 'ence –
I will trek South and make sure
If it's only my fancy or not
That the sunshine of England is pale,
And the breezes of England are stale,
An' there's something gone small with the lot.
(64–9)

I know of no stronger example of how permeable seemingly antithetical ideological positions such as Yeats' nationalism and Kipling's imperialism might become in the 1890s, but they had been almost as permeable for most of the century.

The women poets of the 1890s were many of them more attracted to the noise of the traffic than to waters lapping. I owe to Ana Parejo Vadillo an especially evocative extract from the diary of Michael Field. The passage begins in the London streets. It is Whistler's London, a London turned into a painting by the fog:

> A fog – a glower of yellow, ignoring roofs, carriages, the opposite side of the streets – everything in the dear city except the immediate pavement before one & the sudden passing faces –their flesh tints strangely emphatic for a moment & then dim with disappearance.[12]

The fog endears the city to the two poets as they walk its streets by transforming it into a city of the imagination, a Baudelairean city 'pleine de rêves'. As they turn away from the National Gallery they meet Arthur Symons, 'the "rose-mesh" [the quotation is from Browning's 'Rabbi Ben Ezra'] of Arthur's cheeks and lip, as he met [them], enchanting in the dismal space between one's eyes & the fog'. Symons took them back to his room in Fountain Court, and they examined its contents, the engraving from Carpaccio, the portrait heads of Sarah Bernhardt, Olive Schreiner, Mary Robinson, George Meredith and Coventry Patmore, and the books. Symons showed them the new novel by George Moore and on the shelves they were delighted to notice one of their own volumes. The journal entry is suffused by the two women's confident enjoyment of their place within a republic of letters that, unlike the British state, accepts women as equal citizens. Katherine Bradley and Edith Cooper write as freewomen of the city, free to walk its streets, to inspect its galleries, to read its books, and to converse with their peers, even if the conversation takes place in the rented room of an unmarried poet of doubtful reputation. The city was available as it never had been before to women unescorted by men, giving them the freedom that Amy Levy celebrates, using one of those French verse forms recommended by Gosse, in 'Ballade of an Omnibus' (1889). The bus opens the whole city to women who do not own a carriage and cannot always afford to hire a cab:

> The 'busmen know me and my lyre
> From Brompton to the Bull-and-Gate.
> (11–2)

These were new women, but the life they lived had been imagined for them long before. It was Elizabeth Barrett Browning's Aurora Leigh who had in 1856 first seen the London sun

> Push out through fog with his dilated disk,
> And startle the slant roofs and chimney-pots
> With splashes of fierce colour.
>
> (3, 176–8)

It was Aurora, too, who had shown how a woman writer might mix easily with male friends such as Vincent Carrington, the painter, and Lord Howe, and have her adoring admirers, amongst them Carrington's fiancé, Kate Ward. Aurora had made herself into a professional woman of letters, on terms of easy familiarity with the London literary world, its editors and journalists, critics, and projectors. Elizabeth Barrett Browning had lived her own London life almost entirely confined to the family home in Wimpole Street, but she allows her heroine to live quite differently. She gives Aurora the opportunities that some forty years later her successors were to grasp so eagerly.

Most poets of the 1890s thought of themselves as in reaction against the Victorian age that they knew was ending, whether they were in reaction like Wilde against its narrow ideal of manliness or, like Alfred Austin, against its pervasive femininity. But it was a stance that served to tie them to their predecessors as much as to separate them, because Victorian poets had from the very first defined themselves by their rejection of the culture from within which they wrote. That is why the 1890s may serve equally well as a palinode to the age and, as I have chosen to stress in this chapter, as its epitome. I began this book with three poems, 'The Palace of Art', The Burden of Nineveh', and 'The Crystal Palace', one of them written at the beginning of the period, one in its middle years, and one at its end, all of them poems that describe exhibition spaces. I end with three poems all of which were written at the very end of the Victorian period or still later, poems which have in common only their doubleness.

The poets of the Victorian age were obliged to recognize that poetry no longer enjoyed the cultural centrality that poets of earlier ages could take for granted. Poets occupied an enclosed cultural space, a space isolated, as Clough complained, from the ordinary business of living. It was the novel, it was *Bleak House* and *Vanity Fair*, that had found a way of accommodating all the business of life that 'people, who are not verse-writers, are obliged to have to do with.'[13] In comparison with the novelists, Clough felt, Victorian poets occupied the margins of the nation's cultural life. But, I would want to add, those who lived on the periphery enjoyed a freedom that those who lived at the centre could not easily claim. William Barnes occupied the margins more determinedly than most, not just by living in the West Country, in Dorset, but by writing his best poems in its dialect, and he represents his decision as liberating. It secures his freedom from the economic constraints that weigh heavily on writers who inhabit the metropolitan centre of the nation. As he put is in 'My Orcha'd in Linden Lea' (1856):

> Let other v'ok meäk money vaster
>   In the aïr o'dark-room'd towns,
> I don't dread a peevish meäster.
> (17–9)

Had he been confined to the centre, as the close of the poem makes clear, he would have been unable to look at the world with the meditative delight that prompts his best verse:

> I be free to goo abrode,
> Or teäke ageän my homeward road
> To where, vor me, the apple tree
> Do lean down low in Linden Lea.
> (21–4)

Barnes delights in the marginality that he fixes in his use of dialect, but so too might the Poet Laureate himself as in Tennyson's 'Northern Farmer: Old Style' (1864), and 'Northern Farmer: New Style' (1869). That marginality is one reason why Victorian poetry, though its achievement may be less imposing than the achievement of the Victorian novelists, is, as a poem by William Barnes signals as well as anything, so much more various. It is that variety that I want in the final pages of this book to celebrate.

Ernest Dowson's 'Nuns of The Perpetual Adoration' (1896) contemplates the lives of an order of nuns:

> Calm, sad, secure; behind high convent walls,
>   These watch the sacred lamp, these watch and pray:
> And it is one with them when evening falls,
>   And one with them the cold return of day.
> (1–4)

The nuns safeguard the calm tenor of their lives by excluding the world, and the poem too lives a reclusive life. Even in its title it turns its back on a predominantly Protestant English readership, who might have only a dim awareness that the nuns of the perpetual adoration belong to an order devoted to the uninterrupted worship of the Blessed Sacrament, or that the sacred lamp signifies the presence of the Host in the chapel. The life that the nuns lead behind their walls is a sanctified version of the life lived by Tennyson's Mariana:

> Her tears fell with the dews at even;
> Her tears fell ere the dews were dried.
> (13–4)

Tennyson's twelve-line stanza seems knowingly cognizant of the etymology of the word stanza, Italian for room. Mariana is as enclosed in the poem's seven stanzas as she is confined to the rooms of her moated grange. The eight neatly chiselled quatrains of Dowson's poem work in much the same way. They call to mind the convent cells, each with its pious inmate, or perhaps the beads of the rosary that the nuns finger, and in fingering tell all the days of their lives:

> These heed not time; their nights and days they make
> Into a long returning rosary,
> Whereon their lives are threaded for Christ's sake:
> Meekness and vigilance and chastity.
> (4–7)

The even tenor of such lives is acted out in a diction that seems to disregard difference, so that in the first stanza 'sad' becomes synonymous with 'calm' and 'secure,' and in the second 'vigilance' becomes a virtue like meekness or chastity, which, in an order of nuns devoted to perpetual contemplation, it almost is. Dowson's verse is slow and formal in its movement, like the movements of the nuns themselves, recreating in its repetitions – 'it is one with them … And one with them' – the repetitive rituals that mark out their days.

Dowson clearly suggests an analogy between the convent's rituals and the rituals of verse. Outside the walls 'the roses of the world' are in danger of being 'trod under by the hurrying feet' (19–20), but inside the convent there in no such danger, and the feet of the poem move with the same unhurried pace as the nuns. But for all that the life of the poem seems to share the lives of the nuns, the poet's perspective retains a rather chilly detachment. The convent's life is contemplated from a position outside its 'impenetrable gate' (15). The nuns' way of life has its value in the escape it offers from the 'weary laughter' and the 'sick despair' (14) of life outside the gate. More luridly, the nuns fascinate because of the contrast they offer with another community of women, 'the roses of the world', who ply their trade on the street and whose fate it is to be 'trod under by the hurrying feet' (19–20). It is because the poem seems to live with the nuns, while the poet remains on the street that it preserves its strange double character. The disconcerting consequence is that all the formal devices that Dowson deploys to ensure that the rhythm of the poem imitates the rhythms of convent life can easily be understood as registering mockery rather than respect. One reader might be moved by the spectacle of a worldly poet shocked into rehearsing as best he can the calm dignity of the life of the nuns, but another will find that the poem follows in the nuns' footsteps almost in the same way that Trabb's boy dogs the newly gentrified Pip in Chapter 30 of *Great Expectations*, wickedly imitating his airs. 'Nuns of the Perpetual Adoration' is a poem that seems at once to honour the ceremony of verse and to look askance at it, as if, like the religious rituals that it so closely resembles, poetry were little more than flummery. It accurately represents a number of poems of the 1890s by so very nearly becoming a parody of itself.

In 'The Oxen' (1917) Hardy too imagines a faith that he cannot share, but he is removed from it not in space but in time. It is the faith of his childhood, and he is separated from it by 'years':

> Christmas Eve, and twelve of the clock.
>   'Now they are all on their knees,'
> An elder said as we sat in a flock
>   By the embers in hearthside ease.
>
> (1–4)

It is a domestic scene, the children sitting by the fire, listening to an adult (supposedly Hardy's mother), but the words 'elder' and 'flock' quietly consecrate the farmhouse, making it into a kind of church. The legend is that at midnight, as Christmas Day begins, the cattle kneel, becoming identical for that moment with the wooden cattle in the Christmas crib paying their reverence to the baby, and it does not occur to any of the children to doubt it. The first two quatrains of the poem, each a single, complete sentence, record the memory. The final two quatrains establish how distant the memory is:

So fair a fancy few would weave
  In these years! Yet I feel,
If someone said on Christmas Eve,
  'Come; see the oxen kneel

'In the lonely barton by yonder coomb
  Our childhood used to know,'
I should go with him in the gloom,
  Hoping it might be so.

(9–16)

The legend is a 'fancy', a word that seems to take account of the century-old subordination of the fancy to the imagination. The word allows the miracle a charm that depends on it being so slight, and yet it still carries the suggestion that it was stories like this that made Hardy into a poet. But, even if this is granted, kneeling cattle remain much less of a wonder than the Incarnation, which is why they have the power to prompt a wistfulness so keen that the syntax has to move across the division between the stanzas to accommodate it. The lines work to establish how Hardy is at once very far from his childhood and very close to it. His childhood identity was communal, one of the flock, incorporated in a 'we'. The adult is a sole self, an I, aware of an inner loneliness that as a child he associated only with a building, the isolated barton. It is not a building that we used to know in our childhood, but a building that 'Our childhood used to know', an expression that seems wholly to disconnect Hardy from his childhood self, and yet, as if instinctively, Hardy slips back even as he marks the disconnection into his childhood vocabulary, in which a cowshed is a barton and a valley is a coomb. The poem ends in hope, but a hope defined by its tenuousness (after its first syllable the poem's last line is a long diminuendo), the fossil of an unthinking childhood faith. It is a hope that is at best hypothetical, dependent on a *feeling* that *if* someone asked him to he would go, so that it remains quite unclear whether it lightens or darkens the 'gloom'.

Hardy thought Charlotte Mew 'the best woman poet of her day'.[14] The kinship between the two is clear enough in 'The Farmer's Bride', the title poem of her first volume, which was not published until 1916, although Mew had been a contributor to *The Yellow Book* as early as 1894. 'The Farmer's Bride' is, like most of her work, terse. The story at first seems grimly simple. A farmer has married, he now realizes, precipitately ('but more's to do / At harvest-time than bide and woo' (2–3)), only to find that his young bride responds with horror to his sexual advances. One autumn night she runs away, but she is pursued: 'We caught her, fetched her home at last / And turned the key upon her, fast'. (18–9) Since then she keeps house 'As well as most' (21), and will even 'chat and play', but only if no men are present. She is happiest with animals, 'birds and rabbits' and the cattle, which is unsurprising because the farmer scarcely distinguishes between her and them. The hunt for her after she has escaped is described as if it were a field sport, a hare-coursing: 'All in a shiver and a scare / We caught her'. (17–8) It is at its close that the poem becomes more mysterious:

> The short days shorten and the oaks are brown,
>   The blue smoke rises to the low grey sky,
> One leaf in the still air falls slowly down,
>   A magpie's spotted feathers lie
> On the black earth spread white with rime,
> The berries redden up to Christmas-time.
>   What's Christmas-time without there be
>   Some other in the house than we!
>
>   She sleeps up in the attic there
>   Alone, poor maid. 'Tis but a stair
> Betwixt us. Oh! my God! the down,
> The soft young down of her, the brown,
>   The brown of her – her eyes, her hair, her hair!
> (34–46)

There are the vivid splashes of colour so typical of 1890s poems, and the sharply discrete objects so often found in poems throughout the Victorian period, the leaf, the feathers, the berries, their discreteness underlined by lines the rhythm of which resists the simple ballad tetrameters: 'On the black earth spread white with rime'. The farmer's understanding of life centres on the cycle of the seasons; summer when he first chose his bride, harvest when he married her, the 'fall' when she ran away, and the springtime with which she is associated by virtue of her youth: 'Sweet as the first wild violets, she, / To her wild self'. (32–3) But his marriage knows only one season, winter, the season of frost. On her wedding night 'Her smile went out', 'Like the shut of a winter's day'(6–7). Three years have passed and she has stayed shut, still a maid. The poem ends with the farmer imagining his own Christmas miracle, but no more believing in it than Hardy believes in the miracle of the oxen kneeling. In the early days of the marriage, when they still shared a bed, the farmer remembers her 'Lying awake with her wide brown stare' (13), a brownness that is taken up in the leafless wintertime oaks before it is returned in the poem's last lines with a new and shocking intensity to the bride's eyes and her hair. He still thinks of her as an animal, 'The soft young down of her', but there is tenderness in the thought as well as lust, and it seems harsh to deny that a combination of the two emotions might constitute something like love. The farmer's imagination is haunted by the fragility of the physical barrier between himself and his wife's body, 'but a stair', but it is the barrier that has ensured that all through the three years since he has married her she has remained a bride, the focus of his painfully intense erotic imaginings. Chastity functions in much the same way to generate the erotic charge of Dowson's 'Nuns of the Perpetual Adoration', but Mew's handling of the matter remains enigmatic. It is the condition of unnaturally extended erotic anticipation in which the farmer has lived for three years that has sharpened his senses so that he notices how the 'blue smoke rises to the low grey sky'. He is a coarse west-country farmer, but sexual abstinence has done for him what it did for Tennyson's Mariana: it has made a poet of him, which is why, whether or not we suspect that Charlotte Mew feels a kinship with him that has to do with her own frustrated same-sex desires, it is the farmer's consciousness that intrigues her rather than the consciousness of his pitiable victim, the bride. It is by allowing her poem to feel so much more intimately with the farmer than with his wife that Mew confers on her poem its own strange doubleness, a doubleness that makes it a wholly appropriate poem with which to end this book.

Endnotes

1. 'The Decay of Lying', *Literary Criticism of Oscar Wilde*, ed. Stanley Weintraub (Lincoln, Nebraska: University of Nebraska Press, 1968), p. 182.
2. 'Poems by William Morris' (1868) *Westminster Review*, **34**(2) (October), 300–13, 311.
3. W.B. Yeats, *Essays and Introductions* (London: Macmillan, 1961), p. 494.
4. *Literary Criticism of Oscar Wilde*, pp. 195–6.
5. *Oscar Wilde: Interviews and Recollections*, ed. E.H. Mikhail (London: Macmillan, 1979), p. 445.

6. Alfred Austin (1869) 'Poetry of the Period: Mr Swinburne', *Temple Bar*, **26** (July), 457–74.
7. *Complete Works of Algernon Charles Swinburne*, ed. Sir Edmund Gosse and Thomas James Wise, 20 vols (London: William Heinemann, 1926), 13, pp. 417–27, and 15, pp. 62–119.
8. See the sonnets, 'Thou large-brained woman and large-hearted man' and 'True genius, but true woman!'.
9. See Mary Ann Caws and Gerhard Joseph (2005) 'Naming and Not Naming: Tennyson and Mallarmé', *Victorian Poetry*, **43** (Spring), 1–18.
10. Edmund Gosse (1877) 'A Plea for Certain Exotic Forms of Verse', *Cornhill Magazine*, **36** (July), 53–71.
11. The echo is pointed out by Tricia Lootens, 'Alien Homelands, Rudyard Kipling, Toru Dutt, and the Poetry of Empire', in Joseph Bristow (ed.) *The Fin-de-Siècle Poem: English Literary Culture in the 1890s* (Athens, Ohio:Ohio University Press, 2005), pp. 285–310.
12. Quoted by Ana Parejo Vadillo, 'Immaterial poetics: A Mary F. Robinson and the Fin-de-Siècle Poem' in Joseph Bristow (ed.), *The Fin-de-Siècle Poem: English Literary Culture in the 1890s* (Athens, Ohio: Ohio University Press, 2005), pp. 231–60, 231.
13. *Prose Remains of Arthur Hugh Clough*, ed. Blanche Clough (London: Macmillan, 1888), pp. 356–7.
14. As reported by Sir Sydney Cockerell in his obituary notice of Charlotte Mew, *The Times*, March 29, 1928, p. 21.

Bibliography

1 Introduction: The Victorian Poetry Palace

Current understanding of Victorian poetry owes most to Isobel Armstrong, especially to her *Victorian Poetry: Poetry, Poetics and Politics* (London: Routledge, 1993). The earlier study from which I have learned most is Eric Griffiths, *The Printed Voice of Victorian Poetry* (Oxford: Clarendon Press, 1989). Important later studies include Matthew Campbell, *Rhythm and Will in Victorian Poetry*, and Robert Douglas-Fairhurst, *Victorian Afterlives: The Shaping of Influence in Nineteenth-Century Literature* (Oxford: Oxford University Press, 2002). *The Victorian Poet: Poetics and Persona*, ed. Joseph Bristow (London, New York and Sydney: Crook Helm, 1987) is a well-chosen anthology of Victorian writings on poetics. *A Companion to Victorian Poetry*, ed. Richard Cronin, Alison Chapman and Antony H. Harrison collects a comprehensive array of essays on Victorian poetry. *The Cambridge Companion to Victorian Poetry*, ed. Joseph Bristow (Cambridge: Cambridge University Press, 2000), and Linda K. Hughes, *The Cambridge Introduction to Victorian Poetry* (Cambridge: Cambridge University Press, 2010) offer good introductions to the poetry of the period. For a more wide-ranging introduction to Victorian culture, see *A Companion to Victorian Literature and Culture*, ed. Herbert F. Tucker (Oxford: Blackwell, 1999). On *Sonnets from the Portuguese* see Rhian Williams (2009) '"Our deep, dear silence": Marriage and Lyricism in the *Sonnets from the Portuguese*', *Victorian Literature and Culture*, **37**(1), 85–102.

Reading Victorian Poetry, First Edition. Richard Cronin.

2 Self-Division and the Dramatic Monologue

The modern interest in the dramatic monologue has its origin in Robert Langbaum's seminal *The Poetry of Experience: The Dramatic Monologue in Modern Literary Tradition* (London: Chatto and Windus, 1957). See also Alan Sinfield, *The Dramatic Monologue* (London: Methuen, 1977), and Warwick Slinn, 'Dramatic Monologue' in *A Companion to Victorian Poetry*, ed. Richard Cronin, Alison Chapman, and Antony H. Harrison (Oxford: Blackwell, 2002), pp. 80–98. Glennis Byron's *The Dramatic Monologue* (London: Routledge, 2003) offers a particularly good account of the contribution of women poets to the genre. There are influential essays by Ralph W. Rader (1976) 'The Dramatic Monologue and Related Lyric Forms', *Critical Inquiry*, **3**, 131–51, and by Herbert F. Tucker (1984) 'From Monomania to Monologue: "St Simeon Stylites", and the Rise of the Victorian Dramatic Monologue', *Victorian Poetry*, **22**(2), 121–37, and 'Dramatic Monologue and the Overhearing of Lyric' in *Lyric Poetry: Beyond New Criticism*, ed. Chaviva Hosek and Patricia Parker (Ithaca, New York: Cornell University Press, 1985), pp. 226–43. I am most indebted in my own account of the form to Eric Griffiths, *The Printed Voice of Victorian Poetry* (Oxford: Clarendon Press, 1989). On the publishing conditions that Victorian poets had to confront, see Lee Erickson, 'The Market' in *A Companion to Victorian Poetry*, ed. Richard Cronin, Alison Chapman, and Antony H. Harrison (Oxford: Blackwell, 2002), pp. 345–60. On Barrett Browning's 'The Runaway Slave at Pilgrim's Point', see Marjorie Stone, 'Elizabeth Barrett Browning and the Garrisonians: "'The Runaway Slave at Pilgrim's Point", the Boston Female Anti-Slavery Society, and Abolitionist Discourse in *The Liberty Bell*' in *Victorian Women Poets*, ed. Alison Chapman (Cambridge: Brewer, 2003), pp. 33–55, Sarah Brophy (1998) 'Elizabeth Barrett Browning's "The Runaway Slave at Pilgrim's Point" and the Politics of Interpretation', *Victorian Poetry*, **36** (Fall), 273–88, and Warwick Slinn, *Victorian Poetry as Cultural Critique* (Charlottesville and London: University of Virginia Press, 2003), pp. 56–89. James Thomson's essay on Xantippe is included in his *Essays and Phantasies* (London: Reeves and Turner, 1881).

3 Victorian Metrics

The best general guide to the metrics of Victorian poetry remains the third volume of George Saintsbury's *History of English Prosody from the Twelfth Century to the Present Day* (London: Macmillan, 1910). See also Edwin Guest, *A History of English* Rhythms, 2 vols (London: Pickering, 1838). The most helpful recent studies are Eric Griffiths, *The Printed Voice of Victorian Poetry* (Oxford: Clarendon Press, 1989), Matthew Campbell, *Rhythm and Will in Victorian Poetry*, (Cambridge: Cambridge University Press, 1999), and Yopie Prins, 'Victorian meters' in *The Cambridge Companion to Victorian* Poetry, ed. Joseph Bristow (Cambridge: Cambridge University Press, 2000), pp. 89–113. There is also much of interest, especially on Swinburne's metres, in Prins's *Victorian Sappho* (Princeton: Princeton University Press, 1999). Special mention should be made of Dennis Taylor's *Hardy's Metre and Victorian Prosody* (Oxford: Clarendon Press, 1988), which not only offers the fullest account of Hardy's metrical practice, but includes in its opening chapter a particularly acute summary of Victorian prosody. The most interesting Victorian study of metrics is an essay that Patmore published in various versions, the best edition of which is *Coventry Patmore's 'Essay on English Metrical Law*', ed. Mary Augustine Roth (Washington: Catholic University of America Press, 1961). Stevenson's remarks on metre appear in his essay 'On Some Technical Elements of Style in Literature' included in his *Essays in the Art of Writing* (London: Chatto and Windus, 1905); Newbolt's appear in (1911–2) 'A New Study of English Poetry', *English Review*, **10**, 185–301, 657–72. Anne Jamison gives a brilliant account of the metrics of *Goblin Market* from which I have profited in 'Goblin Metrics', the fifth chapter of her *Poetics en Passant: Redefining the Relationship between Victorian and Modern Poetry* (New York: Palgrave Macmillan, 2009). Two helpful studies of the metrics of *Maud* are Edward Stokes,(1964) 'The Metrics of *Maud*', *Victorian Poetry*, **2**(2), 97–110, and Scott Dransfield (2008) 'The Morbid Meters of *Maud*', *Victorian* Poetry, **46**(3), 279–97. For a modern reading of the speaker of *Maud* as a poet, see Robert E. Lougy (1984) 'The Sounds and Silence of Madness: Language as Theme in Tennyson's *Maud*', *Victorian Poetry*, **22**(4), 407–26. See also Anna Barton, *Tennyson's Name: Identity and Responsibility in the Poetry of Alfred Lord Tennyson* (London: Ashgate, 2008), especially pp. 82–103. For a fascinating account of Clough's metrics, though not a discussion with which I wholly agree, see J.P. Phelan (1999) 'Radical Metre: The English Hexameter of Clough's *Bothie of Toper-na-Fuosich*,' *Review of English Studies*, **50**, 166–87.

4 Long Poems and Short Poems: the Victorian Sonnet Sequence

On the epic ambitions of Victorian poets, see Herbert F. Tucker, *Epic: Britain's Heroic Muse, 1795–1910* (Oxford: Oxford University Press, 2008). On the Spasmodics, see in addition to Tucker's *Epic*, Antony H. Harrison, *Victorian Poets and Romantic Poems* (Charlottesville: University Press of Virginia, 1990), Richard Cronin, 'The Spasmodics' in *A Companion to Victorian Poetry*, ed. Richard Cronin, Alison Chapman, and Antony H. Harrison (Oxford: Blackwell, 2002), pp. 291–304, and the special issue of *Victorian Poetry*, edited by Charles LaPorte and Jason Rudy (2004) dedicated to the Spasmodics, **42**(4). On the Victorian sonnet, see William Davis (1873) 'The Sonnet', *Quarterly Review*, **134** (January), 186–204: Charles Tomlinson *The Sonnet: Its Origin, Structure, and Place in Poetry* (London: John Murray, 1874);William T. Going, *Scanty Plot of Ground: Studies in the Victorian Sonnet* (The Hague: Mouton, 1976); Jennifer Ann Wagner, *A Moment's Monument: Revisionary Poetics and the Nineteenth-Century English Sonnet* (London: Associated University Presses, 1996); Natalie M. Houston (1999) 'Valuable by Design: Material Features and Cultural Value in Nineteenth-Century Sonnet Anthologies', *Victorian Poetry*, **37**(2), 243–72; Alison Chapman, 'Sonnet and Sonnet Sequence' in *A Companion to Victorian Poetry*, ed. Richard Cronin, Alison Chapman, and Antony H. Harrison (Oxford: Blackwell, 2002), pp. 99–114; John Holmes, *Dante Gabriel Rossetti and the Late Victorian Sonnet Sequence: Sexuality, Belief and the Self* (Aldershot: Ashgate, 2005); and Stephen Regan (2006) 'The Victorian Sonnet, from George Meredith to Gerard Manley Hopkins, *Yearbook of English Studies*, **36**(2), 17–34. Hutton's review of Meredith's *Modern Love* is included in *Meredith: The Critical Heritage*, ed. Ioan Williams (London: Routledge and Kegan Paul, 1971).

5 Victorian Poetry and Translation

Lawrence Venuti offers a useful survey of Victorian translation practice in *The Translator's Invisibility: A History of Translation* (London: Routledge, 1995). See also the *Oxford History of Literary Translation in* English, 4, 1790–1900, ed. Peter France and Kenneth Haynes (Oxford: Oxford University Press, 2006). The discussions of FitzGerald's translation that

I have found most useful are Robert Douglas-Fairhurst's in *Victorian Afterlives: The Shaping of Influence in Nineteenth-Century Literature* (Oxford: Oxford University Press, 2002), Erik Gray, *The Poetry of Indifference; from the Romantics to the* Rubáiyát (Amherst and Boston: University of Massachusetts Press, 2005), and Herbert F. Tucker (2008) 'Metaphor, translation, and autoekphrasis in FitzGerald's *Rubáiyát*', *Victorian Poetry*, **46** (Spring), 69–85. On the Sapphic tradition in Victorian poetry see Yopie Prins, *The Victorian Sappho* (Princeton, New Jersey: Princeton University Press, 1999), and *The Sappho Companion* ed. Margaret Reynolds (London: Chatto and Windus, 2000). On Toru Dutt, see Tricia Lootens, 'Alien Homelands: Rudyard Kipling, Toru Dutt, and the Poetry of Empire' in *The Fin de Siècle Poem: English Literary Culture and the 1890s*, ed. Joseph Bristow (Athens, Ohio: Ohio University Press, 2005), pp. 285–310. On Tennyson and Lear, see Richard Cronin, 'Edward Lear and Tennyson's Nonsense' in *Tennyson Among the Poets: Bicentenary Essays*, ed. Robert Douglas-Fairhurst and Seamus Perry (Oxford: Oxford University Press, 2009), pp. 259–75, and Anna Barton (2009) 'Delirious Bulldogs and Noisy Crockery: Tennyson as Nonsense Poet', *Victorian Poetry*, **47**(1) (Spring) 313–30. See John Marshall Gest's translation and notes on the book that Browning purchased in the Florentine market, *The Old Yellow Book: Source of Browning's* The Ring and the Book (New York: Haskell House, 1970). For a full study of the influence of the *Rubaiyat* on Eliot's thought and work, see Vinnie-Marie D'Ambrosio, *Eliot Possessed: T. S. Eliot and FitzGerald's* Rubaiyat (New York: New York University Press, 1989).

6 Victorian Poetry and Life

On the Victorian fascination with sharp detail, see Carol Christ, *The Finer Optic: The Aesthetic of Particularity in Victorian Poetry* (New Haven: Yale University Press, 1975). On the representation by Victorian poets of the visual world, see Jonathan Crary, *Techniques of the Observer: On Vision and Modernity in the Nineteenth Century* (Cambridge, Mass.: Massachusetts Institute of Technology Press, 1990); Kate Flint, *The Victorians and the Visual Imagination* (Cambridge: Cambridge University Press, 2000); and Catherine Maxwell, *Second Sight: The Visionary Imagination in Late Victorian Literature* (Manchester: Manchester University Press, 2008). On Victorian poetry and science, see W. David Shaw, 'Poetic Truth in a

Scientific Age: The Victorian Perspective', in *Centre and Labyrinth: Essays in Honour of Northrop Frye*, ed. Eleanor Cook *et al.* (Toronto: University of Toronto Press, 1983); and Richard Butts (1985) 'Languages of Description and Analogy in Victorian Science and Poetry', *English Studies in Canada*, **11**(2), 193–213.

7 Victorian Poetry and Religion

On Victorian religion see Stephen Prickett, *Romanticism and Religion: The Tradition of Wordsworth and Coleridge in the Victorian Church* (Cambridge: Cambridge University Press, 1976); W. David Shaw, *The Lucid Veil: Poetic Truth in the Victorian Age* (London: Athlone, 1987); and Michael Wheeler, *Death and The Future Life in Victorian Literature and Theology* (Cambridge: Cambridge University Press, 1990). On Tractarian poetry, see G.B. Tennyson, *Victorian Devotional Poetry: The Tractarian Mode* (Cambidge, Mass.: Harvard University Press, 1981); Stephen Prickett, 'Tractarian Poetry' in *A Companion to Victorian Poetry*, ed. Richard Cronin, Alison Chapman and Antony H. Harrison (Oxford: Blackwell, 2002), pp. 279–90; *John Keble in Context*, ed. Kirstie Blair (London: Anthem Press, 2004); and the special issue of *Victorian Poetry*, **44**(1) (2006) devoted to Tractarian poetry, edited by Emma Mason. On Christina Rossetti's poetry, see Alison Chapman, *The Afterlife of Christina Rossetti* (Basingstoke: Macmillan, 2000); and Constance Hassett, *Christina Rossetti: The Patience of Style* (Charlottesville: University of Virginia Press, 2005). On Victorian women poets and the doctrine of reserve, see Isobel Armstrong, '"A Music of Thine Own"': Women's poetry – an expressive tradition', in her *Victorian Poetry: Poetry, Poetics and Politics*, pp. 318–77. On Emily Dickinson, see Martin Greenup (2004) 'The Glimmering Frontier: Emily Dickinson and Publication' *Cambridge Quarterly*, **33**(4), 345–62.

8 Conclusion: the 1890s

Holbrook Jackson's seminal *The Eighteen Nineties* (London: Grant Richards, 1913) is the book from which all later commentators on the period have begun. See also Arthur Symons, *The Symbolist Movement in*

Literature (London: Constable, 1899); Richard Le Gallienne, *The Romantic '90s* (London: G.P. Putnam, 1925); Linda Dowling, *Language and Decadence in the Victorian Fin-de-Siècle* (Princeton, New Jersey: Princeton University Press, 1986); Murray Pittock, *Spectrum of Decadence: Literature of the 1890s* (London: Routledge, 1993); and *The Fin-de-Siècle Poem: English Literary Culture in the 1890s*, ed. Joseph Bristow (Athens, Ohio: Ohio University Press, 2005). On Tennyson and Mallarmé, see Mary Ann Caws and Gerhard Joseph (2005) 'Naming and Not Naming: Tennyson and Mallarmé', *Victorian Poetry*, **43** (Spring), 1–18. On the new freedom of women poets in the city, see Linda Hunt Backman, 'Amy Levy: Urban Poetry, Poetic Innovation, and the Fin-de-Siècle Woman Poet' in *The Fin-de-Siècle Poem: English Literary Culture in the 1890s*, pp. 207–30.

A Note on Texts

Wherever possible poems are cited from *Victorian Poetry: An Annotated Anthology*, ed. Francis O'Gorman (Oxford: Blackwell, 2004). Poems not included in O'Gorman's anthology are cited from the following:

Matthew Arnold, *The Poems*, ed. Kenneth Allott (London: Longman, Green and Co., 1965)

Philip James Bailey, *Festus* (London: William Pickering, 1848)

William Barnes, Poems, ed. Bernard Jones, 2 vols (London: Centaur Press, 1962)

John Stanyan Bigg, *Night and the Soul* (London: Groombridge, 1854)

Elizabeth Barrett Browning, *The Works*, 5 vols, gen. ed. Sandra Donaldson (London: Pickering and Chatto, 2010)

Robert Browning, *The Poems*, 2 vols, ed. John Pettigrew and Thomas J. Collins (London, Penguin, 1981)

Robert Browning, *The Ring and the Book*, ed. Thomas J. Collins and Richard D. Altick (Peterborough, Ontario: Broadview Press, 2001)

Edward Carpenter, *Towards Democracy* (London: George Allen and Unwin, 1905)

Lewis Carroll, *The Complete Works* (London: Nonesuch Press, 1939)

Arthur Hugh Clough, *The Poems*, ed. A.L.P. Norrington (London: Oxford University Press, 1968)

John Davidson, *The Poems*, ed. Andrew Turnbull, 2 vols (Edinburgh: Scottish Academic Press, 1973)

Emily Dickinson, *The Complete Poems*, ed. Thomas H. Johnson (London: Faber, 1970)

Sydney Dobell, *The Poetical Works*, ed. John Nichol, 2 vols (London: Smith, Elder, 1875)

Toru Dutt, *Ancient Ballads and Legends of Hindustan* (London: Kegan Paul and Trench, 1882)

Michael Field, *Long Ago* (London: G. Bell and Sons, 1889).

Edward FitzGerald, *The Rubáiyát of Omar Khayyám: A Critical Edition*, ed. Christopher Decker (Charlottesville: University Press of Virginia, 1997)

W.S. Gilbert, *Patience: An entirely new and original aesthetic opera in two acts,The Savoy Operas*, 2 vols (London: Macmillan, 1957)

Arthur Hallam, *The Writings*, ed. T.H. Vail Motter (London : Oxford University Press, 1943)

Thomas Hardy, *The Complete Poems*, ed. James Gibson (London: Macmillan, 1976)

Gerard Manley Hopkins, *The Poems*, ed. W.H. Gardner and N.H. Mackenzie, fourth edition (London: Oxford University Press, 1967)

A.E. Housman, *The Poems*, ed. Archie Burnett (Oxford: Clarendon Press, 1997)

John Keats, *The Poems*, ed. Jack Stillinger (London: Heinemann, 1978)

John Keble, *The Christian Year, Lyra Innocentium and Other Poems* (Oxford: Oxford University Press, 1914)

Rudyard Kipling, *Rudyard Kipling's Verse: inclusive edition, 1885–1932* (London: Hodder and Stoughton, 1933)

Edward Lear, *The Complete Nonsense and Other Verse*, ed. Vivien Noakes (London: Penguin, 2006)

Amy Levy, *A London Plane Tree and Other Verse* (London: T. Fisher Unwin, 1889)

James Clarence Mangan, *Selected Poems of James Clarence Mangan*, ed. Jacques Chuto, Rudolph Holzapfel, Peter van de Kamp, and Ellen Shannon-Mangan (Dublin: Irish Academic Press, 2003)

John Westland Marston, *Gerald: A Dramatic Poem and Other Poems* (London: C. Mitchell, 1842)

Herman Melville, *Collected Poems*, ed. Howard P. Vincent (Chicago: Packard, 1947)

Charlotte Mew, *The Farmer's Bride* (London: Poetry Bookshop, 1916)

Alice Meynell, *Poems* (London: Elkin Matthews and John Lane, 1893)

Thomas Moore, *Poetical Works*, ed. A. D. Godley (London: Oxford University Press, 1910)

Henry John Newbolt, *Admirals All, and Other Verses* (London: Elkin Matthew, 1897)

John Pierpont, *Anti-Slavery Poems* (Boston: Oliver Johnson, 1843)

Christina Rossetti, *The Complete Poems*, ed. R. W. Crump (London: Penguin, 2001)

D.G. Rossetti: poems are cited from the Rossetti Archive, ed. Jerome J. McGann, http://www.rossettiarchive.org/

Alexander Smith, *Poems* (London: David Bogue, 1853)

John Addington Symonds, *Animi Figura* (London: Smith, Elder and Co., 1882)

Algernon Charles Swinburne, *Major Poems and Selected Prose*, ed. Jerome J. McGann and Charles L. Sligh (New Haven and London: Yale University Press, 2004)

Alfred Tennyson, *The Poems: in three volumes*, ed. Christopher Ricks (Harlow: Longman, 1987)

Augusta Webster, *Portraits and Other Poems*, ed. Christine Sutphin (Peterborough, Ontario: Broadview Press, 2000)

Walt Whitman, *Leaves of Grass*, ed. Jerome Loving (Oxford: Oxford University Press, 1990)

Oscar Wilde, *Plays, Prose Writings and Poems*, ed. Anthony Fothergill (London: J.M. Dent, 1996)

William Wordsworth, *The Poems*, 2 vols, ed. John O. Hayden (Harmondsworth: Penguin, 1977)

William Wordsworth, *The Prelude: The Four Texts (1798, 1799, 1805, 1851)*, ed. Jonathan Wordsworth (London: Penguin, 1995)

William Butler Yeats, *Collected Poems* (London: Macmillan, 1963)

Index

Reading Victorian Poetry, First Edition. Richard Cronin.

Printed and bound by CPI Group (UK) Ltd, Croydon, CR0 4YY

07/07/2026

14916222-0003